love

Lupita

Lupita Tovar

THE SWEETHEART OF MÉXICO

A Memoir

As told to her son

Pancho Kohner

Cover design: Dan Perri

LUPITA TOVAR
"THE SWEETHEART OF MÉXICO"

Copyright © 2010 by Pancho Kohner. 77047-KOHNER

All rights reserved.

All photographs from the author's collection.

Without limiting the rights under copyright reserved above, no part of this publication may be reproduced, stored in or introduced into a retrieval system, or transmitted, in any form or by any means (electronic, mechanical, photocopying, recording or otherwise), without the prior written permission of the copyright owner of this book.

This book was printed in the United States of America.

ISBN:
Softcover 978-1-4500-8456-7

Hardcover 978-1-4500-8457-4

For my grandchildren and great-grandchildren.

And the days dwindle down to a precious few

September. . . November. . .

And these few precious days,

I'll spend with you

These precious days,

I'll spend with you.

—Maxwell Anderson, "September Song"

Acknowledgments

For many years I encouraged my mother to write the story of her life but she kept saying to me, "You should write it."

I procrastinated until one day when, in preparation for an exhibit at the Motion Picture Academy, I showed Alejandra, Fabricio, and Concepción Espasande Bouza my mother's vast collection of memorabilia from her show business career.

"You *must* write Lupita's story," they told me. "Not only for her, but for all the talented people she worked with."

Laird Koenig read my first draft and encouraged me to complete a full-length book. The manuscript then found its way into the hands of family members and friends, all of whom offered constructive suggestions and corrections. My readers included my sister Susan, my children Alex and Melissa, and my friends and colleagues Amy Chai, Arthur G. Solmmsen, Bob Dickson, Duncan Ball, Kevin Brownlow, George Van Noy, Jill Schary Robinson, John Crowther, Joseph Dispenza, Julie Kohner Greenberg, Kent Wilson, Larry Ceplair, Lucy Tovar, Maria Esther Gonzalez, Marvin Zuckerman, Maria Riva, Melanie Downing, Melissa Conway, Patricia Weitz, Paul Davids, Peter Withers, Saul Cooper, Sonya Alexander, Xóchitl Fernández and Rogelio Agrasánchez, Jr.

Kevin Thomas was kind enough to supply the foreword, film historian Lon Davis edited the entire manuscript and encouraged me with his enthusiasm for this project, and Irene Simon made the final corrections with her expertise in five languages.

Long before my commitment to write this book my wife, Maggie, had the foresight to take notes whenever Lupita spoke of her life's adventures. Maggie's clear critical suggestions and unstinting support were invaluable.

Thank you, one and all.

Of course, none of this would have been possible without the subject herself—my mother, Lupita Tovar. She has generously shared the incredible-yet-true accounts of her long life, and remains a patient, good-humored, inspiring individual even in this, her one-hundredth year.

CONTENTS:

FOREWORD by Kevin Thomas
PREFACE

PART ONE
MAP OF MEXICO

CHAPTER 1	BORN UNDER HALLEY'S COMET	1
CHAPTER 2	REBELS HANGING BY THEIR NECKS	5
AUTHOR'S NOTE:	A BRIEF HISTORY OF THE 1910 MEXICAN REVOLUTION	7
CHAPTER 3	A HACIENDA IN TEHUACÁN	9
CHAPTER 4	A DIRT FLOOR AND NO RUNNING WATER	11
CHAPTER 5	"SOME DAY I'LL DANCE ON THAT STAGE"	13
AUTHOR'S NOTE:	"THE PERSONAL ENEMY OF GOD"	17
CHAPTER 6	DISCOVERED BY HOLLYWOOD	19
CHAPTER 7	"I AM MISS TOVAR"	23
CHAPTER 8	"MY PERSONAL SANTA CLAUS"	25
CHAPTER 9	ARRIVING IN A FAIRY TALE	27
CHAPTER 10	MEETING PAUL KOHNER	31
AUTHOR'S NOTE:	A YOUNG MAN TO WATCH	33
CHAPTER 11	"NOT IN A MILLION YEARS!"	41
CHAPTER 12	"GIVE ME 24 HOURS"	45
CHAPTER 13	"ARE YOU A CATHOLIC?"	49
CHAPTER 14	"LA NOVIA DE MÉXICO"	57
CHAPTER 15	*DRÁCULA*	63
AUTHOR'S NOTE:	FOREIGN-LANGUAGE VERSIONS	69
CHAPTER 16	"WOULD YOU LIKE TO BE A STAR?"	71
CHAPTER 17	ALMOST KIDNAPPED	73
CHAPTER 18	*SANTA*	77
CHAPTER 19	"MY FAVORITE FILM"	81
AUTHOR'S NOTE:	*SANTA*, THE FIRST MEXICAN TALKIE	85
CHAPTER 20	A DECADENT PLACE	89
CHAPTER 21	"I CRIED MY HEART OUT"	93

CHAPTER 22	"DARLING, WILL YOU MARRY ME?"	95
CHAPTER 23	"THE MEXICAN ROSE"	99

PART TWO
MAP OF EUROPE

CHAPTER 24	BERLIN—1932	107
CHAPTER 25	PAPA JULIUS	109
CHAPTER 26	THE WEDDING CEREMONY	113
CHAPTER 27	A TERRIBLE EVENING	115
CHAPTER 28	"IT TOOK A LOT OF COURAGE"	119
CHAPTER 29	"COULD I DANCE WITH YOUR NIECE?"	121
AUTHOR'S NOTE:	THE END OF THE WEIMAR REPUBLIC	125
CHAPTER 30	"FRÄULEIN, HALT!"	127
AUTHOR'S NOTE:	A VERY DANGEROUS TIME	129
CHAPTER 31	"LET HER DIE IN PEACE"	131
CHAPTER 32	ADVENTURES IN FILMING	135
CHAPTER 33	ARRESTED AT THE BORDER	143
CHAPTER 34	LUCKY TO ESCAPE	149

PART THREE

CHAPTER 35	STARTING OVER IN AMERICA	153
CHAPTER 36	WITH PAUL IN MEXICO	157
CHAPTER 37	GOOD FRIENDS	161
CHAPTER 38	BECOMING AN AGENT AND A FATHER	165
AUTHOR'S NOTE:	THE EUROPEAN FILM FUND	167
CHAPTER 39	"KAFFEEKLATSCH AT THE KOHNERS"	169
CHAPTER 40	"SHOT WITH HIS BOOTS ON"	171
AUTHOR'S NOTE:	GENERAL SATURNINO CEDILLO	177
CHAPTER 41	SELLING VACUUM CLEANERS	179
CHAPTER 42	DESPERATE TO HELP	183
CHAPTER 43	"THE BATTLE OF LOS ANGELES"	185

CHAPTER 44	MORE FILMING IN MEXICO	189
CHAPTER 45	LIBERATION IN EUROPE	195
CHAPTER 46	BULLFIGHTS AND OLD BOYFRIENDS	197
CHAPTER 47	FRIDA AND DIEGO	199
CHAPTER 48	THE MYSTERIOUS B. TRAVEN	203
AUTHOR'S NOTE:	THE ENIGMA OF B. TRAVEN	207
CHAPTER 49	"FORGIVE ME"	211
CHAPTER 50	FINALLY MEETING B. TRAVEN	213
CHAPTER 51	"YOU CHANGED MY WHOLE LIFE"	217
CHAPTER 52	GRANDMOTHERS	221
CHAPTER 53	THE FIFTIES	223
CHAPTER 54	A MEMORABLE TRIP	225
CHAPTER 55	MAURICE CHEVALIER	229
CHAPTER 56	THE BEL AIR FIRE AND OTHER TRAGEDIES	231
CHAPTER 57	A "BOUTIQUE" AGENCY	235
CHAPTER 58	OUR SCANDINAVIAN FRIENDS	241
CHAPTER 59	A TROUBLED YEAR	245
CHAPTER 60	GRANDCHILDREN	249
CHAPTER 61	LENI RIEFENSTAHL	251
CHAPTER 62	THE FAMILY IN MEXICO	253
CHAPTER 63	COURAGE, HARD WORK, AND DESTINY	257
AUTHOR'S NOTE:	A EULOGY FOR PAUL KOHNER	263
CHAPTER 64	FILM FESTIVALS AND A RETURN TO BERLIN	267
CHAPTER 65	THE GOLDEN ARIEL	271
AUTHOR'S NOTE:	AN EVENING TO REMEMBER	275
CHAPTER 66	ANOTHER BIRTHDAY!	279
FILMOGRAPHY		283
INDEX		291

Photographs and Inserts

Page:

	MAP OF MEXICO
#2	Wedding of Maria Sullivan and Egidio Tovar, 1909
#9	Lucy, Grandmother, Mother, Jorgito, and Lupita (age 8)
#26	*Ilustrado* magazine, Lupita Tovar, 1928
#29	Excercise of option letter
#30	María Alba, Lupita Tovar, and Delia Magaña
#30	Tío Baby and Lucy Sullivan
#32	Paul Kohner, 1929
#34	Carl Laemmle letter to the American consul
#35	PK card—Manager
#35	Erich von Stroheim and Carl Laemmle
#36	PK card—Casting Director
#36	PK card—Personal Representative
#36	Mary Philbin, Carl Laemmle, Junior Laemmle, Conrad Veidt, and Paul Kohner
#37	Mary Philbin and Paul Kohner
#38	Paul Kohner, 1929
#39	*JUEVES de EXCELSIOR* magazine cover
#40	*LA OVACIÓN* magazine cover
#44	Lupita Tovar, 1930
#46	Paul Kohner and Carl Laemmle, 1929
#48	*ILUSTRADO* magazine cover
#50	Antonio Moreno and Lupita Tovar
#50	Lupita Tovar and Antonio Moreno
#51	Paul Ellis, Lupita Tovar, and Antonio Moreno
#52	Lupita Tovar and the cast of *La Voluntad del Muerto* – Paul Kohner and George Melford (front, center)
#53	First screening of *La Voluntad del Muerto*
#54	George Melford, Antonio Moreno, Lupita Tovar, and Paul Kohner
#55	*CINELANDIA* magazine cover
#56	*EL CINE* magazine cover
#57	Lupita Tovar returning to Mexico, 1930
#58	Marquee Cine Balmori, Mexico City
#58	Lupita Tovar at the Cine Balmori, November 30, 1930
#59	*La Voluntad Del Muerto* poster
#62	*ILUSTRADO* magazine cover
#63	*Drácula* newspaper ad
#64	Mexican magazine cover, Lupita Tovar, 1930
#66	Lupita Tovar and Carlos Villarías—*Drácula*
#66	Lupita Tovar—*Drácula*
#67	José Mojica and Lupita Tovar

#68	Lupita Tovar and Carlos Villarias—*Drácula*
#71	Lupita Tovar, Buck Jones, and Frank Rice in *Border Law*
#72	*Border Law* poster, 1931
#74	Lupita Tovar on stage in San Luis Potosi
#76	Lupita Tovar, *East of Borneo* poster, 1931
#77	Federico Gamboa and Lupita Tovar
#79	*NUEVO MUNDO* magazine cover
#80	*MUNDO AL DIA* magazine cover
#82	Lupita Tovar in the opening scene of *Santa*
#84	Lupita Tovar and Donald Reed in *Santa*
#84	Lupita Tovar and Carlos Orellana in *Santa*
#86	Teatro California Marquee, 1932 premiere of *Santa*
#86	*Santa* premiere with Lupita Tovar and Frank Fouce at far right
#87	*Santa* POSTAGE STAMP
#87	LOTTERY TICKET
#88	*LA OPINIÓN* magazine cover
#90	Paul Kohner, Helene and Ernst Lubitsch, and Hans Kraly
#90	Lupita Tovar, 1932
#93	Paul Kohner, 1932
#96	William Wyler, Zita Johann, Lupita, and Ernst Laemmle
#98	*CINE-MUNDIAL* magazine cover
#101	Lupita with the German Olympic team on the S.S. *Deutchland*
#101	"To my sweetheart with all my love, Lupita," 1932
#102	*CINEARTE* magazine cover
#105	MAP OF EUROPE
#106	*FOTOGÉNICAS* magazine cover
#108	Lupita and Paul, Berlin, 1932
#115	Hedy Lamarr, Gustav Machatý, and Paul Kohner
#116	Lupita and Paul, 1932
#118	*ROTOGRÁFICO* magazine cover
#122	Filming a close-up of Rod La Rocque—*S.O.S. Iceberg*—Paul at far right
#123	*Die Weisse Hölle vom Piz Palü* German poster
#131	*S.O.S. Eisberg* German poster
#132	Lupita, 1933
#136	Buster Keaton and Lupita Tovar in *The Invader*, 1933
#137	*Vidas Rotas,* Miguel Pereira, Maruchi Fresno, Enrique Zabala, G. Pollatschik, Lupita Tovar, Francisco de P. Cabrera, and director Eusevio F. Ardavin
#138	Lupita Tovar and Enrique Zabala—*Vidas Rotas*
#138	*Vidas Rotas* — Lupita Tovar
#139	*ARTISTAS HISPANA, Vidas Rotas* magazine cover
#140	*Vidas Rotas* poster
#141	Walter Klinger, Paul Kohner, Marian Marsh, and Luis Trenker

#142 *The Prodigal Son* — French poster
#143 Maria Andergast, Luis Trenker, Marian Marsh, Lupita, and Paul
#146 Colonel von Blomberg's letter
#147 Paul, Helene, Julius, and Lupita
#148 *ALLO PARIS* magazine cover
#154 José Crespo, Lupita, and Carlos Borcosque — *Alas Sobre el Chaco*
#154 Juan Torena, Fortunio Bonanova, and Lupita — *El Capitán Tormenta*
#154 José Bohr and Lupita—*Marihuana,* 1936
#155 Lupita, *Cuando la Vida Florece—When Love Blooms.*
#157 Carl Laemmle, Lupita, and General Saturnino Cedillo
#160 Paul, Lupita, Marian Anderson, Dolores del Río, and Diego Rivera
#163 Ernst, Nina, Talli, Lupita, and Paul
#170 Lupita and Paul, 1941
#172 *The Fighting Gringo* poster
#173 *CINEGRAMAS* magazine cover—*María*
#174 Lupita and Josefína Escobedo in *María*
#174 Sam's Yacht, *Malahne*
#174 Talli Wyler, Lupita, and Sam Spiegel on the *Malahne,* 1960
#175 Lupita and General Saturnino Cedillo
#176 *ILUSTRADO* magazine cover — *María*
#179 Lupita and Gene Autry — *South of the Border*
#180 *South of the Border* poster
#181 Ernst Lubitsch, Albert and Mrs. Bassermann, Charlotte and William Dieterle
#181 Luis Trenker and producer Harry Sokal
#187 *Casablanca* Production Report
#188 Jack Ross letter
#189 Lupita and Sara García in *Resurrección,* 1943
#190 *ESTAMPA* magzine cover
#192 Lupita and Paul Henreid
#192 Warner Baxter, Lupita, Jerome Cowan in *Crime Doctor's Courage*
#193 Susan, Paul, Lupita, and Pancho, 1944
#194 *MÉXICO CINEMA* magazine cover
#197 Antonio Moreno, Lupita, Carlos and Mrs. Arruza
#200 Diego Rivera painting Susan and Pancho, 1946
#201 Diego Rivera painting Lupita's portrait
#202 Portrait of Lupita by Diego Rivera
#203 B. Traven letter Febr. 27.
#204 B. Traven letter Febr. 28.
#206 *Mercedes Lozano Ortega* Screenplay
#209 *REVISTA DE REVISTAS* magazine
#210 *CINEMA reporter* magazine
#213 Emilio Fernández, Dolores del Río, and Lupita
#214 Lupita and Orson Welles

#214	Lupita, B. Traven, and Paul
#216	*CINEMA reporter* magazine
#217	Lupita and President Ortiz Rubio's sons
#217	Lupita and President Manuel Ávila Camacho, 1943
#218	President Miguel Alemán, inscribed to Lupita and Paul
#218	Pancho and President Luis Echeverría Álvarez on the set of *The Bridge In The Jungle*
#221	Paul and Lupita—mud at Stone Canyon
#222	Susan, Grandma Helene, Paul, Lupita, Grandma Lucy, and Pancho
#225	Erich von Stroheim and Lupita
#226	Our Chevrolet in France
#228	Lupita with Artur and Maria Brauner
#228	Pancho, Miriam Bru, Horst Buchholz, and Lupita
#230	Maurice Chevalier, Lupita, and Paul
#237	Lupita, Armando del Moral, and Ricardo Montalban
#237	Lupita, *Maria Elena*
#242	Ingmar Bergman letter
#243	Ingmar Bergman, Paul, and Lupita
#250	My grandchildren, Melissa, Chris, Alex, and Paul
#252	Tom Reed letter
#254	Lupita and Ambassador John Gavin
#255	Frederick, Walter, and Paul Kohner
#257	*Variety* article
#260	Pancho and Paul
#260	Back side of photo (love letter)
#261	Paul, 1928
#267	Lupita and Barry Norton in *Drácula*
#268	Lupita and Juan José Martínez Casado, *Santa*
#269	Angelika and Volker Schlöndorff, Lupita, and Horst Buchholz
#271	The Golden Ariel
#273	*Santa* poster
#277	Lupita, 2006
#281	Lupita Tovar, 1929

Foreword

Lupita Tovar is Hollywood royalty, a woman of beauty and charm, wit and intelligence, warmth and enthusiasm. She is the star of *Santa* (1931), her native Mexico's very first talkie, in which she played an innocent girl seduced, ending up in a brothel, yet holding on to her soul. She is the widow of legendary agent Paul Kohner, to whom she had been married fifty-six years upon his death in 1988. She has lived in a gracious Spanish Colonial-style home in Bel-Air ever since she persuaded her husband that they should buy it in 1936 for twelve thousand dollars. Lupita celebrated her ninety-ninth birthday there with a party attended, along with many others, by the children of David O. Selznick, Ernst Lubitsch, William Wyler, Dore Schary, and relatives of Carl Laemmle, for whom Paul Kohner produced twenty-six films, many of them in Berlin, early in his career.

It's easy to assume that Lupita, with her vivaciousness and effortless noblesse oblige, grew up in a Mexico City palacio or a vast hacienda, so it comes as a shock to learn that in her childhood she lived in homes with dirt floors and no plumbing, the eldest of nine children of a hard-drinking, strict, brutal father and a passive mother. At seventeen she was discovered by the great filmmaker Robert Flaherty and subsequently won a chance to go to Hollywood. She was accompanied there by her doughty Irish-American maternal grandmother, Lucy Sullivan, remembered by her great-grandson, Pancho Kohner, as "a tall, rawboned Irish woman" who reminded him of one of his father's most distinguished clients, director John Huston.

Lupita was working at Universal, dubbing American films into Spanish, when she met Kohner, who subsequently cast her in the Spanish-language version of *Drácula*. Restored and then revived over the past twenty years, the film has brought Lupita a large following among film buffs for her sensual portrayal of the film's leading lady.

Lupita believes in living life to the fullest, and her life has been rich in adventure, glamor, accomplishment, and, at times, danger. She was born at the dawn of the Mexican Revolution, surviving a shooting attack on a train in her youth. Looking back, she realizes that, having spent her earliest years in a country torn by bloodshed, she acquired a fearlessness that bordered on naïveté when Hitler came to power while she and Paul were living in Berlin. For years she was pursued, all the way to Italy and Hollywood as well as Mexico, by the fearsome General Saturnino Cedillo, a politico with a private army of ten thousand men. Lupita has been adored by the elusive B. Traven, author of *The Treasure of the Sierra Madre*, and Ingmar Bergman, among countless others.

After the success of her first Spanish-language film, *La Voluntad del Muerto*, Lupita became known as

"The Sweetheart of Mexico," and in her living room hangs a portrait of her painted by her friend, Diego Rivera. Across its top, Rivera painted a ribbon, bearing the inscription "La Novia de México." On the occasion of the fiftieth anniversary of the original release of *Santa*, Lupita's likeness appeared on a Mexican postage stamp. Between 1929 and 1945 she appeared in thirty films, both American and Mexican, and was the leading lady of both Buster Keaton and Buck Jones. While in Mexico, she was featured in a film version of Tolstoy's *Resurrection*. By then she decided that she wanted to concentrate all her attentions on her husband, whose career as an agent was in ascent, and their two young children, Pancho (who became a producer and screenwriter) and Susan (who became an Oscar-nominated actress). Susan's two sons by her late husband, menswear designer John Weitz—Chris and Paul Weitz—have become a top Hollywood filmmaking team.

For the past two years, Pancho and his wife, Maggie, have been carefully writing down Lupita's fascinating accounts of her life. Kohner has so deftly captured his mother's voice and personality that reading this book is like having a chat with Lupita, a natural storyteller, in her living room. She is the eternal enchantress.

— Kevin Thomas

Kevin Thomas has been reviewing movies for the *Los Angeles Times* since 1962.

Preface

In July of 2007, just shy of her ninety-seventh birthday, my mother said to me, "It took a lot of courage." She was referring to her decision as a young girl to leave her native Mexico with her Irish grandmother for Hollywood, and eventually travel alone to Europe to marry the man she loved; she was also summing up her whole life.

Paul Kohner, her lifelong love, was her complete opposite. A Hollywood movie producer, he came from a different part of the world, a different culture, and a different religion. He was born in Czechoslovakia, in a region known as the Sudetenland, which was part of the Austro-Hungarian Empire. Paul was eight years older than Lupita and far more experienced in affairs of the heart. Before meeting Lupita he had been engaged to Mary Philbin, the female lead in Universal Pictures' *The Phantom of the Opera* (1925).

In 1932, Paul returned to Europe. Six months later, over a long-distance phone call, he asked Lupita to marry him. She said yes and immediately boarded a train to New York, and then a ship to Germany. From there, Paul would take her to meet his parents in Czechoslovakia and be married. Paul and Lupita started their life together in Berlin at the same dangerous time that Adolf Hitler began his rise to power. In 1935, after a "close call" with Nazi border guards, they fled Germany and returned to America.

Lupita was, and is, indisputably beautiful. Her liveliness, and her gift for conversation in several languages, were great assets to my father as a producer and, later, as a talent agent. In the heyday of Hollywood, my parents went out most nights to premieres and to elegant parties in fancy evening dress. In the glittering era of *stars*, they were at the top.

Our family took frequent weekend car trips to Palm Springs, La Jolla, and Carmel. During these rides, our mother would entertain my sister and me by telling us stories of her life as a child. I remember during one drive to Carmel we laughed at the part of a story where she said, "Bullets were hitting the side of the train and *Abuelita* was lying on top of me!" Bullets! People shooting at *our* mother! And the image of our large grandmother, our *abuelita,* lying on top of our ninety-eight-pound mother was very funny. We laughed, which must have seemed disrespectful, because she suddenly stopped telling the story. Then, for a very long time, she refused to tell us more of what her life was like before we were born.

Fortunately, I heard many of these stories years later when Lupita was being interviewed by PBS, the BBC, Deutsches Fernsehen, and many documentary filmmakers trying to recapture what life was like in the early days of Hollywood. Some of these stories she kept in her diaries and others were written down by my wife, Maggie, when we accompanied Mom on long plane trips to Mexico and to Europe. Lupita loves to tell the stories of her life.

Even though she hasn't lived in Mexico since she was eighteen, Lupita's Spanish is impeccable. But her English is unique. I've tried to keep her "voice" as accurate as possible in the written word. When Lupita tells a story, she is a passionate actress performing, and her voice takes on the inflection of each character.

This is the story of how Lupita Tovar was discovered by Hollywood, how she met the love of her life, and how they lived happily ever after. It might sound like a fairy tale, but it's all true. For those of you who weren't lucky enough to hear these stories firsthand, here is Lupita's life. And what a life it has been!

— Pancho Kohner

PART ONE

GOLD WASHING.

MEXICAN PEASANTRY.

The Illustrations by H. Warren, & Engraved by J. Rogers.

BORN UNDER HALLEY'S COMET

My parents named me Guadalupe Natalia Tovar and they called me Lupita, the diminutive of Guadalupe. My Irish mother said that as she was giving birth to me, *dar a luz* (as we say in Spanish), she looked out her window and saw the tail of Halley's Comet. That was in the tropics of Southern Mexico, July 27, 1910. I'll tell you how we got there.

In 1880, my great-grandfather, John W. Slocum, an Irish immigrant, left Michigan in a covered wagon with his two daughters, Lucy and Jenny. John's wife had died and he wanted to start a new life. After a long and tedious journey, they arrived in El Paso, Texas, on the Mexican border. There, John placed his daughters in a Catholic convent school, while he went to work in the silver mines.

A few years later a young friend, John W. Sullivan, paid a visit to the Slocum home, where he met Lucy—it was love at first sight. Though Lucy was only seventeen, they married and headed south over the border to the silver mines in Chihuahua. Their three children, John, Carlos, and my mother, Mary, were born in Mexico. When new, rich, silver deposits were discovered in the state of Oaxaca, they packed up and traveled a thousand miles farther south to the town of Rincón Antonio, which later became known as Matías Romero. From there, John Sullivan often traveled back and forth to El Paso, Texas, where he still had an interest in a silver mine. One time he didn't return. Lucy went looking for him on horseback, all the way back to the border, but she never did find out what had happened to him. Irish Lucy was left alone to raise her three small children as best she could in Matías Romero.

A new railroad line brought commerce to the town, and soon there were several American families living there. At first, Lucy worked nights at the town hospital, but that meant she had to leave her children alone. So, since there were no restaurants in town, and therefore no place for the railroad workers to eat, she started serving meals in her home. Everyone loved Lucy's cooking, especially her American-style lemon pies.

* * *

My father, Egidio Tovar, was born and raised on a hacienda called El Carnero, in Tehuacán, six hundred miles to the northeast. His parents were ranchers. Their children, eight in all, were educated at home by tutors. The Tovars even had their own chapel and a priest, Father Nápoles, living with them. Egidio's sisters—Petra, Virginia, and Margarita—were never allowed to leave the hacienda. The boys were horsemen; the girls learned embroidery and painting, mostly saints for the church.

One morning, quick tempered eighteen-year-old Egidio didn't like the way his shirt had been ironed so he dropped it in a bucket of dirty water.

Wedding of Mary Sullivan and Egidio Tovar, 1909

His mother snapped at him, saying, "Your sister pressed that shirt!"

The argument that followed grew out of hand and Egidio left home. He rode a horse the six hundred miles to Matías Romero, where he found work as an administrator for the new railroad. When Egidio came to Lucy Sullivan's house for his meals, he quickly fell in love with her young, blond, and fair-skinned daughter, Mary.

Egidio's sisters sewed Mary's wedding gown and on August 29, 1909, Father Nápoles came from Tehuacán to perform the marriage ceremony.

One year later I was born: the first of nine children. Three years later, my sister Lucy was born, and a year after that, Guillermo, my first brother; but he died when he was just a few months old. Nine months later, my mother gave birth to my brother Carlos.

When I was five, we moved to the town of Salina Cruz, farther up the coast where my father took over the administration of the hotel by the train station. I remember traveling there in a *carreta* (a two-wheeled cart), with large oxen pulling us.

The hotel had Chinese help, who all had long braids down their backs. The cook was Chinese, too, and since I was always curious, he taught me to eat with chopsticks. We lived in the hotel and I kept a pet armadillo in the yard. One day the cook came running out of the kitchen, waving a large knife and shouting in Chinese. He grabbed me. Then everyone came out to look at the large snake that was dangling from the tree I had been sitting under.

My grandma Lucy had stayed behind in Matías Romero with her sons and her sister Jane, who had married another Irishman named Delahaye. Jane had a daughter and three sons, one of whom they called "Baby" because he was the youngest. The name stuck, so even though his surname changed to Delaha, until the day he died I always called him Tío Baby (Uncle Baby).

* * *

Life was uneventful until my two-year-old brother Carlos died of meningitis; our whole family was devastated. My mother cried and cried. The doctor said it would be good for my mother to take a trip. So, together with my sister Lucy and my Tío Baby, who was now sixteen, we left Salina Cruz by train to visit Grandma. I was delighted. I loved my grandma more than anyone and this would be my first time on a train.

When our train stopped at the town of Santa Lucrecia, the stationmaster came out waving his hands and yelling, "They've kidnapped my son!" He said the rebels had ridden through and there had been wild shooting. "They grabbed my son and took him. He's only fourteen!" This, apparently, was a common occurrence: making boys ride behind them on the same horse, to protect their own backs from bullets.

A revolution had started in Mexico. In the south, where we lived, the fight was led by Emiliano Zapata, whose battle cry was, "It is better to die on your feet than to live on your knees!"

There were soldiers on our train, some riding on the roof, armed and ready to protect us, so nobody was very worried. But, just in case, as our train pulled out of the station, several businessmen came to my mother asking her to put their money in a "safe" place.

We hadn't gone very far when we heard shooting. Racing alongside our train were rebels on horseback, shooting at us! These men were dark from the sun; their skin was like burnt leather. They were naked except for *taparrabos* (black loincloths), leather belts with bullets across their chests, and large sombreros. Mama pulled us down between the seats and lay on top of us. When bullets hit the side of the train making loud *clangs*, I yelled, "I've been hit!" I insisted that I had been shot, but no, I hadn't. It was just the vibrations of bullets that I felt. Our soldiers fired back, adding to the noise. I was afraid, but my heart beat wildly with excitement.

When the rebels finally rode off and our train stopped, the engineer was dead—shot through the eye. A man climbed a telegraph pole but the wires had been cut, so we couldn't send for help. Then one of the soldiers offered to drive the train, but he didn't know how. We went forward and back, and forward again and again. When we finally got to Matías Romero the whole town was at the station; they had heard the shooting in the distance. We stayed there with my grandma Lucy for ten wonderful days.

My uncle John had gone back to El Paso, where he married a girl named Gabriella. Grandma showed me her picture; she was very pretty. My uncle Carlos had married a girl by the name of Dolores Márquez, and moved to Cuba. The next year, when I was seven, Uncle Carlos sent for my grandma and she left to join him in Havana. That was hard for me. My grandma—a strong tall, pioneer woman—was my best friend.

REBELS HANGING BY THEIR NECKS

In Oaxaca there were often earthquakes—bad ones. When the shaking started, I would run out of the house. My sister Lucy never woke up during earthquakes. I remember seeing cows go down on their knees and the earth opening. I've never forgotten those strange sights.

When I was seven, not only did my grandma leave for Cuba, but my father went for a long time to South America on some business venture that had to do with curing hides. He was always very restless. While he was gone, we moved to the edge of town and lived in what had once been the old Sanatorio MacPherson, a clinic that had been replaced by a new hospital in town. We had one half of the building and Mr. Canseco lived in the other half with his two sons who were my age. Mrs. Canseco lived in a little house on the hill above us, where she could watch her family; she had leprosy. The Cansecos owned horses and cows. We children used to put a rope around the middle of a *baccero* (calf); we would climb on and ride bareback until we were thrown off. When my father was there, we weren't permitted to do such things. Things were entirely different when my father was there; he was very strict and wanted Lucy and me to dress properly and stay clean. That meant no playing with the boys and the ranch hands. Also, it seemed that when my father was there my mother was always pregnant. Did I mention that I was the eldest of *nine* children? My newest brother was named Jorgito. Mother was not a very strong woman. Oh, she could draw water from the well and chop wood when needed, but unlike Grandma Lucy, in times of crisis she wasn't very brave or very resourceful.

This was the tropics, and it was very, very hot. Our half of the Sanatorio MacPherson had thick walls of stone on the bottom three feet, and then just chicken wire above to let in the breeze. Whenever Zapatista rebels came, we would first let the horses loose and then we would crawl in a little hole in the granary to hide until we heard a trumpet signaling that the rebels were leaving.

The rebels would often shoot from our house, aiming down at the town. Oddly enough, they never took anything and, foolishly, I wasn't afraid of them. But it must have been dangerous, because as soon as my father came back from South America, we all moved to his family's hacienda in Tehuacán to stay with my aunts.

In preparation for the move, my father sold all of his books except for his favorite, *Don Quijote de la Mancha*. My mother simply gathered our clothes, food, and everything else, in a large sheet and tied the corners together.

We left at two in the morning on an old military train full of soldiers. The train was steam-powered, so we had to stop several times in the dark for wood and water for the boiler. In the morning, our train moved faster; and in daylight we were shocked to see a sight I've never forgotten—Zapatista rebels hanging by their necks from telegraph poles. We counted them until we got to Puebla. I couldn't tear my eyes away. There were dead men as far as I could see.

AUTHOR'S NOTE:

A BRIEF HISTORY OF THE 1910 MEXICAN REVOLUTION

Rebels, *Banditos*, and *Federales* are familiar to us primarily from the movies. Their existence is a consequence of the Mexican Revolution of 1910, a very violent time in Mexico. To put things in some perspective:

The dictator Porfirio Díaz was president of Mexico. The distribution of land as prescribed in the revolution led by Benito Juárez that freed Mexico from the French in 1868 had not succeeded. The peasants still sought control of their land.

In 1910, Emiliano Zapata, a sharecropper in the Cuautla Valley of southern Mexico, began his agrarian revolt, in an effort to help the peasants claim their land. His rallying cry was: "*¡Tierra y Libertad!*" (Land and Freedom.) Zapata led a peasant army to fight the government of President Porfirio Díaz.

In 1911, Francisco Madero's revolutionary army captured the important border town of Ciudad, Juárez. Madero then marched his army south. President Díaz surrendered, recognizing imminent defeat, and Madero triumphantly entered Mexico City and assumed the presidency.

In 1912, President Madero sent General Victoriano Huerta to put down a revolt in the northern state of Chihuahua. The ex-president, Porfirio Díaz, who lived out his days in France, was sentenced to death for treason. His nephew Félix Díaz then started a revolt in the port city of Veracruz.

In February of 1913, Félix Díaz's army attempted a coup in Mexico City.

President Madero quickly appointed General Victoriano Huerta to command the loyalist troops and defend the presidential palace, which Huerta did only because he intended to become president himself.

In the midst of this tumult, United States Ambassador Henry Lane Wilson stepped in and negotiated a settlement. General Huerta assumed power; Madero was placed under arrest and the next day was shot "while trying to escape." The result was a full-fledged civil war.

The northern states revolted, and Governor Venustiano Carranza declared himself chief of the Constitutional Army. In Chihuahua, the assassination of the local governor left a power vacuum, which was quickly filled by Francisco (Pancho) Villa, owner of a butcher shop. In Sonora, the governor appointed Álvaro Obregón as chief of military operations, with fierce Yaqui Indians as the backbone of his army.

In April of 1914, President Woodrow Wilson ordered the landing of eight hundred marines in Veracruz to protect American interests. At the same time Pancho Villa's northern division defeated General Huerta's National Army at Zacatecas. Huerta resigned and fled into exile. Carranza and Obregón triumphantly entered Mexico City in August 1914, and the U.S. forces departed Veracruz in November. When a new civil war erupted, Zapata joined Villa. Their armed peasant masses expelled Carranza and Obregón from Mexico City, and Carranza withdrew to Veracruz.

In 1915, Obregón routed Pancho Villa's army near Celaya, in the bloodiest battle of Mexican history. Zapata's army then left Mexico City, and the United States recognized Carranza's government as the ruling party.

In 1916, Félix Diaz attempted yet another revolution.

In 1917, a new constitution was adopted which addressed ownership of property and protection of wage earners. Carranza took an oath to obey this new constitution. A year later, on his way to Veracruz, he was ambushed and assassinated in the mountains near Puebla.

Zapata was shot by Mexican federal troops in 1919. Today, he remains a folk hero in Mexico.

It was during this turbulent time that Lupita Tovar began her fascinating life.

3

A HACIENDA IN TEHUACÁN

We lived for eight months at El Carnero, the Tovar family hacienda in Tehuacán, which is in the state of Puebla. I missed the heat and rain of the South, but the hacienda was heaven. The kitchen had a high ceiling and brick stoves that burned charcoal. My aunts made marmalade from their own fruit trees in huge copper pots. In a smaller room they made butter and cheese. The main room was enormous, with huge, intricately carved doors.

There were horses and cows and goats. The *vaqueros* would help me onto a horse with no saddle, just a rope bridle. I was seven years old and had the freedom to run and explore all over the ranch. That was heaven!

My father was the youngest of eight children. His mother's name was Guadalupe Cid; I was named after her. She had Spanish blood, and so did my grandfather, Atanasio Tovar; they both died before I could meet them. I inherited my mother's pale Irish skin and my father's very dark hair. As a child, I only knew my aunts and two of their four brothers, Uncle Ramón and Uncle Arturo.

My aunts taught me needlework. Eager to learn, I always felt I was their favorite. On Sundays we went to our own small church. My sister and I dressed all in white and we took spring flowers. When neighbors joined us at Mass, my Aunt Margarita, who had a marked face from small pox, would cover her face with a veil. My three aunts never married, but many years later I found out that Virginia had an illegitimate child, a son named Jorge.

My father could not find work in town, so after several months he had me write a letter to Hazel King Cabrera, an American childhood friend of my mother's from Matías Romero. Hazel was now living in Mexico City, the Distrito Federal, and was married to the general manager of the National Railway Co. My father was too proud to ask for a job himself, so he dictated the letter to sound as though it were coming from me. He got an immediate reply to come to the capital. Father left first to find a place for us to live, and then we joined him.

Lucy, Grandmother, Mother, Jorgito, and Lupita, age eight

A DIRT FLOOR AND NO RUNNING WATER

I was eight when we arrived in the capital, the Distrito Federal, in 1918. After the heat and humidity of the tropics, the change in temperature was a big shock. The capital is at eight thousand feet, and it was a bitterly cold winter. Father was at the station with an automobile and driver from the railway company. As we drove through the city, there was a loud *bang* and I dove for the floor. As it turned out, it was just a backfire.

Father had rented a very small house on Calle de Minería. It had a dirt floor, no furniture, not even running water. At first, we children slept huddled together on the floor, covered with newspapers to keep warm. Lucy was five and Jorgito was two. He died that winter.

My mother was soon pregnant again and, to my delight, she sent for Grandma Lucy. I had missed my grandma terribly. She always had time for me and had the patience to answer my many questions. Grandma returned from Cuba to help, but the baby, named Egidio after my father, died of diphtheria when he was only eleven days old.

Four brothers had died; that was heartbreaking. I must have wondered at how fragile life was. My mother was constantly telling us, "Don't drink the water!" Everything had to be boiled. Diphtheria, meningitis, undulant fever from raw milk, and dysentery from bad water were the primary killers of children. Childhood death was a fact of life, and the small, white, horse-drawn children's hearse was a common sight.

A year later, my uncle Carlos and his wife came back from Cuba. As soon as they returned, Father borrowed money from Carlos and they started a hat business. We moved to a better house on Patriotismo Street; that was where my sister Lucy strangled five kittens that I had rescued from the street. She did it with a cord. I couldn't believe it. I ran to my grandma, crying; I was devastated. That night, when my father found out, all he said was he was glad to be rid of them.

After the hat business didn't work out, my father went into local politics. He was sort of like a ward heeler, a salaried bureaucrat working to get out the vote, even though there was really just one political party.

My father owned a gun, a big *pistola*. He would often get drunk at a cantina with the other politicians and when he came home he would open a window and start shooting. If he heard a noise on the roof at night, he would lean out the window and shoot. The noise was probably just a cat, but he took pleasure in shooting his gun, and he made me learn to shoot, too. "Since you are the oldest, you will learn," he said.

In the backyard, he showed me how to load the *pistola* and hold it with two hands. It was heavy. I shot at the fence and sometimes missed. The neighbors never complained. This was Mexico, after all: everyone had guns.

At home, my father liked to say, "Right or wrong, I am the law here!" There was no reasoning with him. My mother told me that when my father was courting her in Salina Cruz, he shot her dog! That would have been enough for me to say "Get the hell out of here!"

* * *

When I was ten years old, my sister and I went to our first real school, the Fray Pedro de Gante Catholic School, which was run by nuns. Until then, we had been tutored at home. My father had a horrible habit: He would ask us, "What did you learn today?" If we didn't answer quickly enough, he would hit us on the side of the head. So, to avoid that, oh boy, I had to be alert. If father got mad at us, Lucy would cry or faint and fall on the floor. I always had a very good memory; I could read a page and recite it back to you, word for word. But my sister had a terrible memory and she always had difficulty with her schoolwork. Once, I stood outside the classroom window and gave her answers to an important test.

It rained a lot in the capital. We often ran home from school, soaking wet. One night Father came home with a roll of white rubber sheeting, the kind used on hospital beds. He told our Aunt Antonia, who was staying with us, "You are such a good dressmaker—make the children raincoats." They were terribly ugly things, capes with pointed hoods. We had to wear them on the long walk to school and boys used to taunt us along the way. We tried to hide our faces beneath the hoods; we were so embarrassed.

Years later, a man approached me at a party and said, "Lupita, you don't know me, but you and your sister used to pass by my house on the way to school wearing your white raincoats with the pointed hats. We called you the Ku Klux Klan and you threw sticks and stones at us." I had a good laugh at the memory, but it wasn't funny back then.

* * *

Now that father was a *político* working for the government, my father had a fancy car and a driver. He liked to show off. He thought he was a big shot, but he still came home drunk most nights, sometimes vomiting outside the front door. We called it *cantando el guacaro* (singing the *guacaro*), because that's what it sounded like.

The next year we moved to San Pedro de los Pinos, across the street from my aunt Jenny and my great-aunt Jenny, who was my grandma Lucy's sister. Our new house had a wood floor but no real bathroom—just a small room with a hole in the ground and a little kitchen outside. Saturday was bath day. My mother would pump water from a well and heat it over coals. We sat in a tub while she poured it over us. I didn't know any other way, so I didn't mind.

5

"SOME DAY I'LL DANCE ON THAT STAGE"

My father had strict ideas about raising girls. We were not allowed to play outside, not even sports. When he wasn't there, I danced to the music on the radio. I used to dance with a broom while cleaning the house. The radio was our key to the outside world.

When I was thirteen or fourteen, I saw a picture in the newspaper of a beautiful woman wearing an elegant hat. So I chased a chicken, caught it, and pulled off its tail feathers. Then I made a cardboard hat and covered it with the chicken feathers. I thought it was beautiful, almost as beautiful as the one the woman wore in the ad.

Father was always making fun of me, ridiculing me, and this time was no exception. Seeing me in the elaborate makeshift hat, he called me "Empress Carlota."[1]

Whenever the trash collector came by our house, shouting and pushing his handcart, my father would yell, "*Emperatriz*, your carriage is here!" That hurt.

One day I took the streetcar with my mother and Lucy down the Avenida Juárez to the *zócalo*, the central plaza with its cathedral, National Palace, and shops that sold cloth and thread. As we passed the magnificent new Palacio de Bellas Artes, I said to my sister, "You see that? Some day I'll be famous and I'll dance on that stage."

My mother's friend, Hazel Cabrera, had a car and driver. She would sometimes take us with her when she did her shopping. And on special occasions, like a birthday, she would take us to Sanborn's on Avenida Juárez for lunch and a delicious Lady Baltimore cake. Sanborn's was where Pancho Villa used to go for an ice cream sundae, his favorite treat.

I was industrious at an early age. We were only allowed two pairs of shoes for the whole year. When our shoes had holes in them, we filled the holes with cardboard. So, I used to collect medicine bottles from the trash in the neighborhood. I'd wash them and sell them back to the pharmacy for two *centavos* each. I sold old newspapers for ten *centavos* a kilo. I saved my money until I had enough to buy myself a new pair of shoes. I never thought of myself as poor; there were a lot of people in the city with less than we had.

The nuns taught me how to do beautiful needlework. I made lace and intricately beaded embroidery with a needle and I became so good, I won first prize in needlework at school. I made all my own clothes by hand, even my underwear! I knitted a shawl for my grandma and she loved it so much she saved it forever. I was always sewing. Later on, I was even able to knit lovely dresses. I still love hats and shoes; nice shoes have always been my big weakness.

On Sundays, when we went to Mass, I got to wear my best dress, which, of course, my mother had made. We were devout Catholics, and on Christmas Eve I would walk to church with my

---

1   Carlota and Austrian Maximilian von Habsburg ruled Mexico in 1864.

grandma for midnight Mass. My family was strict. We never knew what mood my father would be in when he came home. In the evening, when we heard his key in the lock, we would all stand at attention. We didn't go to movies much, only once in a great while when we would get permission from my grandma. Of course, the movies were in black and white and had no sound, but they showed me a world that I didn't know.

On my fifteenth birthday, my father stumbled in very drunk with the musicians from a cantina. He snapped his fingers at my mother and told her to serve them dinner. I don't know what came over me, but I was tired of seeing my father drunk and bullying my mother. I stood up from the table and said, "My mother is no slave!" He stared at me, swayed a little bit, and snatched a glass from the table, aiming to throw it at me.

"Go ahead! Go ahead and hit me!" I screamed at the top of my lungs.

His face went white; he couldn't believe what had come out of my mouth. He put the glass down and left the house without saying a word. He stopped drinking for a while after that. And my mother treated me with more respect, too. She had just given birth to my sister Sarita and needed my help more than ever.

For my sixteenth birthday, my mother wanted to have my picture taken. My father didn't want to pay for that, but my mother insisted. She took me to have my hair done, and then we went to the photographer. Afterwards, my sister Lucy and I went to church. We were so busy talking we didn't notice that Pepe Ocaranza had been watching our house and had followed us.

Pepe had a crush on me. He was always waiting outside our girls' school, just standing at the side, waiting for me to come out. He was the son of our family doctor. I thought Pepe was kind of cute. He always wore clothes that were a little too big for him. On the way home from school the Ocaranzas' maid would slip me notes from Pepe that I would hide behind a picture on the wall. But my mother found them and threatened, "*¡Te voy acusar con tu Papá!*" (I'm going to tell your father!)

Pepe knew it was my birthday. When we went into the church, he sat behind me. When we left, he still followed us. A few blocks from my house, I turned and he was right there. We gazed at each other for a moment, too scared to speak. Then we shyly said good-bye. That was the first time I had talked to him.

When Lucy and I came home, there was my father, waiting. I had barely closed the door when, without saying a word, he hit me. I mean, he punched me with his fist and knocked me to the floor. As usual, when my father lost his temper, Lucy fainted in a dead heap.

"Where were you?" he shouted. I wasn't given a chance to explain; before I could get up, he took off his belt and beat me with it. My mother was behind him, not saying a word. I curled up and protected my face with my hands. He had used his belt on me before, but this time he used the end with the buckle. My grandma came running and stopped him and helped me up. I could hardly stand.

Then he threw me out of the house.

"*Go*—get out! Get out of this house!" he shouted, shoving me toward the door.

But Grandma Lucy stood there, blocking him, and yelled back at him, "If she goes, *I* go!" He looked at her and knew that she meant it.

All this was because a girl, Rogelia, had told lies about me. My uncle and his wife had adopted this girl, who always wanted to go with us wherever we went. But this time I had said, "No." When my father came home and asked where I was, Rogelia had answered, "She must be with her sweetheart."

I couldn't walk for two weeks. I had to be taken to be examined by Dr. Ocaranza, Pepe's father. My back still had big welts.

"How did Lupita get hurt like this?" he asked, as he examined my marked back.

My mother said quietly, "She fell down the stairs." I couldn't even look at her.

"No," he said. "I don't believe that. This girl has been beaten, brutally, and I must notify the police." So my mother started to cry and pleaded, "Please don't do that; don't say anything." She grabbed his arm and said, "I promise; it won't happen again."

He paused, and then said, "If this happens again, the police have to be notified."

Nothing changed. If I forgot to do a chore, my mother would warn me, "I will tell your father, I will tell your father," and the minute he came in, she started telling him all the things I had or had not done. I had not swept the floor, I had not hung the laundry and so on, nothing really bad, but he would still get angry. He never used words—just his hands. I started to think that maybe I wasn't his daughter. My friends' parents didn't treat them like this.

* * *

There was a big change in my life when one morning I was told that I didn't have to go to school that day.

"Why?" I asked.

"The school is closed," is all my mother would say. My sister and I just stared at each other. We wanted to go to school. School was the best part of our day.

All the priests and nuns disappeared. It was so strange not to be able to go into a church. When my sister Mary was born, she had to be baptized in a hut in a village where a priest was hiding.

AUTHOR'S NOTE:

"THE PERSONAL ENEMY OF GOD"

In the 1920s, the political power and vast wealth of the Catholic Church promoted within Mexico an anticlericalism of unprecedented ferocity. Mexico may be a land where barefooted Indian women burn candles and offer gifts to figures of *La Virgen Morena* (the Dark Virgin), but it is also the land where churches were burned, where priests hid for their lives, and where a powerful, half-crazed state governor had cards printed describing himself as "The Personal Enemy of God."

This governor, Tomás Garrido Canabal of Tabasco, was supported by—and his activities were legitimized by—an even more powerful man—President Plutarco Elías Calles, who held office between 1924 and 1928, and then ruled through puppet presidents until 1934.

President Calles was inaugurated on November 30, 1924, and quickly plunged Mexico into a severe religious crisis. Calles and the federal government were against the worldly power of the Catholic Church and opposed its influence over Mexican people. The 1917 Constitution had outlawed monastic orders, prohibited religious organizations from owning property, and reduced clergy to the status of second-class citizens by taking away their right to vote.

President Calles now was determined to eliminate every trace of Catholicism from Mexico. On June 14, 1926, he signed a decree designed to put teeth in the constitutional articles; it spelled out in specific terms the penalties for violations. Among them: five hundred pesos for wearing clerical garb and five years imprisonment for criticizing the laws or inducing a minor to join a monastic order. In retaliation, the clergy, with the backing of the Vatican, closed the churches.

The trouble came when President Calles attempted to enforce the laws in strongly Catholic west-central Mexico, particularly the state of Jalisco. This triggered the terrible 1926–29 Cristero War. Shouting their battle cry, "¡*Viva Cristo Rey!*" (Long live Christ the King!), a motley assortment of ranchers, Catholic students, workers from Guadalajara, and Indians from Jalisco's north held off President Calles's federal army for three years. More than 56,000 soldiers died, and 30,000 civilian and Cristero lives were lost.

In 1934, Calles backed the presidential candidacy of Lázaro Cárdenas, who proved to be both the most honest and the most radical president in Mexican history. Now rich and increasingly corrupt, Calles soured on land reform, calling the Revolution a "political failure." Guessing that Calles wanted to remove him, Cárdenas struck first. On April 9, 1936, he had Calles arrested and dumped over the Texas border.

Later, Calles was allowed to return to

Mexico by President Manuel Ávila Camacho, Cárdenas' moderate successor. Calles lived quietly in Mexico City until his death in 1945, at the age of sixty-eight. As if to symbolize the decline of rabid anticlericalism that had gripped Mexico in the heyday of Calles and Garrido, and The Personal Enemy of God; the new president, Manuel Ávila Camacho, publicly announced that he was a religious believer.

President Calles is best remembered as the founder of the Partido Nacional Revolucionario, the party that went on to rule Mexican politics for seventy years.

In 1926, with the church-run schools closed, Lupita went to a non-parochial school. It was there that her prayers were answered.

6

DISCOVERED BY HOLLYWOOD

We moved again, this time to a house near the Jardín Pombo in San Pedro de los Pinos. From there it took my sister Lucy and me one hour to walk to our new school, the Parque Lira. We would watch the streetcar pass us by, but we never had any money to ride. Since it was too far to walk home at noon, we brought our lunch, a *bolillo* (a roll), with a scrambled egg inside, and an apple. We sat under the trees in the park and had a picnic with our friends, Julia and Clemencia Martínez. We talked about our dreams for the future; Lucy, Julia, and Clemencia all wanted husbands; I wanted to dance.

The Parque Lira School remained open because it was not run by priests and nuns. Our lessons now included dancing and rhythmic gymnastics; we hadn't had these activities with the sisters. I loved the change. From then on I wanted to be a dancer. It never crossed my mind to be an actress; my earliest desire was to dance. Dancing made me feel free!

* * *

In 1928, during a school vacation, I read in the newspaper, *El Universal Illustrado*, that a movie director from Hollywood, Mr. Robert J. Flaherty, was coming to Mexico City. He was in charge of a contest, in which the winner would receive a contract with Fox Film Studios. I don't know why, but I kept the paper.

When we returned to school after our ten-day vacation, I was rushing from the classroom to change for gymnastics and dance class when I bumped into the school principal, Mrs. Kraus. She was standing with two American men, who looked slightly uncomfortable and out of place. I excused myself, terribly embarrassed, and kept on running. But Mrs. Kraus called me back and introduced me. The visitors smiled politely. One of them took my hand and examined both sides, saying something to the other man that I did not understand. Then I rushed to my locker to change into my black bloomers, white sailor blouse, long black stockings and tennis shoes.

The whole school was already assembled when I got to the gymnasium. The girls were standing alertly in rows.

"Lupita, please move to the front," Mrs. Chafino, our physical education teacher, said firmly. I was one of her best pupils. When I danced I always imagined myself as a beautiful ballerina, floating through the air. I took the lead. "Girls, do your very best. We have foreign visitors," Mrs. Chafino announced as she moved to the sidelines.

I glanced around, looking for the visitors. Mrs. Kraus was approaching with the Americans who smiled broadly when they spotted me.

My hips usually swayed from side to side when I walked. I didn't really realize how it looked; it was just natural for me. Now, each time I passed in front of the visitors with my walk, they made comments to each other and smiled at me. Bertha, the girl behind me, understood English, so she started to tease me.

"These are very rich oil men from Texas who are looking for a wife," she said. "Next they will look at your teeth like they do when they buy a horse."

A couple of days later my father received a telegram from the principal of the school requesting that he come to her office to discuss something about me.

We were having our *merienda* (a light supper), when my mother silently handed my father the telegram. My father exploded! He demanded, "What have you done? What kind of trouble are you in?" I opened my mouth to speak, but nothing came out. "I will not be embarrassed!" he said. "Your mother will go and find out what this is about!" He got up from the table without eating, slamming doors on his way out. My father wasn't tall but he was imposing; he carried himself like a spring, wound tight even when he wasn't mad.

That night as I was falling asleep, my father came into my room and started yelling at me again, "Tell me the truth, what have you done?!"

Grandma came to my rescue. "Leave the girl alone!" she said. "What is it with you people that you always think the worst?"

The next day my mother walked with me to school, clutching my hand tightly. I was carrying my one-month-old sister, Mary. We walked in silence, like we were going to a funeral. I kept telling myself, "My grades are very good. I have nothing to fear."

We walked up the long driveway of the Parque Lira. When we got to the top, my whole class was outside making so much noise I could not understand what they were saying. I led my mother to Mrs. Kraus's office; then I went outside with the baby to see what was going on. My classmates ran up to me, excitedly saying, "Don't you know? You're going to Hollywood to be a movie star!" I held the baby closer, my mouth open in shock.

Moments later I was summoned back to the office. My mother was crying. Mrs. Kraus took my arm and sat me down. I handed the baby to my mother and smoothed my skirt. "Your mother feels very bad that you had such a hard time at home yesterday," Mrs. Kraus said. "She has explained to me how your father reacted to our telegram." Mrs. Kraus reassured my mother, saying, "Lupita is a wonderful girl, first in her class. You have nothing to worry about with this girl." Stern Mrs. Kraus had a twinkle in her eye. "Lupita, our American visitor last week, Mr. Flaherty, is a film director from Fox Studios in Hollywood. He wants permission from your parents to make a screen test of you. He will also test two other girls from this school. A teacher will accompany you and, of course, your mother, if she wants to go."

We walked back home where my father was already waiting, looking very serious, his jaw clenched in anger. I walked past him with my eyes downcast, and I took the baby to the bedroom to change her diaper. My heart was beating so fast, I could hardly concentrate. When I went to the table, lunch was waiting, and so was my father.

"What is this all about?" He had changed his tone since my mother had told him about the interview.

"I think it's about a contest," I said, and went to get the newspaper I had kept.

He read it carefully; then placed the paper on the table. He looked at me hard and said, "Do you want to do this test?"

"I would like to see how they make movies," I said, trying not to sound too eager.

"Well, if your mother goes with you, I have no objection."

That was it, he had decided. He started eating, and I was too happy to say anything.

The next morning I awoke early. I was already waiting for my mother by the door when she got up. We walked again to the Parque Lira. I was a few steps ahead of her, willing her to hurry. When we arrived at school, we were taken by car to a film studio in Chapultepec. It was really just an empty warehouse with broken windows. Once there, the other girls and I were ushered into a room, where a man put makeup on us and fixed our hair. When I looked in the mirror, I hardly recognized myself.

I looked older and sophisticated. I wondered what Pepe would think if he saw me like this. I knew instinctively my father would not approve.

We were taken into a big room, where there were bright lights and a large camera on a tripod. Ernest Palmer was the cameraman. I found out later he had photographed *7th Heaven* and *Street Angel* in Hollywood. Contrary to his name, his assistant, Stanley Little, was a very tall man.

A handsome Mexican gentleman, Manuel Reachi, was the interpreter. He was a writer and film producer who had been married to Agnes Ayres, Rudolph Valentino's co-star in *The Sheik*. Later, Manuel Reachi married Carmen López Figueroa, whose family owned the newspaper, *El Excelsior*.

Mr. Flaherty directed the screen test: "Turn left, turn right—you are happy and excited. That's it! Now you're very sad." He had me cry by telling me that my mother had died! He had me fix flowers in a vase and then filmed a close-up of my hands; he was fascinated with my hands. They looked like everyone else's hands to me, but even Mr. Palmer, the cameraman, commented on them.

Then they wanted me to put on a bathing suit. My mother didn't want to allow that, but they calmed her down, saying they would send everyone out of the room. They had several bathing suits to choose from; my mother chose the biggest, ugliest one. When I came out of the dressing room wearing just the bathing suit, my mother got angry again and shooed the remaining people out. Mr. Flaherty told me what to do and then he had to go out of the room, too. The cameraman had a black cloth over the camera and himself so he could only see me through the lens. My mother was very old-fashioned, even for 1928.

When we finished, Mr. Flaherty seemed pleased. Manuel Reachi said, "Well, kid, I may see you in Hollywood." Everything was moving so fast, I didn't know what to think. The next day at school, my friends asked me a thousand questions. I had to describe in detail what had happened.

Two weeks went by and my life had returned to normal. Then one evening my father came home late. He looked very serious. He took off his coat and pulled out a document from his pocket. He put it down on the dining-room table and said a Mr. Ben Logan from Fox Studios had come to his office with this contract. Mr. Logan had told my father that several thousand girls had been interviewed, sixty-five girls had been given screen tests, and I had won first prize. I had been chosen to go to Hollywood. I was stunned! My mouth felt dry. I could barely swallow.

"Go ahead and read it. You may have the satisfaction of knowing you won, but I'm sending it back." I didn't believe what I was hearing. He couldn't have meant that.

I took the contract to my room and carefully read the Spanish translation. It was a contract for seven years with an option every six months, starting at one hundred and fifty dollars a week! My father didn't make that in a year! I could not sleep that night, thinking this was a chance in a lifetime—maybe I could become a star! But I knew only a miracle could help me with my father. Once his mind was made up he never changed it, and I had been taught to obey him without question.

In the morning, my father left without saying a word. I went to school with a heavy heart; I felt like I was going to die. I told my friends and teachers what had happened—that my father was returning the contract. They could not believe that he would do such a thing. Everybody gave me advice, but I knew it was useless. There was nothing I could do. My father was in control of my life; if I had been a boy, things might have been different.

The next few weeks were awful. If I was slow doing my chores, my father would say, "Wake up, Gloria Swanson, you are not in Hollywood." I had to fight back tears. Some of the girls at school teased me, asking, "When are you going to Hollywood?" and "Did your contract arrive yet?"

The contract had arrived, my father had rejected it, and that was that.

We moved again, this time to a house that belonged to some relatives at Venecia 19, in the Colonia Juárez. The house was nicer, but I didn't care; I was still so disappointed by my father's decision.

It was the end of September, and it was still very hot. At times I felt like I couldn't breathe. This was my last year of school. Afterwards, I would be expected to stay in the house, take care of the younger children, cook and mend socks. My father would never allow me to get a job outside of the house. My father did not even allow us to have friends.

7

"I AM MISS TOVAR"

A few weeks later, my father was late coming home again. When we sat down to dinner he had an announcement. Fox had sent a second contract, this time offering to pay an additional twenty-five dollars a week for a companion. I couldn't believe it. There was also a letter from Alfonso Pesqueira, the consul of Mexico in Los Angeles, urging my father to reconsider: "Your daughter has been chosen to represent Mexico in the United States. This is quite an honor for her, to represent her country."

Father's friends told him that that this was an opportunity for me to learn English and, if it didn't work out, I would be back home in six months. That convinced him.

He handed me the contract and said, "If I don't say anything in the morning when I leave the house, you can sign it."

I put the contract under my pillow and lay awake for hours, praying for a miracle. The next morning I got up very early and set the table for breakfast. My father came downstairs and didn't even say good morning. I held my breath as I brushed his hat and handed it to him as I did every morning. After I closed the door behind him, I thought I was going to faint. My mother started to cry. All I could think about was signing that paper!

At one o'clock the doorbell rang. I opened the door while holding my baby sister in my arms. There was a well-dressed man at the door, a lawyer from Fox Studios. He introduced himself, "I'm Roberto Bell, from Fox Studios. Is Miss Tovar in?"

"I am Miss Tovar," I said, promptly. I knew I looked really young in my school uniform.

"No," he said, "your older sister."

"I am the oldest," I insisted.

"Please call your mother," he said, sounding unsure of himself.

My mother came to the door. She was shaking. "She is the oldest," she whispered.

"My God, she is only a child," Mr. Bell said under his breath. He shook his head. "Well, I have a contract for you to sign."

Grandma went with us into the dining room, where I sat at the table and put my name on several papers.

"When would you like to leave?" Mr. Bell asked, smoothing back his thinning hair. Mr. Bell was far from good looking, but to me he looked like a Greek god.

"As soon as possible," I said. "Before my father changes his mind."

"Who will go with you?" he asked. My grandma spoke up, in a strong voice, "*I* will."

"Well, today is the thirteenth of November. You'll need time for a passport and your wardrobe." He handed me three hundred dollars in cash and said, "I will notify the studio you'll be leaving by train on the nineteenth, arriving on the twenty-second. You'll be met in Los Angeles by the studio people. Good-bye and good luck."

My father must have been waiting around the corner, because two seconds later he came in. I handed him the money. He counted it and put it in his pocket.

"I need a passport," I said.

"And she needs proper clothes," my grandma added.

"We'll go after lunch," he said, and headed for the dining room.

He took me to the *lagunilla* (the flea market), where everything was stolen and cheap. He bought a dress that was too big and too mature for me, a pair of shoes, a hat that made me look like a fireman, and a pair of silk stockings; that was my wardrobe.

When we came home my mother looked through the purchases and said, "She needs a coat!"

I will never forget the coat she gave me. It was a peculiar shade of brown with spots, but I didn't say anything. Everything went into a small bag, with my underwear and two cotton dresses from school. It wasn't much, but I was ready to go!

My mother's friend, Hazel King Cabrera, was very fond of me. She arranged for my grandmother and me to travel on her husband's private Pullman car to the border, where we would transfer to an American Pullman car. With the influence of Mr. Cabrera, my grandmother and I would be well taken care of.

Even as we boarded the train and waved good-bye to my family, I was still worried that my father would change his mind. As the wheels started to turn, steam was released; it sounded to me like *escape, escape*.

Pepe had heard that I was leaving and managed to sneak on board without my father seeing him. He found us in our private Pullman car. He said he wanted to see me once more, to say good-bye. It was awkward. He looked so sad and Grandma was watching us. "Good-bye, Pepe," I said, quietly. When he got off at the next station on the outskirts of the city, I was very confused. I was excited to be leaving, but I knew I was giving up something, too.

Now, as we headed north, the powerful locomotive picked up speed. We were flying like the wind, and as I looked out the window, my heart was racing; I felt like I was riding a horse at full gallop.

* * *

It took us three days to get to Ciudad Juarez, across the border from El Paso, Texas. El Paso was where Grandma had married John W. Sullivan, thirty-five years earlier. My grandma was a sturdy, capable woman, but she didn't talk much. She hadn't spoken English in many years; now she was especially quiet.

An eager young man whom my father knew met our train and helped us through customs. Then he helped us board our train to Los Angeles. This time we had just a tiny compartment with beds that folded down from the wall. I was mesmerized as I looked out the window. In New Mexico, we crossed over the Continental Divide. That night we saw the lights of Tucson, Arizona, and early the next morning we passed over the Colorado River into California. First there was desert, then, as we got closer to Los Angeles, there were miles and miles of orange groves. When we stopped in San Bernardino, we bought oranges at the station; they smelled and tasted like heaven.

8

"MY PERSONAL SANTA CLAUS"

December 1, 1928, when our train arrived in Los Angeles, no one was there to meet us. We were close to Lincoln Park, the birthplace of the City of Angels, where Spanish was still the common language, but we had no idea where we were. We were alone and lost. We waited for about an hour, watching the station empty out.

Finally I said, "*¿Abuelita, que hacemos?*" (Grandma, what do we do?)

She said, "Well, you have the contract."

There were several taxis parked in front of the station but Grandma was very shy, and I couldn't speak a word of English. I took out my studio contract and showed it to a cab driver. The driver nodded; we got in the car and he drove us to Sunset and Western, to the Fox Studios. My father had given us a little money, so I paid the driver.

We must have looked terribly out of place as we went into the offices with our suitcases. I went to the front desk with my contract. The receptionist looked at it and said, "Just a minute. Take a seat." She pointed to a bench, so we sat down and waited. We watched as people came and went, and after what seemed like a long time, my name was called. I showed another girl my contract. She took one long look at me and then disappeared. She returned with Mr. Jimmy Ryan, who was the casting director. He introduced himself and talked to my grandma. He had gone to meet us, but his car had broken down on the way. When he finally got to the station, we were already gone. He was very apologetic. And he was terribly pleased that my grandma was Irish and spoke English.

Mr. Ryan showed us into his office and, after a few minutes, a Mrs. Bauer came in. She was going to be my interpreter. She spoke some Spanish, but not very well. We were taken to another building to meet the president of Fox Studios, Mr. Winfield Sheehan. He was a big man, older and serious looking; he couldn't hide his surprise when he saw my young face. Then he held my hands and said, "Well, I recognize these hands." He was fascinated with my hands. Then he studied my face again and seemed pleased with what he saw. "Would you like to see your screen test?" he asked. Mrs. Bauer translated for me.

"Yes, please," I answered. I was curious to see how I looked onscreen.

Mrs. Bauer took us to a small projection room, where I sat next to my grandma. The lights went out and the test came on the screen. With makeup, different clothes, and a lace mantilla over my head, I didn't recognize myself. I looked very sophisticated. The test was long; I blushed, I laughed, I got angry, I turned this way and that. I did everything Mr. Flaherty instructed me to do. In the end, he had even filmed a close-up of my hands, which apparently made an impression on Mr. Sheehan.

After watching the test, Grandma and I were taken to the St. Francis Hotel on Hollywood Boulevard. It was a very fancy place, not at all like the Hotel Salina Cruz that my father used to manage.

At the hotel, Grandma received a beautiful bouquet of flowers from Mr. Sheehan. She and I had dinner in the coffee shop downstairs and went to bed early, exhausted. The next day I was picked up by Mrs. Bauer and taken downtown to a dentist to have my teeth checked. The studio was very thorough; I guess they wanted to make sure they got their money's worth.

These men—Jimmy Ryan, Mr. Sheehan, and everyone else at Fox—looked very American to me, but I found out they were all Irish! That explained why they were so nice to my grandma, Lucy Sullivan.

* * *

Robert J. Flaherty, who discovered me and brought me to Hollywood, is often called the father of documentary filmmaking. He is best known for directing and photographing *Nanook of the North*, a classic film about Canadian Eskimos. To this day, I say a silent prayer to Mr. Flaherty, my personal "Santa Claus."

Ilustrado magazine, Lupita Tovar, 1928

9

ARRIVING IN A FAIRY TALE

Going to the studio was like stepping into a fairy tale. At noon in the commissary I saw pirates, Indians, and even ballerinas. There was an aura of mystery and glamour around the actors. They were like something out of a storybook, so beautiful and well dressed. The first stars I met were Charles Farrell, Virginia Valli, Olive Borden, Janet Gaynor, George O'Brien and his wife, Marguerite Churchill. They were all under contract to Fox Studios. They welcomed me and made me feel like I was part of the "family."

The studio had a grooming class for newcomers, and a young woman, Miss McKenna, was assigned to me. She taught me how to walk, enter a room, sit, cross my legs, and how to hold a cup of tea. I was told the public wanted to see a glamorous actress. You always had to look nice, with clothes pressed and makeup and hair done.

They sent a publicity man from the studio who told us: "Actors are in glass houses—always on display. Your public expects you to look your best." He himself was always properly groomed.

Every week I collected a check for one hundred-fifty dollars. Mrs. Bauer, from the studio, took me to the Bank of America and helped me open an account. I kept fifty dollars for Grandma and me to live on and sent the rest to my father in Mexico.

The studio wardrobe department would dress us in gorgeous evening gowns for publicity pictures. If you were a big star and went to a premiere, the opera, or the symphony, the men dressed in white tie. For the ladies, a corsage and a lovely studio dress for a royal entrance and a glamorous exit. Jewelry was loaned to the stars, too. You were told never to play with your hair, never be sloppy, always wear white gloves, and always wear a hat. "You must look like a lady," was the message that was drilled into us.

Quite a few girls were already well groomed. I had no money, but I always managed to look well dressed. I made my own clothes and, for special occasions, I found a cheap dressmaker to copy clothes I had seen in magazines. My dress may have cost fourteen dollars, but I walked as if I wore a thousand-dollar dress. I always wore gloves. We were encouraged to learn by watching the more experienced actors. I taught myself how to put on makeup by watching Janet Gaynor and Mary Astor at the studio. In Mexico, I hadn't even owned a lipstick!

I was now "Miss Tovar." (Nobody ever called you by your first name.)

Even though I wasn't in Mexico to graduate, at the end of the year the Parque Lira School sent me my medals and my high school diploma. My friends had been writing, wanting to know what my life was like in Hollywood. Even Pepe wrote, sending me long romantic letters and poems. Pepe was in love with me, but love was not on my mind at all.

On New Year's Eve of 1928 I was invited to a party by Alfonso Pesqueira, the Mexican consul. He sent a man from his office, Ernesto Romero, to escort me. Ernesto was a very nice man, very polite—and very short. He was the technical advisor for the studios, for whenever a picture mentioned Mexico.

That New Year's Eve was the first time in my life that I went to a party and the first time that I danced with a man! Quite a few men asked me to dance that night. I was not used to so much attention. I sat with the consul and his wife and I met some of the prominent Mexican families of Los Angeles. I had a lovely time. When I got home that night, I tried to describe to Grandma what it was like—the party, the people, the food, and the music. I was so happy, and I could tell she was happy for me.

After the holidays, Grandma and I moved to a small bungalow on Harold Way, which was closer to the studio. Grandma soon made friends with Jacobita Villavicencio, a lady who lived nearby. The two of them got together every afternoon and played a card game called *Malia*, and had coffee afterwards. I went to the studio every day, where I did screen tests for the publicity and makeup departments. During breaks, I would watch all the actors on the set, and tried to mimic their actions.

Mrs. Bauer was supposed to teach me English, but she always talked to me in her broken Spanish. I was, in fact, teaching her more than she was teaching me. Everybody was extremely kind to me. I was walking on air. What a difference this was from my previous life.

I started taking dance lessons with Eduardo Cansino who was from Sevilla, Spain. He and his Irish wife, Volga Hayworth, became my close friends.[2]

The studio had a lot of actors under contract, not just stars. Whenever a new film was announced, there was competition to be assigned any role, no matter how small. I finally got my first role in *Joy Street*, a silent picture with Lois Moran. The story was set in Switzerland in a boarding house that was built on a stage at the studio. My second small part was in *The Veiled Woman* with Lia Torá, an actress from Brazil, and a Russian actor, Ivan Lebedeff, who was very debonair and wore a monocle. As these were silent films, it didn't matter where you were from or what language you spoke.

Just before the end of my six-month option, Mr. Flaherty called and said he would like to see me. He came to visit and told us that he was planning on making a picture in the South Seas, away from the Fox studio. He said he would like to test me, but I couldn't tell anyone.

We did the test one night in a small studio. Two days later he came to see us again and said to my grandma, "The test is very good; Lupita photographs like a million dollars. She is a natural and has an air of innocence—just what I need in this film." He went on to say, "I know Fox will not exercise their option on her. They're using the girls they've brought from Spain and Argentina who are a little older and have established relationships with directors. Just keep quiet and when they notify you that they will not take up their option, I will announce my picture with you. I've had differences with the studio and they wouldn't let me have you if they were aware of what I'm going to do." If what Mr. Flaherty said was true, and the studio did not take up my option, my weekly checks would stop. Grandma and I would have to go home! That thought was terrifying.

On the last day of my contract, late in the afternoon, Mr. Ryan's secretary called me to come to the office. I was prepared to hear bad news, but when I went in, Mr. Ryan asked me nicely, "What's new?"

"Nothing," I said, innocently, "I'm learning English and taking dancing lessons."

He said, "Very good." He opened a folder and pulled out a piece of paper, pointing to a line. "I want you to sign here," he said, his tone warm. "The studio has decided to renew their option and you'll get your next increase in salary. Isn't that great?"

I was surprised, but I said nothing. "We'll find something for you, don't worry," he said. "Next week you'll do a new screen test."

I did this test, but it was a waste of time. The director had already made up his mind to hire a girl from Argentina. She was older than me and did not go around with a chaperone.

---

[2] Their daughter, Margarita Carmen Cansino, grew up to become an actress and changed her name to Rita Hayworth. She was a great beauty and became known as "The Love Goddess."

> May 7, 1929
>
> Miss Guadalupe Tovar,
> Fox Film Corporation,
> Hollywood, California.
>
> Dear Miss Tovar:
>
> This will confirm our mutual agreement entered into on this date whereby Fox Film Corporation agrees to exercise their option for your services and this notice is to be regarded as if same had been served on you on the day and date specified in your contract.
>
> Therefore: In accordance with paragraph Third of contract entered into between you and Fox Film Corporation dated November 3, 1928, we hereby notify you that we are exercising the option granted us for a further period of six months commencing May 19, 1929, in accordance with the terms and conditions specified in said contract.
>
> Will you be good enough to acknowledge receipt of this letter by affixing your signature to copy attached at place designated, and return same to undersigned.
>
> Yours very truly,
> FOX FILM CORPORATION
> by _____
> General Superintendent.
>
> This will acknowledge receipt of the original of this notification, and also confirm our agreement as set out above:
>
> _Guadalupe Tovar_
> _Lucy S Sullivan_

Exercise of option letter. ©1929 Twentieth Century Fox. All rights reserved

Somehow, the studio had found out about Mr. Flaherty's plans and that he had tested me. They renewed my option to get even with him. He chose Raquel Torres from Hermosillo, Mexico, to replace me and go to Tahiti with him. The film, *White Shadows in the South Seas*, won an Academy Award for Best Cinematography.

The studio kept me busy doing makeup tests, and close-ups of my hands were used in a film with Sue Carol and Nick Stuart. My hands became popular before *I* did. When Nick Stuart was making love to Sue Carol in *Girls Gone Wild*, it was *my* hand, not Sue Carol's, he was playing with. I thought my hands were nice, but I still didn't see what was so special about them.

* * *

That summer of 1929, Fox was having a grand opening of a new theater in San Francisco. They were making a big fuss about it and, as we were contract players, they sent Delia Magaña, María

Alba, and me to be part of the festivities. Delia was another girl whom Mr. Flaherty had tested; she had won second prize, but she was soon sent back to Mexico. Maria Alba was from Barcelona, Spain. I was nineteen, but this was the first time I had gone anywhere without my grandma. We went by train with Mrs. Bauer as our chaperone.

Maria Alba, Lupita, and Delia Magaña

On the day of the theater opening there was a huge parade through downtown San Francisco. I was riding in a convertible with Stan Laurel and Oliver Hardy, when I heard somebody shouting, "Lupita! Lupita! ¡Soy tu Tío Baby!" Uncle Baby was running alongside our car! I yelled the name of my hotel to him.

I hadn't seen Tío Baby since I was eight years old. He was with us on the train ten years before, when we had gone to visit my grandma and the rebels had shot at us.

My uncle came to see me at the hotel. He looked older, but he was just as warm and kind as I remembered. He told me he was married to a girl named Frances who was also from Mexico.[3]

Tío Baby and Lucy Sullivan

When I got back from San Francisco, I got a big surprise. There was a large billboard outside the studio announcing the following:

The King of the Khyber Rifles, with newcomer Lupita Tovar.

---

3   Tío Baby raised his family in San Francisco, where he was a social worker. I loved my uncle. He visited often, and sixty years later, when he was dying, my son, Pancho, and I went to say good-bye. We took him a bottle of his favorite scotch. Barely able to lift his head, he smiled and said, "Thank you, I think I'll take this with me."

10

MEETING PAUL KOHNER

Evenings and weekends, Grandma and I would go strolling down Hollywood Boulevard, which was close to our one-bedroom bungalow on Harold Way. We would go to the Pig 'n Whistle, where we always sat at the counter. I would have a strawberry ice cream sundae, and Grandma would have apple pie and coffee.

I soon got a part in Raoul Walsh's silent film, *The Cock-Eyed World*, with Victor McLaglen, Edmund Lowe, and the French actress Lili Damita, who married Errol Flynn. I was enjoying these small roles. I learned a lot by watching the other actors.

Silent pictures were fun because you didn't have to worry about dialogue; you could say anything. We had music on the set to help us get in the mood of the scene. Everybody was happy and enjoying it.

Then in 1929, talking pictures seemed to happen overnight, and everyone was suddenly worried about his or her voice. The studios started bringing in stage actors from New York. Fox Studios had announced, "*The King of the Khyber Rifles,* with Lupita Tovar," but now it was going to be a "talkie." As I couldn't speak English well enough, Myrna Loy got the lead with Victor McLaglen, and I ended up with a very small part. The title was changed to *The Black Watch*. John Ford directed that film.

* * *

For the first six months of my contract, the studio had paid me one-hundred-fifty-dollars a week, and for the last six months the studio paid me one-hundred-seventy-five-dollars a week. That was a lot of money in 1929. But every week I sent most of it home to my father, keeping just enough for my grandma and me to live on. Now I was worried. Acting in talking films was going to be very different, and I wasn't trained. And although I had been trying hard, I could just barely speak English.

To add to my worries, in October the stock market crashed. It seemed like everyone had been investing in stocks, and when the stocks lost their value a lot of people were in serious trouble. There were stories of men committing suicide by jumping out of windows. Soon there were long lines at public soup kitchens. There were men milling about at the studio gate looking for any kind of work they could find. I was worried; I didn't want to think about going back to Mexico, but if the studio didn't pick up my option, I didn't see any other solution.

Jimmy Ryan, the Fox casting director, was a good friend, and he was also worried about me. One day he called me to his office and said, "Lupita, I'm very concerned that your next option will not be taken because we're bringing in people from the theater for talking pictures. Which is a shame because I think you could have a very bright future."

He was very nice about giving me the bad news. But then he said he did know one way I could keep working. "Universal Pictures is dubbing films into Spanish," he said. "I'm going to give you a letter to the man in charge."

The next day I made sure I looked my best. I dressed in my nicest dress, hat, and gloves. Universal Pictures was in the San Fernando Valley. I walked five blocks in my high heels to the streetcar, then, when I got off at Cahuenga Boulevard, I walked several more blocks to the studio on Lankershim Boulevard.

The secretary at the main desk was very pleasant. She took my letter from Jimmy Ryan and told me to wait. I sat quietly in the reception room for a long time.

Men kept passing by, staring at me. One tall, handsome young man went by three times, craning his neck each time to get a look at me. At one point after he walked away, I had a peculiar feeling that somebody was staring at me. I looked around and saw the same man looking at me through the crack of the door. I was very nervous; I didn't like being stared at.

Another man, older and reeking of cigarette smoke, came over and said, "Young lady, how would you like to go to a party tonight?"

"No, thank you, I don't go to parties," I said, looking away from his wandering gaze.

"You'll get one hundred dollars just for going there," he said.

I said, "Thank you, no!" I was starting to get nervous. I wasn't used to getting party invitations from strangers, and this man definitely made me uncomfortable. So, I got up and said to the secretary, "I have to go home now. I'll leave this letter for Mr. Kohner with you. Here is my telephone number, and if you will be so kind, please call me and tell me when I should come back." I got out of the office as fast as I could and walked all the way to Cahuenga to take the streetcar back to Hollywood. My feet hurt, but all I could think about was getting home.

I told Grandma what had happened. "It was scary," I said. "I think we should go home." Grandma said I shouldn't be so quick to decide: "They may call you to come back."

"I won't go back alone," I said.

I called Mrs. Cansino, the wife of my dance teacher, and I asked if she would go to Universal with me if they called.

She said, "Of course, I'll be happy to. I know how frightening it is to go to one of these appointments alone, particularly if you're new to a place."

The very next day I got a call from the secretary at the studio to meet with the head of the Foreign Film Department. The executive wanted to see me at three that afternoon. Mrs. Cansino drove me there.

When we got to the studio, we were given directions and we walked to where there were several bungalows. The lot was bustling, with people everywhere. On the door of one of the bungalows was written, "Foreign Film Department, Paul Kohner." The name meant nothing to me. The secretary showed us right in to Mr. Kohner's office, and I got a shock! The man behind the desk was the same young man who had been staring at me the day before. He stood up and, grinning like a Cheshire cat, said, "Haven't we met before?" "No, sir," I said, promptly. I was shaking; I turned around and whispered to Mrs. Cansino in Spanish, "This is the man I told you about."

Paul Kohner, 1929

AUTHOR'S NOTE:

A YOUNG MAN TO WATCH

Paul Kohner was just as adventurous as Lupita. Paul was born in Teplitz-Schönau, Czechoslovakia, on May 29, 1902. His father, Julius Kohner, published a weekly film magazine, the *Internationale Filmschau*, and opened a movie theater, a *Kino*. He was known as "Kino Kohner." (In Teplitz, it was typical for people to be identified by their profession.) Julius and his wife, Helene, had three sons: Paul, Frederick, and Walter.

Teplitz had excellent schools, an opera house, a symphony orchestra, and a library that compared favorably to the best in Prague. The population of thirty thousand was predominantly German and Czech; Catholics, Protestants, and Jews lived together harmoniously.

In 1920, Julius Kohner was going to the resort town of Karlsbad, three hours away, to interview Carl Laemmle at the Hotel Pupp. However, he sprained his ankle while running to board the train and his son, Paul, asked to go in his place.

Carl Laemmle was a self-made man from the small town of Laupheim, Germany. He immigrated to the United States in 1884. After working as a bookkeeper, he bought nickelodeons and expanded into film distribution. He soon formed the Universal Motion Picture Manufacturing Company and went on to produce more than four hundred films.

When Paul got to the Hotel Pupp, he was told that Laemmle was not giving interviews. Paul had had the foresight to have a business card printed. He wrote a note on the back, "If I have taken three hours to come here; surely you can spare three minutes to see me."

Laemmle took an immediate liking to Paul. He invited him to lunch with his family, including his seventeen-year-old daughter, Rosabelle. By the end of the day, it was Laemmle who was interviewing Paul. He offered Paul a job in his New York office, which Paul immediately accepted.

Paul Kohner arrived in New York at the same time as William Wyler, in 1920. Willy, as he was called, was from Mulhouse in the Alsace region of Germany, on the border with France; Willy's mother was a distant cousin of Carl Laemmle, who believed strongly in nepotism. Eventually there were *seventy* Laemmle relatives on the Universal payroll. The Universal Manufacturing Company had its headquarters in the Mecca Building on Broadway, just north of Times Square.

Paul and Willy found rooms for seven dollars a week on Eighty-Sixth Street. They became lifelong friends, bonding over their adventures of being poor immigrants in the big city. They weren't paid much, and every week they had to pay back part of the cost of their boat passage to New York. One night when they were cold, broke, and hungry, they went to a Jewish synagogue, which was at least heated. Paul opened his prayer book, given

Universal Film Manufacturing Co.

CARL LAEMMLE, President

"GRAND HOTEL PUPP,"
Karlsbad, Czecho-Slovakia,
August 30, 1920.

To:

The American Consul,
Prague, Czecho-Slovakia.

Dear Sir,-

This is to inform you that I have promised the bearer of this letter, Mr. Paul Kohner, of Teplitz-Schonau, Czecho-Slovakia, a position upon his arrival in America. I will make good my promise to him inasmuch as I have taken an interest in this young-man and hope to make a good American citizen out of him in due time. I will see to it that while in my employ he will be self-supporting.

Thanking you for any assistance you may be able to render Mr. Kohner in obtaining the necessary papers, pass-port, and so forth, I remain,

Very truly yours,

Carl Laemmle

Laemmle letter to the American consul

---

to him by his aunt Clara, and out fell a note from her and some money—a miracle! The note read, "If you have opened this book, you deserve a reward."

Paul and Willy went to movie theaters, where they showed a letter of introduction that stated that they were the New York representatives for Julius's Czech movie magazine, the *Internationale Filmschau*. This often got them in for free. These were silent films and the subtitles helped them to learn English. Universal Pictures published a trade paper for exhibitors and theater owners and Paul studied this to further improve his English.

On his own, Paul started corresponding with the editors of European newspapers and magazines. He wrote stories in German about Universal films that were in production and films that were soon to be released. He translated the company's internal trade paper, adding gossip from the local papers about the movie stars. One day he went to Carl Laemmle's office with a batch of foreign publications containing stories he had written. Laemmle was furious, demanding to know how much Paul had spent to generate this publicity. Paul then showed him the checks he had received for his writings. To Paul's chagrin,

Laemmle took the checks, but he also gave him a promotion; he would be in charge of foreign publicity with an office of his own, and he got a raise from eighteen dollars to twenty-five dollars a week. Paul immediately asked if he could have his name on the door and quickly had cards printed with his new title.

> **Paul Kohner**
>
> MANAGER
> FOREIGN PUBLICITY DEPT. 1600 BROADWAY
> UNIVERSAL FILM MFG. CO. NEW YORK CITY

Willy asked Paul if he could translate these same stories from German into French, which having come from the Alsace, he spoke well. The two wrote and translated at night and sent their articles to European publications. Published stories came back, often with pictures they had sent of stars and, when they were lucky, pictures of Carl Laemmle. They went to see Laemmle and showed him the results of their work. Paul asked if Willy could join him in the Foreign Publicity Department. The "Foreign Department," Paul's invention, was soon copied by rival studios and marked Paul Kohner, at twenty-five, as a young man to watch.

Laemmle loved to gamble and he was now betting on a big-budget film called *Foolish Wives*, directed by and starring the Austrian actor Erich von Stroheim. Von Stroheim was known as "the man you love to hate," because of all the villainous roles he played during the Great War. The film budget rose from $200,000 to $750,000, and kept on rising. Paul suggested that they capitalize on their ballooning cost by putting up a giant electric billboard on Times Square to boast of the weekly budget of the picture to date. That summer of 1921, the crowds in Times Square saw the weekly cost of *Foolish Wives* pass one million dollars. The publicity that this created helped make a hit for the studio and Paul went from Laemmle's protégé to trusted advisor.

Erich von Stroheim and Carl Laemmle

When Erich von Stroheim was in New York, Paul interviewed him, and he must have made a good impression. That von Stroheim's mother was Czech probably helped their connection. It was Stroheim who put in a good word with Laemmle to allow Paul to transfer to Hollywood—the West Coast—where the movies were actually filmed.

Paul started as a third assistant director on Westerns, although he was as unfamiliar with horses as he was with the dice players on the set who regularly took his salary.

In 1922, he was assigned to travel around the Western states in a Model T Ford to check on what theater owners wanted in the way of stories. He showed sample reels of upcoming productions and got firsthand reactions that he cabled back to Carl Laemmle.

Paul was quickly promoted to casting director, then to production supervisor and personal representative of Carl Laemmle.

Casting Director and Personal Representative cards

Mary Philbin, Carl Laemmle, Junior Laemmle, Conrad Veidt, and Paul Kohner

Erich von Stroheim, now Paul's friend, introduced Paul to Mary Philbin. Von Stroheim had directed her in *Foolish Wives*, and again in *The Merry-Go-Round* (1923). Paul and Mary fell in love, but tried to keep their relationship a secret. They knew Mary's parents would object; they were staunch Catholics.

In 1926, while Mary was starring in Paul's production of Victor Hugo's *The Man who Laughs*, Paul proposed to her. Ecstatic, Mary accepted, but they still had to keep their engagement a secret until she felt it was safe to tell her parents. The film was a box-office success and Mary was praised by the critics for her role as Dea, the blind girl.

When Mary announced her engagement, her family was outraged and asked for a meeting with Paul. Everything was going reasonably well until Mary's father brought up the subject of religion, and Paul answered that he was a Jew. Although her father liked him, Mary's mother could not accept this and convinced her ex-husband that Paul would force Mary to convert to Judaism. A heated argument started between Mary's parents and Paul. Mary was in tears and insisted that, although she wanted to marry Paul, she would never abandon her faith. Paul understood and insisted he had no intention of converting her. But Mary was given an ultimatum by her parents: Marry Paul and she would be disowned! She returned the ring and told Paul that she loved him, but could not marry him.

Mary Philbin and Paul Kohner

Paul was devastated, but his disappointment may have been tempered by the knowledge that while he was in Europe on his annual trip to see his parents, Mary had been two-timing him, dating Guinn "Big Boy" Williams, a star in Westerns. Mary Philbin never did marry. She died in 1993, at the age of eighty-nine.

Paul Kohner, 1929

JUEVES de EXCELSIOR magazine cover

La Ovación

11

"NOT IN A MILLION YEARS!"

Mr. Kohner introduced himself and shook hands with Mrs. Cansino and me. He asked us to sit down and said, "This letter from Mr. Ryan is the most complimentary letter I have ever received. Do you speak English, Miss Tovar?" His eyes seemed to look right into me.

"Very little," I said.

He looked at the pictures I'd brought. Then he asked if there was any film of me.

"Yes, I worked in two pictures at Fox," I said, in my accented English.

"I'll get the film tomorrow," he said. "I'd like you to come back for the screening. May I have your phone number?" I told him, and he wrote it on the back of one of my pictures, saying, "I'd like to keep these."

"They are for business!" I said quickly. Somehow I was afraid he would keep them for himself.

"Of course, and now, ladies, I'd like to take you to dinner."

"No," I quickly replied.

Mrs. Cansino said, "That's very kind of you, sir, but I must return home to my family and Miss Tovar's grandmother is waiting for her."

He walked us to the door and said, "Until tomorrow afternoon." He looked at me with so much tenderness, I didn't know what to think.

I didn't even say good-bye. I had never met a company man with such manners before.

On the way home, Mrs. Cansino said, "You are going to marry this man."

"*What?*" I said. "Not in a million years. He scares me!" Then, after a while, I asked, "What made you say that?"

"The way he looked at you," she said.

The next afternoon, we went back to his office for the screening of my film. He was very happy to see us. He led us into the small screening room and sat next to me. The lights went down and the film started. I noticed that he was not looking at the screen, but at me.

"You must look at the screen, or you'll miss me," I said. He just smiled.

When the picture was over we went back to his office.

"Very nice," he said, "You're very photogenic. Now, how about dinner?"

"No," I said. "I must go with Mrs. Cansino."

He looked at me and asked, "What is your grandmother's name?"

"Lucy Sullivan," I answered nervously. He was already dialing my number. Before I knew it, he was on the phone with my grandma.

"Mrs. Sullivan," he said, "I am a producer at Universal Pictures. Your granddaughter is in my office and I would like your permission to take her to dinner."

There was a pause. Grandma must have said that I had gone out without a coat because then he said, "Do not worry. I will see that she does not get cold and I will take her home very early."

I grabbed the phone from him and said in

Spanish, "Grandma, what have you done? I didn't want to stay!"

"He sounds like a gentleman," she said. "And he says he will bring you home early. I am sure it will be all right." I hung up and said to Mrs. Cansino, "Please stay."

She said, "I can't—my children are waiting for me. I'm sure Mr. Kohner will take very good care of you."

The three of us walked to the commissary, where we said good-bye to Mrs. Cansino. Mr. Kohner and I went in to where a group of young men were already sitting. They stood up and Mr. Kohner introduced me to William Wyler, Robert Wyler, Kurt Neumann, and Ernst Laemmle. They all smiled and made comments about me in German. I could hardly speak English, so you can imagine—German! I was scared to death.

Mr. Kohner asked, "Would you like some caviar?"

I said, "No." I had never seen caviar, never. He ordered caviar for me. I tasted it. "*Phew*," I said with distaste.

"Aren't you going to eat it?" he asked.

"No," I said, "I'm not in the mood tonight. It tastes so fishy." At that moment, Willy and everybody else dug into that caviar. They were talking in German and having fun. Mr. Kohner ordered chicken for me; he didn't even ask what I liked. When it came, he started cutting the chicken for me. I said, "Mister, I can cut it myself." He was treating me like a child. Then Mr. Wyler went to the counter and bought me a box of candy. And each one of them then went and bought me a present.

I said, "Thank you. Please, it's getting late."

Mr. Kohner drove me home in a big LaSalle and I sat way over next to the door.

He said, "Who is going to sit in the middle?"

"No one," I answered.

When he met my grandma, he kissed her hand, which I learned was the European way. Then he said to me, "How would you like to work tomorrow night?" I was taken aback.

"I'm dubbing a picture into Spanish and it just occurred to me I don't have the voice for the leading lady. I'll send my car for you at six o'clock."

He said goodnight, kissed my grandma's hand again, and left.

"Grandma, what do you think?" I asked.

"Oh, he is a very fine gentleman, with lovely manners." She was impressed and, I had to admit, so was I.

The next evening I was picked up by John Auer, a young Hungarian who was Mr. Kohner's assistant. I was taken to the dubbing stage, where there were several actors from Spain and Latin America. I watched as a film was projected on the screen and the actors, reading lines from a script in Spanish, tried to match the way the American actors had spoken their lines in English. Our accents in Spanish were all different, but no one seemed to mind. It took a little while for me to get it right, but I learned quickly. The film was *Shanghai Lady* and the star was Mary Nolan.

At midnight, the assistant said, "Break for dinner!" I did not know where they were going so I stayed on the stage, alone. About twenty minutes later, Mr. Kohner came in and said, "What are you doing here?"

I was sitting there in the dark. I said, "I'm waiting for them to come back."

He asked, "Aren't you hungry?"

I said, "No." The truth was I had no money.

He said, "Come with me." And he took me with him to the commissary.

We sat at the counter with the rest of the actors. All eyes were on me, the quiet little girl who came in with the boss. They were having big dinners, plates filled with steak and chicken.

He asked again, "Won't you have something?"

I said, "Just coffee." I was really very hungry, but had to pretend I wasn't.

I think he knew the truth. He ordered a big steak for himself and when it arrived he insisted I have a bite; but when he fed me with his fork, that really got some looks.

We went back to the stage and Mr. Kohner went back to his office or home. I didn't know which. I only saw him at dinner time.

The next night an assistant handed me a ticket and said, "This is for your dinner. You just give it to the cashier." If I had only known the studio was feeding everybody, I would have never refused the night before!

The dubbing lasted three nights, from six in the evening to six in the morning. On the last night, one of the women asked if I had a car.

"No," I answered.

"How do you get home?" she asked.

I said, "The studio car takes me home."

"You must have good connections," she said, looking at me from head to toe as she walked away. I resented that, and at midnight, when Mr. Kohner came to take me to dinner, I told him, "I better not sit with you. I don't want any bad gossip."

"Did somebody say something to you?" he asked. I was very embarrassed, which he noticed. Suddenly, as everyone was leaving for dinner, he said, "Just one minute. If you are wondering why Miss Tovar gets special treatment, it is because she is a guest from another studio and we promised to take care of her. I hope that is clear." There was dead silence.

He had dinner with me and afterwards walked me back to the stage. We had to finish the film that night, so we worked late. I was dead tired when I got home and went straight to bed. The next day the phone rang and Grandma answered. It was Paul Kohner. I made signs to her that I was asleep, so she told him, "She is asleep now."

"Just tell her I called," he said. Two days later he called again. This time I answered.

"You did not pick up your check," he said.

"No, I did not know where to go," I explained.

"I'd like to see you," he said. "Can you have lunch with me at the studio?"

"Yes."

"Good, I'll send my car for you."

When I came to his office, he said, "John Auer will go to the cashier for you." We headed for the commissary. In the daylight I couldn't help but notice how tall he was and how wavy his hair.

His friends were already there and we had lunch together. When we went back to his office, John Auer said, "Manny asked how come she gets twenty-five dollars a night instead of the usual fifteen."

Mr. Kohner said, "Because that's what she gets!" He snatched the check from John and handed it to me. Then he said, "I'll call you at six-thirty."

I thanked him and left. I took my time getting home, looking in shop windows, but not daring to buy anything. Even at twenty-five dollars a night, the work was only for three nights, and now it was over.

Ernesto Romero was at the house when I got there. He was the man from the consulate who used to take me to the consul's parties. My grandma had told him that we were thinking of going back. He said I should stay, maybe change my name, and look for a job doing something else until I could get another role in a movie. My grandmother asked if he would like to stay for dinner and he immediately said, "Yes." Then somebody appeared at the door. It was Mr. Kohner. I was surprised. I introduced him to Mr. Romero. "I told you I would call for you at six-thirty," he said.

"Oh," I said, blushing, "I thought you would call on the phone."

"Well, I'm sure your friend will not mind keeping Mrs. Sullivan company. I have Mr. Sigmund Moos in the car. He's having dinner with us." Mr. Moos was an older gentleman, a friend of Mr. Kohner's from the studio who, from then on, often accompanied us, sort of like a chaperone.

I hesitated, so he said, "Please come."

I made up my mind. "Grandma, I will be home early after dinner." I said goodnight to Mr. Romero and left with Mr. Kohner, who was determined not to leave without me.

During dinner at Musso and Frank's Grill, Mr. Kohner asked me carefully, "Is that man your boyfriend?"

I said, "No, I met him at the consulate. The consul introduced him to me and said, 'Mr. Romero will escort you to our New Year's Eve party.' He comes to visit and sometimes takes my grandma and me for a ride on Sundays. Once he took us to Santa Barbara, and on Easter Sunday he took us to the Hollywood Bowl. We don't know anyone else here."

After dinner we walked down Hollywood Boulevard. On the way home Mr. Kohner said to Mr. Moos, "I'd like you to meet Mrs. Sullivan; she's a fine lady."

We went in and, to my chagrin, Mr. Romero was still there. It was a very awkward situation. We sat down and Mr. Moos asked Mr. Romero a lot of questions. Mr. Romero was a technical advisor. Whenever a picture was made with a Mexican background, the consulate assigned him as their representative to make sure everything was authentic.

Finally, Mr. Moos got up and said, "I think it's time for all of us to go and let the ladies rest." Mr. Kohner was quiet, waiting for Mr. Romero to stand up and say goodnight. Then they all left at the same time. When I finally closed the door, Grandma said, "Mr. Romero was very upset that you went out with Mr. Kohner. He said I should not have allowed it."

"He has no right to say anything," I said, a little angry. "He's not my boyfriend."

Grandma said, "He's in love with you."

"Well, that's just too bad because I am not in love with him or with anyone."

Lupita Tovar, 1930

12

"GIVE ME 24 HOURS"

I started to think about my financial situation, and I told my grandmother, "Since I sent all the money I was getting from Fox to my father, we really have nothing left."

She reminded me, "Well, the rent is paid until the end of the month and we have free passes for the train back to Mexico."

Neither one of us was eager to go home. I hated the idea. I had arrived with such high hopes and the thought of going back to my father's house and his dominance was unbearable. We decided to see what would happen in the next few days. I felt lost. I did not know any agents, and I had little to show for my year in Hollywood.

Several days later, when nothing had changed, I said to Grandma, "I think we should go home."

Reluctantly, she agreed.

"I'm going to the studio today to thank the people who have been so nice to me."

I went to Universal, to Mr. Kohner's office. His secretary said, "Do you have an appointment?"

I said, "No, I've just come to say good-bye and to thank Mr. Kohner for being so kind and for giving me the job." She went into his office and Mr. Kohner immediately came out; he seemed excited to see me.

"Did you get a call from the casting office?" he asked.

I said, "No, I came to say good-bye. I'm going home to Mexico."

He said, "Oh, no, you can't do that!" He pulled me into his office and closed the door.

I explained, "I must go back. I sent all the money I've earned at Fox to my family so they could buy a house. It never entered my mind that Fox would not renew my option. They would have kept me had it not been for the talkies."

"Have you told your family?" he asked.

"No. Not yet. I'm going to write them this evening."

"Don't," he said. "Please give me twenty-four hours before you do *anything*."

He was very upset. He called his secretary, Mrs. Fry, and said, "Please call Mr. Laemmle's office. I would like to see him as soon as possible."

But before I could find out what this was about, I said, "Good-bye," and went home.

The next day I got a call from Mrs. Fry.

"Mr. Kohner would like to talk to you." She sounded so formal.

I said, "Yes?"

"One moment," she said, and then Mr. Kohner got on the line.

"Hello," he said, "how are you today?"

I told him I was fine.

"I'm calling to tell you that since you're still a minor, tomorrow morning at ten o'clock a man from the legal department will pick you up and take you to court so a judge can approve your signing a new contract."

I was speechless. I was getting a new contract and I could keep working! I was so excited I didn't know what to say.

He said, "Hello, are you there?"

I said, "Yes! I will be ready."

"I want to see you in my office afterwards, so you will be brought back to the studio."

"Yes, I understand, until then," I said. "Goodbye." I hung up and screamed, "Grandma! Grandma! I'm getting a new contract tomorrow!"

It was a miracle! We hugged each other and danced in a circle.

Apparently, Mr. Kohner had told Mr. Laemmle that they were wasting half the studio, because at six o'clock in the evening the lights were turned off until six the next morning. Mr. Kohner said that they should hire an additional crew to come in at night and, with Spanish-speaking actors using the same wardrobe, sets and equipment, they could shoot the same film in Spanish for very little money. Latin audiences would be eager to see and hear films in their own language. Mr. Laemmle accepted the idea, so Mr. Kohner quickly took advantage of the moment and told him, "There's a beautiful girl at Fox who's not happy there, and she's thinking of going back to Mexico."

Laemmle quickly said, "Kohner, don't let her get away!"

This was quite a gamble on Mr. Kohner's part because, even though he was a favorite of "Uncle Carl," Carl's son, who was called "Junior," was competing for Mr. Kohner's position as head of production. If this idea of filming a second version of the same story did not pay off, Mr. Kohner's job would be in jeopardy.

The next day at ten on the dot I was picked up by a studio lawyer who introduced himself and said, "Miss Tovar, I'm here to take you to court to get your contract approved." I don't remember having any conversation with him, but I remember he handed me a copy of my contract after it was signed in front of a judge (because I was underage). I did not know how much money I was getting, or for how long. The important thing was that I had a contract for a film called *The Cat Creeps*, which was a remake of a silent film called *The Cat and the Canary*. In Spanish it was called *La Voluntad del Muerto*, which translates as *The Will of the Dead Man*.

As we left the courthouse, the lawyer said, "Now I'm supposed to take you back to Mr. Kohner."

When I arrived at the studio I went to Mr. Kohner's office. I walked in and said, "Mr. Kohner, I am so happy. Thank you."

He stood up from his desk and said, "You're going to start the picture in three weeks."

"I *am*…?" I had tears in my eyes, and I was trembling.

He came closer and put his arms around me and in a very soft voice said, "You sweet thing." I felt safe and relieved. After he dried my tears he said, "My name is Paul, Lupita—call me Paul." Our eyes met and I realized then that he was smitten with me.

But he was still all business. "We'd better go and see Vera West at the wardrobe

Paul Kohner and Carl Laemmle

department."

As we walked across the studio lot, we ran into Junior Laemmle and Paul introduced me. Junior immediately wanted a date with me that night. When I said no, he asked, "Do you know who I am?"

I said, "Yes, you are the son of the president of Universal, but I already have a date with Mr. Kohner." When I said that, Paul laughed like the dickens.

At the wardrobe department Paul introduced me to Miss West: "This is the young girl who will play the lead in the Spanish version of *The Cat Creeps*." Miss West had the sketches for Helen Twelvetrees who would play the same character, Anita, in the English-language version.

Paul looked at them and said, "I'd like something different for Miss Tovar. You can see the two ladies have different personalities."

"Yes, I see what you mean, Mr. Kohner. As soon as I have some sketches ready, I'll show them to you for approval. I'd like to take Miss Tovar's measurements so we can make a dummy." Paul turned to me and said, "Please come back to my office when you are finished here."

We had lunch at the commissary, again with his friends Ernst Laemmle, Kurt Neumann, and Willy Wyler. Then Paul took me to meet Leroy Johnson, head of publicity, and Jack Freulich in the portrait department.

Jack said, "We'll need some nice portraits of our new leading lady, so please make an appointment for a sitting."

Then we went to makeup, where Jack Pierce said, "She's okay, no problem here; straight makeup, no need for a test."

By now I was exhausted; it had been a very exciting, busy day. We walked to Paul's office and he said, "May I take you to dinner to celebrate?"

I said, "No, thank you very much. My grandmother is waiting to hear all about today. And I have an appointment with Mr. Freulich for pictures early tomorrow. He told me to go to makeup first. Thank you for all you are doing for me."

"How are you getting home?" he asked.

"On the streetcar," I said.

"I'll ask John Auer to drive you. I'd like to take you myself but I still have a lot of work to do."

When I left, he was standing at the door, still watching me.

ILUSTRADO magazine cover

13

"ARE YOU A CATHOLIC?"

The next three weeks I went to Universal Studios every day. I was kept very busy with wardrobe fittings, camera tests, and publicity photo sessions. I met the director of *La Voluntad del Muerto*, George Melford; he had directed *The Sheik* with Rudolph Valentino. I also met the rest of the cast: Andrés de Segurola from Barcelona, Roberto Guzmán, a Mexican like me, Lucio Villegas who was from Chile, and Paul Ellis from Argentina. I was especially thrilled to meet Antonio Moreno, the Spanish leading man who was a Hollywood matinee idol. He was not so young anymore. He was forty-four, but still very handsome, with flashing black eyes. I never dreamt I would ever meet him, and here I was playing opposite him!

One day at a wardrobe fitting when Paul Kohner and George Melford had approved everything, Paul said, "When you're through here, please come to my office for some tea."

Mrs. Fry made tea and set out some delicious cookies.

When we were alone, Paul took my hand and asked me, "Are you a Catholic?"

"Yes, aren't you?" I answered, assuming everyone was a Catholic.

He shook his head and said, "No. Does that matter?"

I said, "No. We are all God's children, whether you are a Catholic or not."

"I was engaged to a Catholic girl," Paul said sadly. "Her family wouldn't allow her to marry me."

"Then they must be very stupid," I said.

He smiled a warm smile; everything was all right. In Mexico I had never known anyone with a religion other than mine. At Fox, it had seemed everyone was Irish Catholic.

* * *

The script was translated and adapted in two weeks by Baltazar Fernández Cué, and on the night of July 8, 1930, with much anticipation, we started the Spanish-language version of *The Cat Creeps—La Voluntad del Muerto*. It was a mystery about a man who makes his heirs wait twenty years for the reading of his will.

The English-language version was directed by Rupert Julian during the day and the Spanish version, directed by George Melford, was filmed at night. We had a break for supper around midnight; that's when Paul always showed up. We worked until seven in the morning. We worked Saturdays, too. In the beginning it was very difficult to sleep during the day with all the street noise, but I got used to it.

I was always watching the other actors. I had no trouble remembering my lines, but I never knew where the camera was. In one scene, in which I was supposed to be sleeping, a hairy hand came out of nowhere and took a necklace from around my neck. I was genuinely scared and screamed bloody murder. I wasn't thinking. I had forgotten that I was *acting*, so when I saw this hairy hand I just got scared. Antonio Moreno hadn't spoken Spanish in a long time, so the dialogue was difficult for him.

But he was wonderful, always watching out for me. Sometimes when I did the wrong thing, everybody laughed. Then somebody would say, "Please have an interpreter tell her what Mr. Melford said."

Antonio Moreno and Lupita Tovar

George Melford was marvelous and very patient; we called him "Uncle George." I loved that man. He understood me and was patient with my lack of English. Whenever I could, I wrote down the words I didn't know so I wouldn't forget what they meant the next time. Enrique Tovar Ávalos was the dialogue director. He helped make all our different accents—Mexican, Spanish, and South American—sound as similar as possible.

One day Mr. Laemmle went to see the dailies and, by mistake, they put on the Spanish-language version. They stopped the projection but Mr. Laemmle said, "No. Go on, I want to see them." Afterwards, he called Paul to his office. "Kohner," he said, "I just saw some dailies of the Spanish picture. They're much better than the English version. What are you doing that's different?"

"Mr. Laemmle, when we come in at night we change the set lighting to look like candlelight, and we spray cobwebs all over, and my actors are very expressive and natural."

"I really like the girl, Kohner—she's very good. I tell you what; I'd like you to supervise

Lupita Tovar and Antonio Moreno

the English version, too. But I guess that's not possible … you can't work day *and* night without any sleep."

"Don't worry about that," Paul said, "I have a couch in my office. I don't have to be on the set all night; I can go to my office and lie down. If I'm needed I'll be available, but you'd better talk to Rupert Julian and see if he is agreeable to accepting my advice."

Paul took over the supervision of both pictures. Sometimes, when he dropped in on our set at five in the morning, he looked terribly tired.

On my twentieth birthday, July 27, 1930, Grandma and I invited Paul and his friends Willy and Bob Wyler, Ernst Laemmle, and Kurt Neumann to lunch in our bungalow on Harold

Way. That's when I found out that Paul lived in a boarding house just a few blocks away. Grandma made *arroz con pollo* (rice with chicken) and her famous lemon pie. Paul gave me a small bottle of Chanel No.5 perfume and Bob Wyler gave me Shalimar. Of course, I wore the Chanel No.5 until it was all used up, even though I preferred the Shalimar. Paul gave me Shalimar from then on.

Paul decided to get an apartment of his own. One Sunday evening he came to take me to dinner. He had arranged for John Auer to take Grandma and her friend, Jacobita, to the movies. As usual, Paul came with Mr. Moos, but then we would quickly drop Mr. Moos off and Paul and I would continue on our date. That night after dinner Paul asked if he could take me to see his new apartment. I was reluctant, but he wanted to show me something he had bought at auction.

When we got to his apartment he showed me his purchase, a Russian samovar.

He asked, "Would you like tea?"

"No," I replied, looking nervously around the apartment.

"Coffee?"

"No," I said. I had never been in a man's apartment alone, and this made me feel particularly anxious.

"Would you like a glass of water?" he asked.

"No."

"Do you like poetry?" he asked, getting some water for himself.

He pulled a book from a shelf and started to read poetry to me, in a loud voice, with all his heart, in German! I could hardly understand English, let alone German, but he seemed to like poetry so much, and he was such a gentleman, that I sat there and listened to him attentively. When I told him it was time to go home, he reluctantly closed the book and led me out to his car, holding me by the elbow.

What we didn't know was that Willy and Ernst had convinced the people in the apartment next door to let them listen through the wall. The following day at the studio they made terrible fun of Paul.

Paul Ellis, Lupita Tovar, and Antonio Moreno

Lupita Tovar and the cast of *La Voluntad del Muerto;* Paul Kohner and George Melford, front center

We finished *La Voluntad del Muerto* in six weeks. After a week of rest I was called in to do publicity pictures and interviews. There was going to be a special screening of the film at the studio and the invitations said "black tie." I bought myself the nicest outfit I could find; I spent one whole week's salary on it. It was a beautiful dress, very elegant. It was made of white pressed velvet trimmed with white fox fur. I loved furs.

The preview was at the studio's Projection Room Seven. When Paul and I arrived it was full of European and Spanish-speaking guests; the men were all dressed in dinner jackets. There were special guests: the two sons of Pascual Ortiz Rubio, the president of Mexico, along with Alfonso Pesqueira, the Mexican consul, and film star Rámon Novarro.

Before the picture started, Paul proudly got up and said to the guests, both in English and (reading from a card) Spanish, "You are about to witness a miracle! Tonight, into this room came a completely unknown girl, and when she leaves, she will be a star." I looked around to see who he was talking about.

I was very nervous. I had not seen any of the film. During the screening I grabbed Paul's arm and I had my knees up to my chin the whole time. When the lights came back on there was tremendous applause. I was curled up in a ball, emotionally exhausted, tears rolling down my face. Afterwards there was a party, where everybody came and congratulated me. Paul was beaming with pride.

"They all say I've got a winner and that you look like a star," he told me.

First screening of *La Voluntad del Muerto*

Paul drove me home. When I turned around at the door to say goodnight, he said, "I would like to kiss you. May I?" I pointed to my cheek. But he wanted to kiss me on the lips.

"*No*," I said, "I don't want to get pregnant!" I got scared and said, "You'd better go—Grandma is waiting. Goodnight!" I ran into the house and locked the door.

The next day my embarrassing experience with Paul was all over the studio. Oh, how they laughed!

When I was sixteen, my father had told me my mother wanted to talk to me about "the birds and the bees," but when I went to her she just cried and refused to tell me anything. Mexican girls in general didn't know anything about men or sex in those days. Many marriages were unhappy because girls thought that what their husbands wanted was "dirty." They would often go home to their mothers, scared. A friend of mine had run home on her wedding night; her husband had gotten angry during his attempted lovemaking and they had a terrible fight!

Paul asked Annie Weitzfelder, his doctor's wife, to talk to me. I brought her a small bunch of flowers and we had coffee. She talked to me as if she were my mother, something my mother never did.

"Didn't your mother ever tell you how babies are made?" she wanted to know.

Mrs. Weitzfelder explained to me that you don't get pregnant by kissing, but it could lead to it. I felt silly.

The day that Paul finally took me in his arms and our lips met, I had a strange, happy feeling. I knew then that I was in love. The next day Paul sent me beautiful roses with a card that simply said, "I love you—Paul."

* * *

Paul took me to my first Academy Awards evening. It was in the dining room of the Biltmore Hotel in downtown Los Angeles. Clark Gable, Claudette Colbert, and all of the Hollywood stars were there that evening, looking spectacular. That night *All Quiet on the Western Front* won the Oscar for Best Picture. It was a Universal production and Paul had been involved in making it. George Arliss won Best Actor for *Disraeli* and Norma Shearer Best Actress in *The Divorcee*. Willy Wyler, Janet Gaynor, Erich von Stroheim and his wife, Valerie, were at our table. Prohibition was still in effect and everyone drank bootlegged liquor from coffee cups. Erich, who wore a monocle and had a dueling scar above one eye, carried a hollow cane; the top unscrewed and he poured whiskey out of it. Erich insisted that I drink with him. Every time he tipped his head back to drink, I would throw my drink over my shoulder. Everyone saw what I was doing but Erich did not, and he was amazed that I did not get drunk.

It seemed like such a short time ago that I had been in the corridors of the Parque Lira School in my black bloomers, sailor blouse, long black stockings, and tennis shoes, running to my gymnastics class, where Mrs. Chafino told me to move to the front. Dancing around our gymnasium, we must have looked like the awkward school girls that we were. And yet I had been plucked out of that life and brought to this fantasy world of movie stars and ice cream sundaes and a tall, dark, handsome man who loved me and took care of me.

About a week after the preview of *La Voluntad del Muerto*, Paul told me that the studio wanted me to go to Mexico for the opening of the movie. I couldn't wait to go. I had not seen my family in almost two years.

* * *

The day before I left for Mexico with my grandma, I went to the studio. Leroy Johnson in the publicity department told me again how important it was to always be properly dressed and well groomed to make a good impression with the press and the public.

I stopped by Paul's office to say good-bye and he surprised me with a few words in Spanish. He was taking lessons at night from our dialogue director. I was secretly pleased. He gave me a large photo of himself; on it he had written: "Lupita, remember, fame is fickle, come back unchanged."

George Melford, Antonio Moreno, Lupita Tovar, and Paul Kohner

CINELANDIA y FILMS

Abril 1929

Lupita Tovar
FOX

14

"LA NOVIA DE MÉXICO"

I left Los Angeles on the train with my grandma. The trip was very hot and long. On the third day, when we arrived at Buenavista, the Mexico City central railway station, there was a great commotion. The train kept going back and forth, changing tracks. I looked out the window but couldn't tell what was going on. I asked the conductor, "What's happening?"

He said, "It seems a very important person is on board, maybe in the next car. I think it's the Hollywood movie star, Lupita Tovar."

Suddenly, I couldn't breathe. "Lupita Tovar—but that's *me*!"

I looked at my grandma; her face was full of pride for me.

On the platform, waiting for me, were my mother and father, my sisters Lucy, Sarita, and Mary, and my second brother to be named Guillermo. All my school classmates and teachers and even the Boy Scouts of Mexico were there!

I saw my old boyfriend, Pepe. I hadn't seen him in almost two years. Seeing him made me realize how young and inexperienced we were then. I wondered if he had changed.

When I stepped off the train the Boy Scouts beat their drums. I saw on the front of the locomotive a huge banner that read: "HERE COMES LUPITA TOVAR."

There were people with flowers, and photographers taking pictures. The representative from Universal Pictures, Mr. Juan de la C. Alarcón, introduced himself and welcomed me. I was in tears. I could never have dreamed this would happen. I was a young girl who had gone out in the world and been very fortunate. Now I was home and everyone was welcoming me back with open arms!

Lupita Tovar returning to Mexico City, 1930

The crowd followed us like a swarm to the car. A motorcycle escort led us to my parents' modest apartment on Danubio Street. With the money I had been sending my father (a small fortune in those days), they had moved from the old house.

We climbed the stairs to their third-floor apartment, my little sisters staring at me the whole time. Mary was the youngest; she was just five months old when I left. Sarita had been four and Guillermo just six. I picked up Mary and said, "I'm your sister."

"No," she said, "you are Lupita Tovar, the actress." It sounded strange to me.

After dinner my father went out to play dominoes at the cantina, and that's when the questions started. I spent the evening telling my family everything that had happened to me in Hollywood. I told them about the important actors I had been introduced to and how nice everyone was. I did not tell them about my producer. I didn't think they would understand or approve. I was so excited I could not sleep that night. The next day, November 20, 1930, was the opening of *La Voluntad del Muerto* at the Cine Balmori.

That evening I came out of the apartment with Mr. Alarcón, dressed in my elegant white dress with the white fur. I could hardly get through the throng of photographers waiting outside. He had hired two cars; all of my family was going.

When we arrived at the theater, the Boy Scouts were playing their drums, and photographers' flashbulbs blinded me. My knees shook as I walked in. I felt like I was going to faint.

Carlos Noriega Hope, the editor of *El Universal Ilustrado*, the most important newspaper in Mexico, greeted me at the entrance to the theater. He was master of ceremonies that evening. Carlos escorted me to a dressing room filled with flowers. Then he walked onstage, said glowing words about me, and brought me out.

Lupita Tovar at the Cine Balmori, November 20, 1930

Marquee Cine Balmori, Mexico

There was tremendous applause. I had never been on a stage before. White pigeons were released and bouquets of flowers were handed to me. This was more than a dream come true. This was truly a miracle.

I looked at the sea of people and saw my family and many familiar faces from school. Pepe was sitting in the front row. I stood there petrified, a lump in my throat. I tried to say how happy I was; I never imagined I would get such a welcome.

The picture started and I went back to the dressing room. Halfway through the film, a phone call came from Hollywood. Paul had gathered Mr. Laemmle and a group of artists to talk to me over a loudspeaker. Among the people with him

58

La Voluntad Del Muerto poster

congratulating me was Ramón Novarro. I thought my heart was going to jump out of my mouth! Paul talked to me several times. I heard later that Carl Laemmle had turned and whispered to Paul, "This was all so you could talk to the girl, wasn't it?"

When the picture was over, there was a tremendous ovation. I was supposed to attend a dinner in my honor, but my father grabbed me by the arm, muttering, "No, this is enough. We're going home." He hated publicity and all the fuss they were making over me. He didn't like all the men looking at me. Many of them were very handsome and dressed in tuxedos. I had no choice but to go home with my father. I was disappointed, but it was still a terribly exciting evening.

During the following days I made personal appearances in the different theaters where *La Voluntad del Muerto* was showing and I was mobbed every time. Mr. Alarcón arranged everything. At each theater I walked on stage to say hello to the public and let them know how honored I was to be there.

Pepe followed us around like a little puppy. He had started medical school but he skipped classes to be with me. All this time Pepe had been writing letters to me in Los Angeles—love letters with poems. He was trying to court me from two thousand miles away. But what chance did he have when Paul was constantly at my side, taking me out in the evenings, sending flowers and candy to my grandma and me?

The next day I paid a visit to my aunts. They had a publicity photo of me dressed in skimpy clothing on display, but they had draped it in lace to make me look more respectable. It looked odd and funny.

I was given a lunch by all the theater exhibitors at Xochimilco, the floating gardens in the lagoon outside the city. That was when the press gave me the title "*La Novia de México*," or "The Sweetheart of Mexico," just as Mary Pickford was called "America's Sweetheart."

After that I could not go out on the street without being followed by shoeshine boys and the boys who sold newspapers. They would call out, "There goes my *Novia!*"

Then Mr. Alarcón said the theater owners in the city of Puebla had extended an invitation for me to visit. We left in the morning, and halfway to Puebla we were met by hundreds of students on bicycles; they had come out to escort me to their city. The streets were lined with people (many carrying bouquets of flowers) waiting to see me.

Another lunch was given in my honor. I was sitting at the head of the table with the mayor of Puebla and his special guests. There were many speeches, and then suddenly there was a commotion at the door. It was an Indian looking distraught, dressed in his loose, white cotton outfit, and straw hat. He wanted to see me. It got quiet and I said, "Let him come in." I stood up as he walked slowly toward me, hat in hand. He knelt down and kissed the hem of my dress, then looked up and said, "You look just like her, Doña Lupita." I was speechless. Then he walked backwards until he reached the street. It was very moving.

Mr. Alarcón said, "You're dressed in white and everybody is calling, 'Lupita, Lupita!' (The diminutive for Guadalupe). So he probably thinks you are the *Virgen de Guadalupe*." Nobody laughed. Somebody made another speech and a toast to "*La Novia de México*." I found myself constantly wiping away tears.

Afterwards, I visited the local soldiers' barracks. They had a new machine gun they wanted me to christen. They played the drums and, when I smashed the bottle of champagne over the gun, I cut my left hand. It was bleeding so I held it up, but blood still dripped on my white dress. They wrapped a handkerchief around my hand and praised my courage, but Mr. Alarcón was very worried. We drove immediately back to Mexico City, where a doctor put in several stitches.

Of course, the press made a big fuss about this little accident, which did not sit too well with my father. He said to me, "You are not going back to Hollywood. When you finish this circus performance, you are going to stay home!"

I told him defiantly, "I'm sorry, Father, I have a contract with the studio and I will return there to work." There was no way I could go back to the life I had before. Instead of buying a nice little house as he had promised, my father had used the money I sent to buy a *pulquería* (a lower-class bar). My father had a nasty temper; he fought with everybody. I truly believe he would have killed me with one of his beatings if I hadn't left home.

"You will obey me!" he said.

I asked Mr. Alarcón and a representative from Universal to talk with my father. They asked him if he would pay the studio back what they had invested in me if he forced me to stay. This was *business*, the man explained, and the studio would sue. My father relented and said I could return to Hollywood.

When I left Mexico again, my father made a terrible scene; he still wanted me to stay at home. Grandma and I caught a taxi to the train station with my father's shouts and threats still in our ears. I cried for days on the train; my eyes were swollen from crying. For several months the letters I sent home were returned unopened. He disconnected their phone so I couldn't even call my mother.

15

DRÁCULA

When we returned to Los Angeles, Paul was at the train depot with flowers; I was so happy to see him. It felt so good to be in love. His secretary, Mrs. Fry, had found a very nice two-bedroom furnished bungalow for my grandma and me to rent on Highland Avenue. Until then, she and I had been sharing a bed.

The publicity department was very pleased with the results of my trip. Mr. Alarcón had sent them all the newspaper clippings and photographs. They said they had never seen such publicity. They couldn't get over the success of the picture. Paul, of course, was ecstatic; he had "discovered" me, after all.

Mr. Laemmle was shown all the publicity from Mexico. When he saw it he said, "My God. This must have cost a fortune, all this publicity for the girl." Then he was told that not one penny had been spent; that the press was running after me and that they had given me the title, "The Sweetheart of Mexico." The next day I was called to the studio to see Mr. Laemmle. He told me he was very proud of me and said, "You will start immediately on *Drácula*!"

Dracula was the first of a series of sound horror films that were extremely successful films for Carl Laemmle and Universal Studios. They followed with *Frankenstein* (1931) and *The Mummy* (1932).

In Mexico I had become a star overnight, thanks to Paul and to Mr. Alarcón, who was responsible for the publicity campaign. He and his wife, Josefina, had accompanied me everywhere and protected me in every way. He had even tried to intervene with my father, who became very jealous because I followed Mr. Alarcón's advice.

Drácula newspaper ad

In the meantime, Paul slowly took charge of my life. When he saw how little I had after working for Fox for one year—no clothes or anything—he insisted I save some money and not send so much to my father.

We often had lunch at the studio commissary,

usually with his friends, Willy, Bob, Ernst, and Kurt. There never was any gossip about us, even though I never had a date with anyone else. It quickly became known around the studio, "If you want to keep your job, leave the Mexican girl alone!"

Then one day I got a call from a reporter from *El Universal,* the leading Mexico City newspaper. Virginia Fábregas, a stage actress, had gone back to Mexico and told the press that Paul and I had secretly tied the knot! I denied the rumor saying, "When I marry, it will be to a Latin, of course!" That was the headline in *El Universal* the next day.

The reporter came to see me. I told him that Mr. Kohner was just a good friend for whose help with my career I was deeply grateful, but we were *not* engaged. I went on to assure the reporter that I had no intention of getting married while I was still working in films. The newspaper printed that, too.

The reporter called Paul and he was quoted as saying, "There is nothing further from the truth. Miss Tovar is just a good friend whom I respect, and if I have helped her career it is because she is talented and deserves my help. Anything further is absurd."

Things were a little awkward between us for awhile after that. Paul and I had never talked about marriage; why should we? We were happy just as we were.

Then things got even worse. One evening after work I went to Paul's office from the set and without any warning, he said, "Mexican girls get fat after they marry." I was speechless. I didn't know what to say. I answered, "There are no fat people in my family!"

I *had* been enjoying the chocolates Paul kept giving me and the ice cream sundaes at the Pig 'n Whistle. Perhaps this was just Paul's clumsy way of saying, "Don't get fat!" Or was he thinking ahead about our relationship? I went on a diet right away, quickly dropping back down to my usual ninety-two pounds.

* * *

The English-language version of *Dracula* was to star Bela Lugosi, Helen Chandler, and David Manners, and it was to be directed by Paul Leni. But Leni died suddenly of blood poisoning and Tod Browning took his place. George Melford was hired to direct the Spanish-language version, with a cast including Carlos Villarias, Pablo Alvaréz Rubio, Barry Norton (from Argentina), Carmen Guerrero, Manuel Arbo, Eduardo Arozamena, and me. We used the same sets and the same script translated into Spanish, but a completely different crew, led by cameraman George Robinson. Paul was the supervising producer of both films, but his heart was with our version.

At the end of the year we started filming. Again we shot at night, while the English-speaking cast filmed during the day. The American version had started two weeks earlier so we were able to use the sets they had already finished with. I worked hard to get every line perfect. I felt more secure in my work and everybody at the studio treated me like family. I was happy. It couldn't get better than this.

Even though this was my second starring film, I was still nervous about my performance. I would enter a set and play my scene, but with the lights so bright I still couldn't tell where the camera was or where I was supposed to look. George Melford didn't speak Spanish but somehow I understood him. We had the same dialogue director as before—Enrique Tovar Ávalos—and the script girl was Mexican. Outside of that, the crew all spoke English. There was one Mexican electrician who worked high up in the rafters; his name was Tommy Valdez. He used to watch me from the catwalks and around midnight he would sometimes drop a little something down for me, like a Hershey bar, which I really appreciated.

Only Carlos Villarías, who played Count Drácula, was allowed to see dailies. He was encouraged to be as "Lugosi-like" as possible. The rest of us were on our own. Paul wanted our film to be better than the English-language version. George Robinson, our lighting cameraman, lit our sets with creepy shadows and added cobwebs everywhere. My nightgown was much sexier than the one Helen Chandler wore and, perhaps because we were filming at night, our actors seemed even more menacing.

We worked long hours and Saturdays, too, so I used to meet Paul and his friends on Sunday evenings for dinner and a movie. Paul was so sweet to me. His manners were very old-fashioned; he treated me with respect and was very protective.

We had tremendous respect for our director, George Melford. He was like a god to us. But there was some tension on the set because we knew we were competing with the American *Dracula*; we felt pressure to perform better than them. We were trying so hard. We finished our film in only twenty-two nights; the American version took seven weeks.

I never met Bela Lugosi at the studio; he and the other actors left before we arrived in the evening. But I did meet Mr. Lugosi one Sunday at Ernst Lubitsch's house. He was talking with another Hungarian actor, Victor Varconi, who later worked in Paul's films *The Doomed Battalion* and *The Rebel*. When Paul introduced me as Eva in the Spanish-language version, Mr. Lugosi looked me up and down, and smiled approvingly. I heard that after the success of *Dracula*, he kept a coffin in his bedroom—but maybe that was just publicity.

It seemed to me that everyone in the Spanish-speaking community of Los Angeles knew what we were doing. *La Voluntad del Muerto*, Universal's first Spanish-language talkie, had been a great success and this film was going to be even better. So many people were treating me like a star. Ramón Novarro, the "New Valentino," invited me to dinner parties at his house—with Paul, of course. Ramón had starred in *Ben-Hur*, *The Student Prince in Old Heidelberg* (with Norma Shearer), and was filming *Mata Hari* (with Greta Garbo).

Lupita Tovar and Carlos Villarías—*Drácula*, 1931

Lupita Tovar—*Drácula*

José Mojica invited me to his house in Santa Monica, where he lived with his mother. José was a handsome leading man who also wrote novels, and he had a beautiful singing voice. After his mother died, José entered a monastery and became a Catholic priest. When he returned to acting ten years later, he always played the role of a priest.

In April of 1931, after we finished filming *Drácula*, I was sent back to Mexico to do publicity for the film. My grandma accompanied me again. This time we stayed at a hotel. When I visited my family, the moment I opened the door my mother warned me, "Your father will be home any minute!"

"I'd better go then," I said, heading for the door. I didn't want to make any trouble for her, but then through the door came my father. I went to him, put my arms around him, and kissed his cheek. He was like a stone statue.

"Just tell me what I have done wrong?" I asked, my voice quavering. "What is it?"

He told me that I had disobeyed him by continuing to act. We made peace but when he said, "Come back, and stay here at the house," I said, "No," firmly. "Because after three days there will be trouble between us again."

My father did not understand the need for publicity, which was a big part of my job. For all his machismo, his bravado, he was a very shy, private man.

Drácula was another huge success in Mexico. I went from theater to theater, making personal appearances. I talked to many reporters. They were kind and they often wrote gracious notes, thanking me for interviews.

José Mojica and Lupita Tovar

Lupita Tovar and Carlos Villarías—*Drácula*

AUTHOR'S NOTE:

FOREIGN-LANGUAGE VERSIONS

The foreign markets were very lucrative for American companies, even for silent films. Title cards were translated into all languages where the film might be shown. "Foreign-language" or "second-language" versions were an even bigger success. They could be shot quickly and cheaply by using existing sets. There were no high-salaried contract players to pay and there was virtually no overhead. It became a booming industry.

The reviews for *La Voluntad del Muerto*, the first movie "Filmed in Spanish," were great. One newspaper reviewer in Los Angeles wrote: "In the film, Lupita carries a candle, while everyone south of the border carries a torch."

Unfortunately, no print of either *The Cat Creeps* or *La Voluntad del Muerto* (the Spanish version) exists today. The primitive projection and storage capabilities, especially in Latin America, together with the equatorial heat and humidity, meant that few prints of any film survived. To compound the problem, movies were filmed on unstable nitrate film stock that had a tendency to spontaneously combust. *Drácula* was one of the few to survive long enough to be transferred to "safety" film stock.

In 1977 the American Film Institute made an archival print of *Drácula* for a Universal Studios retrospective at the Museum of Modern Art. The footage that made this possible was discovered in a New Jersey warehouse. But by this time the nitrate negative had begun to decompose, especially the third reel. The only other existing print was found at the *Cinemateca de Cuba*, which graciously allowed that third reel to be copied. Archival copies were then struck from a new negative as a preservation project of the Motion Picture Division of the Library of Congress, UCLA Film and Television Archive, and Universal Studios.

David J. Skal in his book, *Hollywood Gothic*, compares the two versions of *Dracula*. His conclusion is that the Spanish version is completely different from the Bela Lugosi version, and far superior.

Skal writes: "The cinematography has a fluid look with a complex depth of focus creating a menacing atmosphere. The Spanish version did not have to contend with the Hays Office censorship and has a sensuality that adds eroticism. It is more chilling and evocative than its English-language counterpart. Count Drácula has the ability to transform himself into a wolf, bat, or just vapor; he can walk only by night, casts no reflection, and is practically immortal as long as he nourishes himself on fresh blood; he withers at the sight of the Christian cross and is allergic to garlic. But he sets women swooning in a most un-Victorian fashion. When Drácula attacks Eva in her bedroom, he covers her with his cape like a huge bat while the American film settles for a fade-out. Lupita Tovar's Eva becomes sexually animated as the vampire overtakes her. In Tod Browning's American version, the same character seems merely dazed. The actresses in the American film are a bit school-marmish as compared to the Spanish vampires who let their hair down and wear low-cut gowns. Mina's near see-through negligee is quite astonishing, even for a pre-Code film."

Paul Kohner, George Melford, and cameraman George Robinson worked well as a team. They had an editing Moviola on the set so they could view what the other crew had already shot. Often they would compose shots and camera moves to be the mirror opposite of the English-language version. The American version took seven weeks to film and the Spanish version, which at one hundred and two minutes, runs twenty-seven minutes longer, took just three weeks, and cost only sixty-six thousand dollars to produce.

Between 1929 and 1939, one hundred and sixteen Hollywood feature films were made in Spanish. Of those, sixty-seven were dual versions or remakes of silent films, while forty-nine were from original screenplays.

16

"WOULD YOU LIKE TO BE A STAR?"

I started working in English-language Westerns and a couple of comedy two-reelers. One was *El Tenorio del Harem* with Slim Summerville and Tom Kennedy. Another was *Caprichos de Hollywood* with Laura La Plante, Andrés de Segurola (who was an opera singer), and Juan Torena. Both were directed by Kurt Neumann. These were only short films, but this was 1931; America was about to be plunged into the Great Depression and I was happy to be working.

Next I had a co-starring role in Louis King's *Border Law* with Buck Jones, Frank Rice, Jim Mason, and Don Chapman.

Lupita Tovar, Buck Jones, and Frank Rice in *Border Law*, 1931

Then I played in a very old-fashioned story, Noel M. Smith's *Yankee Don*, starring Richard Talmadge. Richard was born in Switzerland and had an accent, so he left acting and became an action director.

Frank Fouce was an assistant director I had met at Columbia Studios. When they were casting the Spanish version of Lionel Barrymore's *Ten Cents a Dance* with Barbara Stanwyck, Frank suggested me for Barbara's part. So I went to Columbia Studios to do *Carne de Cabaret*, which was the title of the Spanish version. It was directed by Eduardo Arozamena and W. Christy Cabanne. Ramón Pereda and René Cardona starred opposite me. Our Spanish-language version took just two weeks. One "take" was all we were allowed, so we had to get it right the first time. This was one of the last films to get away with sexy innuendos before the studios started censoring their own movies to keep the government from interfering.

* * *

One morning as I was about to leave the house, I got a phone call from Mr. Juan de la Cruz Alarcón, who had just arrived from Mexico City.

"What a surprise!" I said. "But I'm just leaving for work at Columbia Studios." I went to the studio alone now; I was twenty-one and Grandma no longer had to go with me.

"Then I'll see you at lunchtime at the studio," he said.

Mr. Alarcón came to the set, waiting a little until we finished a scene, and then we went to lunch at the studio commissary. All the while he had a mysterious smile on his face as though he were keeping a secret. After we ordered, it came out. He asked me, "How would you like to star in the first talking picture to be filmed in Mexico?"

"I'd love to!" I said immediately.

"The story is called *Santa*. There is a group in Mexico who will arrange the financing," he explained. "I'm here to find a cameraman, sound equipment, and a director. You will be the star and the rest of the cast will be Mexican. How would you like to have Antonio Moreno as director?"

"I'd like that very much. In *La Voluntad del Muerto* he helped me a lot."

"Fine, I'll talk to him," he said. "I'll get in touch with you as soon as we're ready."

I was so excited. I couldn't believe it. What an opportunity: to work in Mexico and in a starring role!

Paul was in Europe. The studios didn't make many pictures in the winter, even in California, and most people were taken off salary for a couple of months. After producing a picture called *A House Divided,* with Willy Wyler directing Walter Huston, Paul took this opportunity to visit his family. I wrote to him about my visit from Mr. Alarcón and the possibility of making the first talkie in Mexico. He wrote back, warning me to be careful about the Mexican offer because Mr. Alarcón had never produced a picture before.

Border Law poster, 1931

17

ALMOST KIDNAPPED

After I finished *Carne de Cabaret* at Columbia I was again asked to make personal appearances in various cities in Mexico. I was happy to do so and eager to see my family again. This time Paul thought it would be better if his secretary, Mrs. Gertrude Fry, accompanied me; my grandma was getting older, and she had arthritis (although she never complained).

A month later, Mrs. Fry and I went to Mexico on a publicity tour. We were accompanied by a very nice gentleman from the Columbia office, Mr. Urbina, who took good care of us.

We traveled north from Mexico City by train to San Luis Potosí for the opening of the film. There was a family I knew there, the Corderos; they used to come to visit us with their son Nicolás, who was my age. His mother, Sara Cordero, was American and spoke English with my mother and my grandma.

Nicolás came to our hotel to invite me to their home for Sunday lunch. That night he brought his family to the show. I had a moment to say hello to them, but then I was taken to a radio station to give interviews as part of the film's promotion.

The next day Nicolás picked us up and, after a tour of the town, he took us to his home. The whole family was there, and the table was beautifully set. We had just sat down to eat when there was somebody knocking at the door, insisting to see me. Nicolás told the man I should not be disturbed. He came in anyway. He was dressed in a military uniform.

The man said, "I have come to pick up Miss Tovar."

"What?" I said. "*No.*"

"General Cedillo, my general, is expecting you for lunch."

"Nothing doing," I said. "I don't know this man. I've never heard of him. I don't remember receiving any invitation from him."

The man was insistent: "I have orders from General Saturnino Cedillo to bring Miss Tovar to him!" To Nicolás he said, "Would you explain to the young lady it is better that she goes."

Nicolás said quietly, "Lupita, you'd better go. Mrs. Fry, I'm very sorry, but you've got to go. Just stick with her and don't let her out of your sight."

What I didn't know was that General Saturnino Cedillo was a feared man in Mexico. He was a político with his own private army of ten thousand men. Mrs. Fry and I were brought to General Cedillo's very large house in the city. When we entered I saw there were armed soldiers standing at attention along both sides of a large room. At the end of the room we saw a tall, dark, serious, Indian-looking man; this was the general. He came forward to meet me and, as we walked together past the soldiers, there was a drum roll and the soldiers presented arms. But the general was only watching me; he was trying to devour me with his eyes! The general was intimidating. He was a very large man. He insisted on showing me his ballroom full of floor-length mirrors and Louis XIV chairs lined up against the walls. Then, in an inner courtyard, we got into his open car and were driven to his hacienda outside of town. Mrs. Fry had to go in another car with one of the general's aides and with Mr. Urbina from Columbia Pictures, who had hurriedly come looking for us.

At the general's hacienda, long tables had been set outside for lunch. There were a lot of people waiting for us, and they did not look happy.

After lunch we were taken to a large field, where the general kept his airplanes. He had six small American planes and he ordered one of his pilots to perform for us. The pilot took off and flew very high, then he killed the motor and started it again, and flew upside down. It made me very nervous to watch.

Then the general wanted to show me his supply of machine guns and ammunition. He led me inside a large warehouse and closed the door behind us. Mrs. Fry pounded on the locked door, but the general ignored her. The general did have storerooms full of guns and bullets, of which he was very proud. I was relieved when we came outside again.

I told him, "I must go back to the hotel to rest before the show this evening."

That evening at the theater when I made my appearance, the stage was again covered with beautiful flowers, with the largest basket from the general.

Lupita Tovar on stage in San Luis Potosi, 1931

After another radio interview, I returned to the hotel. We were supposed to leave the next day for Torreón.

In the middle of the night, Mrs. Fry woke me: "Get up, Baby, don't bother to get dressed. Just put your coat on over your pajamas. We have to go now!"

She threw my things in the suitcase and she and Mr. Urbina rushed me down the back stairs and into a taxi at the rear of the hotel. It was still dark when we sped off.

We kept going until we got to the next town that had a railway station. There, Mr. Urbina got us some coffee and arranged for a place for me to dress before boarding the train. I didn't find out what had happened until we were in our suite at the hotel in Torreón.

Mr. Urbina had talked with one of General Cedillo's aides the previous afternoon at the general's hacienda, and he had run into him again that night in the lobby of our hotel.

The aide had told him, "Get that nice young girl out of town. Cedillo is up to no good." It was the aide who had advised us to make our escape.

Mr. Urbina had hurried to tell Mrs. Fry about the plan, but found a soldier guarding my door. He talked to the soldier, saying he was my manager. The soldier said he had orders to guard my door all night. He wasn't budging.

"That's fine; I'm just going next door to see Miss Tovar's companion."

Mr. Urbina knocked on Mrs. Fry's door, telling her he'd like to give her the itinerary for the next day.

"It's important that I see you!" he said.

Poor Mrs. Fry was very proper, but she let Mr. Urbina into her room. She was horrified to hear what was going to happen but understood that we had to sneak out of the hotel. Mr. Urbina went out and talked to the soldier again, saying, "It's going to be a long night. Miss Tovar is already asleep. Why don't you go down for a drink and I'll keep watch for you until you return. Take your time. I have something to read." And he gave the soldier some money. Meanwhile, we got ready and sneaked out the back way. I got in the car and we left in a hurry. Both Mr. Urbina and Mrs. Fry were scared, which made me scared, too. The general must have been furious when he found out what had happened.

After the opening in Torreón, we had a request to go to Tampico on the coast and do a special appearance for the victims of a terrible flood. A small plane came to pick us up. The pilot's name was Jimmy Shultz, a charming young American. It had been raining in Tampico for ten days. I made the appearance on stage, and it was still raining when Jimmy flew us back to Torreón the next day. He promised to call when he came to Los Angeles, but he never got the chance. The weather was so bad that he crashed and died on his way back to Tampico. I found out about it when we arrived by train in Mexico City. I was shocked; I kept thinking it could have been us. We were so lucky.

When we returned to Los Angeles, Paul was waiting for us at the station with flowers. I was very excited, and told him all about the trip. In the car, he looked at Mrs. Fry and asked softly, "Is it true about the pilot?" She nodded grimly.

"What an irresponsible thing to do, to send her by plane in bad weather. From now on there will be no flying for you, young lady."

Paul phoned me the next day. He was going to produce a picture in English, *East of Borneo*, and I would play the native girl. The director was George Melford. My co-stars were going to be Rose Hobart, Charles Bickford, Georges Renavent, and Noble Johnson. I was delighted. I played a barefoot native girl of the South Pacific islands, wearing very little clothing and very dark body makeup. There were a lot of visitors on that set.

In July of 1931, Paul left on his yearly six-week trip to Europe to visit his family, and I went to Mexico to play the lead in *Santa*, the first talkie ever filmed there. I had no idea, then, how that film would change my life.

Lupita Tovar *East of Borneo* poster, 1931

18

SANTA

It was late summer of 1931 when I arrived in the capital of Mexico. I did not know that the book *Santa* had been a bestseller for many years. Right away at the studio I met the author, Federico Gamboa. He was very sweet; he gave me an inscribed copy. The story was well known, even to my father.

Federico Gamboa and Lupita Tovar

When I arrived home with the book and announced, "This is my next film," my father immediately shouted, "That book does not come into my house!" I hadn't read it; I thought it was about a saint, not a prostitute! Trouble again. The whole time I worked on *Santa* I stayed in a boarding house for American teachers at Chilpancingo 59, which was run by Mrs. Ibáñez, a sweet older lady. Grandma and I had a very large room. It was a quiet place, very peaceful, and the food was delicious.

Juan de la Cruz Alarcón had taken such good care of me when I did the publicity tours for *La Voluntad del Muerto* and *Drácula*. At that time he had been the representative of Universal Pictures in Mexico. Now he had formed *Compañía Nacional Productora de Películas, S.A. de México*, to produce *Santa* and other Mexican films that told stories of our culture.

Before we started filming, Mr. Alarcón drove Federico Gamboa, Carlos Noriega Hope (who had adapted the screenplay) and me to the village of Chimalistac. There we met Emeteria, the Indian woman whose life had been Federico's inspiration for *Santa*. She was an older woman now and I was to play her in her youth. I still had no idea what I was getting into.

Santa was a very popular novel. First published in 1903, it had been performed on the stage and had already been filmed years before during the silent era. In the story, Santa is a young *campesina*, a girl from a small village in the Mexican countryside. She falls in love with Marcelino, an army officer played by Donald Reed, who seduces and then abandons her. Santa's brothers find out about the affair and kick her out of the house (as is customary in Mexico—you do something wrong and that's that; out of your home you go). Santa goes to the big city and wanders the streets. She tries to enter a church for refuge, but it's locked. A madam sees her and asks, "Do you have a place to go?" When she says, "No," the madam gives Santa her card. That night when Santa can't find anyplace else, she goes to the madam's bordello. In Mexico it's called a "house of tolerance."

The madam, Doña Elvira, was played by Mimí Derba; she had already produced and directed her own silent films. Carlos Orellana was the wonderful actor who played Hipólito, the blind pianist who falls in love with Santa. We did something awful to him. I had the idea to break an egg and put the skin of the egg inside his eyes to make him look like a blind man.

Santa becomes the most famous courtesan in Mexico. Eventually, she meets a bullfighter, Jarameño, played by Juan José Martínez Casado. The bullfighter falls in love with Santa and wants to marry her. She leaves the bordello to live with him in the city. They are happy for a while, until one Sunday afternoon when he goes to the bullring and she stays home. Marcelino, the army officer who had seduced her, happens to walk by the bullfighter's house and sees Santa on the balcony. He bribes the maid to let him in. He surprises Santa, but she tells him that her bullfighter is the only decent man she knows, the only man who has ever taken care of her.

Meanwhile, the bullfight is canceled and Jarameño comes home early. He finds Santa with Marcelino. Not giving her a chance to explain, the bullfighter, of course, throws her out. She has no place to go but back to the bordello.

Then Santa gets sick and she's thrown out of the "house of tolerance." She sends a message to Hipólito, the blind piano player who is in love with her. Hipólito takes her to his modest rooms, where he lives with his young *Lazarillo* (blind man's guide) named Jorge, who was played by the son of the assistant director, Ramón Peón. Hipólito sends for a doctor. Santa has cancer and needs an expensive operation. Hipólito begs the doctor to help and gives him all his meager savings. They operate (they filmed a real operation), but she dies on the operating table. The movie ends with Hipólito praying at Santa's grave.

* * *

The sound engineers on this first Mexican talkie were the Rodríguez brothers, Joselito and Roberto. Their family had moved from Mexico City to California so their sons could study in Los Angeles. Joselito studied electrical engineering while Roberto was more interested in cinematography. The brothers were in love with the movies. Together, they invented and built a portable sound recorder. When Mr. Alarcón heard a demonstration of their invention in 1931, he convinced them to return to Mexico to be part of the filming of *Santa*. The family sold their bakery, loaded their delivery truck with all their recording equipment, and drove to Mexico City.

One Sunday morning Joselito and Roberto came for me in their big sound truck. "Come with us," they said, "we're going to visit the president!" We felt we were going to make history with our film, so the president should welcome us with open arms. We drove right up to Maximilian's castle in Chapultepec Park, where President Ortiz Rubio now lived. Of course, we were not allowed in, but we had a good time and we laughed a lot.

The next year, after *Santa* had become a big success, President Ortiz Rubio asked me to autograph a photo for him. I told him about our attempt to visit him in the castle, and he had a good laugh.

NUEVO MUNDO
Una Revista Mexicana

LUPITA TOVAR
SANTA

**ABRIL N° 7
UN PESO**

MUNDO AL DIA
5 CTS — 44 PGS

Para "Mundo al Día" con un cordial saludo. Lupita Tovar — Hollywood

19

"MY FAVORITE FILM"

Santa was one of the best experiences of my life. We started filming November 12, 1931, in the village of Chimalistac, San Angel. We filmed the interiors on the same stage in Chapultepec, where I had made my first screen test for Robert Flaherty. It was not at all like the Hollywood studios. There were holes in the walls and in the roof, and often they had to tie blankets over the camera to deaden its sound. But there was tremendous enthusiasm and pride among the crew and the actors. We knew that, with this talkie, we were starting something that was important to our Mexican film industry.

The producers didn't have much money. They were supposed to pay me one hundred and fifty dollars a week; it eventually became one hundred and fifty dollars *a month*. It didn't matter; I was just happy to be in that film. One of the producers was Francisco (Pancho) Cabrera, whom I would meet again in Spain.

Alex Phillips was our cameraman. A big, tall man, he had been born in Canada, but his parents were Greek. He could carry the huge camera and tripod over one arm. Alex had worked with several Mexican actors in Hollywood, among them Emilio Fernández, who went on to become one of Mexico's great directors. These Mexican actors had told Alex all about our country, so when Mr. Alarcón approached him with an offer to be the cinematographer of *Santa*, Alex immediately said, "Yes." Instead of traveling by train, he drove the two thousand miles, and along the way he fell in love with Mexico. He also fell in love with Alicia Bolaños, a cousin of the Rodríguez family. They married, and Alex never left Mexico.[4]

Antonio Moreno had already acted in more than a hundred films but this was his first time directing. One day he was filming a close-up of me and he was telling me what to think of and what to feel.

I said, "Tony, you know what I am thinking of right now? A beautiful roast turkey." The crew laughed at that. It was three o'clock in the afternoon and we hadn't had a lunch break. We worked long hours, but nobody complained.

I had absolutely no experience in the situations I had to act for this story. The first part of the film, where the girl is very innocent, was fine. That was very natural for me. But to perform the other part—the courtesan—that was difficult. I had never seen such people. I hadn't even gone to a nightclub!

Tony said, "There is a group of women extras in the back room. I want you to copy the way they walk, the way they behave." He said, "Watch them. Watch the way they look at men; their walk is very important."

I had never seen or heard of such a place as a bordello. The first time I had even danced with a man was in Los Angeles at the Mexican consul's New Year's Eve party. It was a strange experience for me, having been so sheltered, to play a "lady of pleasure."

Santa was my favorite film because we were like a family on the set. We did everything together. It was a group of people helping one another, and we had fun.

---

[4] Their son, Alex, Jr., became a cinematographer and filmed several of my son Pancho's movies in Mexico and in Hollywood.

Agustín Lara, who composed the music for *Santa*, drank and took drugs. He often disappeared for days. Our pianist, Maestro Cereijo, knew him and would find him for us. The first time he brought Agustín to the set to watch the filming I thought he looked very strange. He was very skinny and had a crooked mouth. At the end of the day as he sat down at our piano and began to compose his theme for the movie, his eyes never left me. And as he played, Maestro Cereijo quickly wrote down the notes.

Agustín Lara's theme song for *Santa* became very popular and it was identified with me. For many years, whenever I entered a restaurant in Mexico, the musicians would immediately play the movie's theme. These are the lyrics:

En la eterna noche, de mi desconsuelo
Tú has sido la estrella, que alumbra mi cielo.
Yo he adivinado, tu rara hermosura.
  Has iluminado mi negrura.
Santa, Santa mía, mujer que brilla en mi
  existencia.
Santa, sé me guía, en el triste calvario de vivir
Aparta de mi senda, todas las espinas calienta
  con tus besos, mi desilusión
Santa, Santa mía, alumbra con tu luz mi
  corazón

English translation:

In the eternal night of my troubles
You have been the star that lights up my sky
I have divined your rare beauty
You have lit up my darkness
Santa, my Santa, you are the light of my
  existence;
You lead me in the painful trial of my life,
You clear the thorns from my path,
And with your kisses you warm my disillusioned
  heart.
Santa, my Santa, your light illuminates my
  heart.[5]

During the filming of *Santa*, Pedro Rubín, who was a famous dancer, asked me to be his partner

Lupita Tovar in the opening scene of *Santa*

---

5   "Santa" by Agustin Lara. Copyright © 1932 by Peer International Corporation Copyright Renewed. All Rights Reserved. Used by permission.

at a charity event on the stage of the Palacio de Bellas Artes. I was scared to death, but of course I said yes. We practiced the tango on the set. Pedro would say, "Just follow me. Don't worry."

That night the theater was sold out. I had never performed on a stage before an audience. I was not a dancer! As we danced "El Choclo," an Argentine tango, I didn't know if I was coming or going. And I was not dressed correctly. I wore a white strapless gown; Pedro wore a gaucho outfit! We did the dance and the applause was tremendous!

Had it not been for the difficulties with my father, I would have been tempted to stay and make Mexican films. I loved Mexico, my school friends, and my family. But I knew that I couldn't stay, because sooner or later there would be more trouble. I had been taught to respect and obey my father, but my life at home would be intolerable. Besides, I had fallen in love with Paul Kohner. Even when he was in Europe, we wrote to each other every day. When Paul returned, he called me from Los Angeles. He was very disappointed that I would not be back for Christmas; I couldn't leave until we finished filming. I missed him terribly.

Lupita Tovar and Donald Reed in *Santa*

Lupita Tovar and Carlos Orellana in *Santa*

AUTHOR'S NOTE:

SANTA, THE FIRST MEXICAN TALKIE

Santa is considered the *Gone With the Wind* of Mexican Cinema. The story had first been made as a silent film in 1918, directed by Luis G. Peredo. It was remade twice after Lupita's 1931 version—in 1943 with Esther Fernández, and again in 1969, starring the actress Julissa. In 1978 Televisa produced a twelve-part television series of *Santa* starring Tina Romero. None of these versions was as successful as the 1931 early-sound version.

Federico Gamboa, who wrote *Santa*, was born in 1864 in Mexico City, and died there in 1939. He was a novelist, poet, playwright, and diplomat. He was also a journalist and a director of the Mexican Literary Academy. He wrote *Santa* as a naturalistic novel in the style of Émile Zola. In the book, Gamboa concentrates on the lowest and darkest side of human nature; he emphasizes the crude and the obscene. He describes the lives of his characters in graphic detail. His language and descriptions are much truer to the lives of the Mexican lower class than portrayed in the movie. Unlike in the movie, when Santa is first seduced she becomes pregnant and miscarries in her fourth month. Gamboa writes in lurid detail of how her mother finds her as she is drawing water from the well in the town plaza, "That's when the pain strikes her, and then the hemorrhaging, as her dog licks the blood from her legs." After she has been thrown out of her home, Santa works in progressively worse brothels and she enjoys her work; she is promiscuous. And only in the book does her friend, the blind piano player Hipólito, rape her in sexual frustration. These were subjects not discussed in Mexico at the turn of the century. No wonder this book was a best seller; and no wonder Lupita's father didn't want *Santa* in his house.

In 1937, Paul Kohner acquired an option to co-produce an English-language version of *Santa* with his friend Joe Pasternak; but when seven years elapsed without a production, the rights reverted to the Gamboa estate.

Agustín Lara wrote many film scores and over six hundred songs. The theme song he composed for *Santa* became a classic. Agustín was Mexico's most prolific and most loved poet/musician; he was well known throughout the Spanish-speaking world. He is best known for the songs "Granada" and "María Bonita." In 1944 he married movie star María Félix. After that marriage ended in divorce, he married three more times.

Rogelio Agrasánchez, Jr., wrote in his book, *Mexican Movies in the United States*:

> The newly refurbished Teatro California reopened on May 20, 1932, for the Los Angeles premiere of Mexico's first sound picture [*Santa*]. This gripping drama, based on Federico Gamboa's widely read novel of the same name, had sprouted many stage adaptations and even a silent film with Elena Sánchez Valenzuela in the lead. The new version, starring Lupita Tovar and directed by Antonio Moreno, met with enormous success in Mexico City and was applauded by audiences throughout the United States.
>
> Among the artists attending on opening night at the Teatro California,

Teatro California Marquee, 1932 premiere of *Santa*

Santa premiere with Lupita Tovar and Frank Fouce at far right

in Los Angeles, were Lupita Tovar, José Mojica, the comedians Laurel and Hardy, Ramón Pereda, Luana Alcáñiz, Julio Pena, Juan Torena, Paul Ellis, Carlos Villarías, Barry Norton, Mona Maris, Ernesto Vilches, José Crespo, Mimí Aguglia, Adriana Lamar, and Conchita Ballesteros. These were some of the actors who had come from many countries to work in the Hollywood Hispanic productions.

Also presiding at the event was Rafael Calderón, distributor of the film; Frank Fouce, local exhibitor; Juan de la C. Alarcón, producer; and the film critics Gabriel Navarro and Esteban V. Escalante. The Hispanic community of Los Angeles, aware of the importance of this premiere, turned the Teatro California into a celebration of Mexican cinematic efforts. The entrance to the theater sparkled with bright lights as the crowds surrounded their film idols to chat with them or get their autographs. Huge portraits of Lupita Tovar, Antonio Moreno, and Carlos Orellana hung from the marquee.

Every few years there is a celebration in Mexico commemorating the filming of Santa. The first celebration was for the 20th anniversary in 1951. On the 40th anniversary in 1971, the Mexican Press Association awarded Lupita the Diosa de Plata (The Silver Goddess) at a ceremony attended by President Luis Echeverría.

On the 50th anniversary of Santa, a commemorative postage stamp was issued. And in 1996, on the 100th anniversary of Mexican Cinema, a lottery ticket bore Lupita's likeness.

Sound engineer Roberto Rodriquez was there for the 60th anniversary with his nephew, Pepe Romay, who has done so much to keep the memory of that first sound film alive. Raúl de Anda was also there; he had just a small part in Santa, dancing with Sofía Álvarez in the bordello. Raúl went on to act, write, direct, and produce films, and Sofía became a very well-known actress.

Santa was immensely popular because Mexican audiences could relate to the story. It portrayed their lives, their customs, and their traditions, right or wrong.

POSTAGE STAMP

LOTTERY TICKET

LUPITA TOVAR.
Primera dama joven mexicana de la Pantalla, quien está ahora contratada con la compañía "Universal" haciendo películas en español.

20

A DECADENT PLACE

When Grandma and I returned to Los Angeles in January of 1932, Mrs. Fry had found us another furnished bungalow on Highland Avenue, very close to the Hollywood Bowl. We had given up our place on Harold Way, as we had been away almost four months. We had very few possessions—just our clothes and a few books. I was still cautious about spending money; what I didn't send back to my father I saved in my bank account.

The four months without Paul had seemed like an eternity. Now that I was back, he resumed his courtship. Summer evenings Paul would drive over from the studio and we would walk to the Bowl, an outdoor amphitheater, to hear a concert. We sat under real stars and the moon and listened to the orchestra. It was very romantic; we would hold hands. (We always held hands, all our lives together.)

Word got back to Hollywood about my starring role in *Santa* and I was offered more roles, mostly in Westerns. That meant getting up at four-thirty in the morning to be on the set at sunrise. Once, on a Western, they put me on a horse and the horse galloped away with me! They were trying out a pistol and the shot had scared the horse. Buck Jones rode after me. At full gallop, he pulled me off my horse and onto his. I came back lying across his saddle, head down, and the skirts all over. They brought me a glass of water and asked, "Miss Tovar, are you ready to do that again?"

I said yes, without hesitation. I was known for being a good trouper.

On weekends, Paul would take me to dinner and to the theater or, of course, to the movies. When I wrote to my family it was difficult to describe what my life was like—it was so different from theirs.

I bought a new Ford, a little two-door coupe. When the dealer delivered it on a Saturday, I asked him, "How do you turn it on?" He showed me and then he left. He didn't ask me if I knew how to drive.

I got in and, when it started, I was moving! I drove slowly around and around the block, hoping it would run out of gas. Finally, a neighbor saw my predicament. He jumped in and turned it off. The next day he showed me how to drive the car. On Monday morning I drove from Highland Avenue to Cahuenga Boulevard, to the Universal Studios. At the entrance, where the guard was, I couldn't stop. I kept on driving around the lot. When I finally stopped, they took the car away from me and wouldn't let me drive it until I finished the picture I was working on. In the meantime, they had a studio car pick me up and take me home every day.

Having our own car gave Grandma and me independence that would have been unimaginable in Mexico. We drove to the beach; we drove downtown; we drove everywhere. We loved our life in California. I was twenty-two years old and couldn't have been happier!

I worked with director Kurt Neumann in his short film *Estamos en París*, with Slim Summerville and Eddie Gribbon. And then I did the Spanish introduction for *The King of Jazz (El Rey de Jazz)*, with Paul Whiteman, again directed by Kurt Neumann.

* * *

One evening Paul took me to the Embassy Club, which was on top of a building at the corner of Hollywood Boulevard and Highland Avenue. It was very elegant; the men were all in formal wear. As usual, Paul had sent me a corsage. We had dinner and danced. Many of Paul's friends were there, including Ernst Lubitsch, his German wife, actress Helene Kraus, and the writer Hans Kraly. Lubitsch had brought Kraly over from Germany to write screenplays for him.

Paul Kohner, Helene and Ernst Lubitsch, and Hans Kraly

Paul and I were dancing near where Kraly and Helene Lubitsch were dancing, when suddenly Ernst came running onto the dance floor, his face a mask of anger. He was much shorter than Kraly, but he swung and slapped Kraly across the face with tremendous force. They were right next to us, so we couldn't escape their argument. Ernst had just found out that Kraly was having an affair with Helene!

Well, it was a big commotion with lots of shouting. At one point, Lubitsch turned to Paul and shouted: "Kohner, did you know this?" And when Paul didn't answer immediately, he demanded, "How could you not tell me?"

"Mr. Lubitsch," Paul said, "I thought you knew." It seemed that everyone knew what had been going on.

That night when Paul took me home, he said, "If a reporter or anyone asks you what happened tonight, just say you don't know anything." That was easy; I didn't know anything about what was going on with these people.

Lubitsch divorced Helene. He moved out of their house in Bel-Air and lived for a long while at the Beverly Wilshire Hotel. Hans Kraly continued writing scripts, mainly for director Sidney Franklin. He wrote the screenplay for Sidney's *Private Lives*, from Nöel Coward's play. The film starred Norma Shearer, Robert Montgomery, and Reginald Denny, and was a big success.

Hollywood was a wild and sometimes decadent place. Couples divorced and married their friends' wives and husbands, like a fast game of musical chairs. In Mexico, a very Catholic country, divorce was unheard of and not tolerated.

I didn't understand these people.

* * *

Lupita Tovar, 1932

Kurt Neumann directed me again, this time in *El Tenorio del Harem* with Slim Summerville, Tom Kennedy, Eduardo Arozamena, and Manuel Arbó.

Then in March of 1932, I was interviewed by A. Edward Sutherland, who was going to direct *Mr. Robinson Crusoe* for United Artists. This was the company owned by Charlie Chaplin, Mary Pickford, D.W. Griffith, and Douglas Fairbanks. The picture would star Douglas Fairbanks, who was also producing. It was going to be filmed in Fiji and Tahiti in the South Pacific. I got a call for an audition with Douglas, who was married to Mary Pickford. He liked me, I guess, because I got the part and I signed the contract. Soon after that, Douglas invited me to a party at Pickfair. He asked whom I would like as my escort.

"I'd like you to invite Paul Kohner," I told him. "He is a producer at Universal Pictures." It was a big thing to be invited to one of these parties. The Fairbankses were the pinnacle of Hollywood society and their house, Pickfair, was a mansion, large and elegant, like an English country estate.

At the party I danced with Ronald Colman, who was known as the quintessential Hollywood-Englishman. It was like a dream. When he looked down at me, my knees shook. All the Hollywood stars were there, and Douglas introduced me as his next leading lady! I danced with Clive Brook, the English stage actor, who was now a leading man in Hollywood films. When Paul and I left, the valet called out in a loud voice, "Miss Lupita Tovar's car!" Paul didn't like that very much.

The next day at the studio, Junior Laemmle was jealous. He had never been invited to "Pickfair." He called Paul a "social climber." Paul just laughed.

The following week, Douglas Fairbanks invited me to a late afternoon party by the pool at the United Artists studio backlot at Santa Monica Boulevard and Formosa Avenue. When I got there, everyone was naked! Even Eddie Sutherland was naked in the pool! I turned and ran. I felt so naive.

Then I found out I was going to be the only woman on that South Pacific island; there wasn't even going to be a makeup woman! No women and thirty men on a faraway location! I told the studio, "Suppose I get sick or something. No, I'd like to have a companion. I won't go without a chaperone." The studio refused my request, saying that I had already signed the contract. I insisted and, in the end, I got out of the contract and their lawyer gave me a small check anyway, to keep me quiet, I guess. María Alba took my part. María was married to the casting director at Fox.

I was very upset, but then I got a dozen yellow roses with a note:

Dear Miss Tovar,
You don't know how right you are
to turn down this film.
You have my admiration and
respect.
—Mary Pickford.

She knew how disappointed I was, but I had done the right thing and I wouldn't regret it. She knew what happened on remote film locations, especially where her husband was concerned. When the picture was over and everyone returned to Hollywood, María Alba's husband divorced her and she went back to Spain. The film was not a success for the studio.

The next time I saw Mr. Fairbanks was in Tijuana. Paul and I were there for a charity event. I walked into the casino and there he was with his whole entourage. I just nodded and went on my way; we didn't speak. I did remain on good terms with Mary Pickford, however. I met her again years later, when Paul and I were married. She was divorced from Douglas Fairbanks and was with Buddy Rogers. Mary reminded me of my wise decision not to go on location with Douglas Fairbanks.

The only other time that I had an unpleasant experience at a studio was at M-G-M. I was asked to come in for an interview on a Saturday afternoon at five o'clock. On Saturday afternoon there was not a soul on the lot. In those days, you wore gloves and a hat. I went to the executive's office, and right away he said, "Take off your gloves." So I took off my gloves. He said, "Stand up." So I stood up. He looked me up and down and said, "Come on, come on—show me your legs." I began to lift my skirt, but it wasn't enough for him.

"*Higher*," he demanded.

"No, sir," I said, and I got my purse to leave.

"Come here!" he said. He chased me around the desk. I ran out of his office and out of the studio.

That evening Paul asked me, "Well, how was your interview at M-G-M?" I told him what happened, and shortly after I heard that L. B. Mayer had fired that man.

I was happy; I was working a lot and everything was going well. Paul and I were in love; he was the perfect gentleman, and my grandma approved of him.

* * *

Then one evening in May of 1932, Paul told me out of the blue that he was going to Germany. Universal had blocked currency there and films could be made more cheaply in Europe than in Hollywood. He was going to be in charge of production in Berlin, and he didn't know when he would be coming back. His father was very ill—a problem with his gallbladder—and he would probably have to have surgery; Paul wanted to be closer to him. He went on to say that he was in no position to make a commitment to me. He had to see what would happen in Germany before he could make any plans for our future.

"Please understand," he said quietly.

I felt like the bottom had fallen out of my world. I felt as though I had been punched in the stomach! Paul tried to hand me a ring. My English was not so good. I did not understand how he could offer me a ring and yet not make a commitment. I refused to take it, and I ran upstairs, sobbing. Paul called my grandma and asked her to keep the ring for me, saying that it was very difficult for him to explain things to me, and he hoped it wouldn't be too long before he could make good.

21

"I CRIED MY HEART OUT"

I had never gone on a date with anyone else. Paul had seen to it that nobody could get near me. At the studio it was quietly understood that he was my boyfriend. Paul liked to show me new things and I was always happy and ready to go anyplace he took me. He took me to concerts, to the opera, and to all the important openings and dinners, always with another couple, usually Willy Wyler and his date. This new life was so exciting for me—so totally different from anything I had imagined growing up in Mexico. I loved every minute of it.

Sunday afternoons, Paul would often take me for coffee to Ernst Lubitsch's house. There I met Greta Garbo and many of the Europeans in Hollywood. They all spoke in German, but I tried to figure out what they were saying. I was never bored. Now all that came to an end.

I had been photographed often at the studio by Freulich and other portrait photographers. I had given Paul some of these large glamour photos with inscriptions like, "To Paul, darling, I love you," and, "To Paul, with all my love." Now Paul, who liked to sit for portrait photos himself, gave me a very serious photo with the inscription,

> Every day, I'll love you more,—
> today more than yesterday—
> but not as much as tomorrow…
> Chin up, darling, we'll come thru all right.
> April 30th 1932 —Paul.

Paul Kohner, 1932

When Paul left for Europe, I went to see him off at the train station. Dr. Weitzfelder and his wife, Annie, came with us. They had taken me under their wing. When I saw the train leave the station, my heart sank. I thought that was the end of my life. For days I couldn't think straight. I lost so much weight that people asked me if I was sick.

* * *

My friend Frank Fouce, who had helped me get the part in Columbia's *Carne de Cabaret*, came to see me with his wife, Anita. Frank was now promoting and distributing films. He wanted me to go with them to the Mexican border towns with prints of my movies and make personal appearances on stage. We would split the money fifty-fifty. I was not working at the time, so I agreed.

The three of us squeezed into Frank's small car and took off. We would check into a hotel in Mexicali or Tijuana. Frank would take the print of the film to the theater while Anita helped me dress in my Mexican costume, and stayed with me backstage. Frank managed the box office, and he was the master of ceremonies. I would make a little speech before and after the film and answer questions from the audience.

Back at the hotel, we were usually famished. Frank would order some dinner and we would divide the pesos. We did this for about three weeks. One time on the way to showing *La Voluntad del Muerto* in a small town just over the Mexican border, we drove through a brush fire that swept across the road. In those days, film stock was made of extremely flammable nitrate. The print, which was in the trunk of the car, could have easily caught fire, as it did sometimes in projection booths!

I finally got a call from the casting office at Universal and I got a small part in Raoul Walsh's *The Cock-Eyed World*. The film starred Victor McLaglen, Edmund Lowe, and Lili Damita.

The months went by slowly. Paul wrote and told me that his father was recuperating from surgery. He also told me he was busy preparing to film *S.O.S. Iceberg* in Greenland with Leni Riefenstahl and WWI flying ace Ernst Udet.

One Sunday afternoon, I was invited for coffee at the house of Henry Blanke, a producer friend of Paul's; he was married to a German girl, Ursula. I was very happy to go.

There were many Europeans there, whom I'd met before with Paul. Suddenly, Ursula Blanke said to me in a loud voice for everyone to hear, "You'd better forget about Paul. He is dating my sister, Crystal, and I'm sure they will get married in Berlin."

I was speechless. Everybody stared at me, eyes full of pity. I slowly took my purse and left without saying a word. I went home and cried my heart out.

"I don't believe it," Grandma said, putting her arms around me. She told me that Paul had left the ring with her for safekeeping and I should not pay attention to that Ursula woman. I didn't know what to believe, but I stopped answering Paul's letters and I started to go out on dates.

Ernst Laemmle had already taken me out to dinner and movies several times, but I really didn't think of those evenings as dates. Then one night when he brought me home, he gave me a ring. On the inside was engraved, "*Te amo*" (I love you).

I tried to give it back to him, telling him sincerely, "Ernst, I think of you as a friend, just a good friend."

Ernst said, "Wear it anyway. You know, Paul isn't coming back."

I didn't want to hurt his feelings, so I kept it. But I dismissed what he said about Paul not coming back. A few weeks later, Ernst asked for the ring back. On a trip to Hawaii with writer Preston Sturges he had met a beautiful Hawaiian girl. I was relieved, and we were able to stay friends.

22

"DARLING, WILL YOU MARRY ME?"

Dick Shire, a Universal Pictures executive, invited me to one of his famous house parties. His secretary called and told me one of the drivers from Universal would pick me up. It was a summer evening and the party was around the swimming pool. Everyone was drinking, and pretty soon somebody pushed John Huston into the pool, fully dressed! Others followed and, before I knew it, Huston was running after me with just a towel around his waist, through the tennis court and garden. I got away and hid in the bushes, shaking; then I sneaked into the house and called Ernst to rescue me!

I went out to the road and waited until I saw Ernst's car. He blinked his lights on and off so I would know it was him. When I jumped in the car and told Ernst what happened, he gave me hell: "How can you be so dumb as to go to a wild Hollywood party—alone?"

"I didn't know," I said. "Dick Shire's secretary called and said Mr. Shire would like to invite me to a party at his home and I was to be picked up. I thought it was a regular get-together."

"For your information," Ernst said, "when they have this kind of party, they go through a studio list of young unattached girls who can entertain the guests. *Don't* accept any more invitations like *this*!"

I said, "Of course not—thank you." When I got home I went straight to bed, pulling the covers up to my chin.

At six the next morning the phone rang. It was Dick Shire.

"Lupita, are you all right?"

"Yes," I said, reluctantly.

"When did you go home?"

"Early," I said.

"Jack Oakie said he saw Huston chasing you around like a madman, then you disappeared, and so did Huston, and then there was a car accident, so I was very worried about you. Do you know where Huston went?"

"No," I said. "I phoned a friend to pick me up. I've been asleep."

"Well, I'm glad you're all right."

That afternoon John Huston called, but I refused to talk to him.

Ernst found out that Huston had gone to the party with Greta Nissen and her husband, Weldon Heyburn. On the way home they had landed in a ditch! "Heyburn has a broken collarbone," Ernst told me. After that experience I played it safe by just going to the movies with Grandma or to dinner with Ernst.

Paul wrote to Annie and Dr. Weitzfelder to please see what was going on and to tell me to answer his letters. I didn't know what to say.

After I made a test at Columbia Studios for a Western, Harry Cohn—who was the head of the studio—asked to meet me. He was curious about me, but polite. I got the part. To celebrate, Ernst took me dancing at a nightclub and our names made it into Louella Parson's gossip column: "Petite Lupita Tovar and Ernst Laemmle seem to be an item. They were seen dancing and enjoying themselves at Mocambo."

The next week, I got a telegram from Paul: "What about Ernst? Please answer." Somebody had sent him the newspaper clipping.

William Wyler, Zita Johann, Lupita, and Ernst Laemmle

The previous Sunday, Frank and Anita Fouce had taken me, in my Mexican costume, to San Pedro, the Los Angeles harbor town. Before showing my film, I was on stage, just talking and telling stories. The audience was mostly sailors. My share from the box office that night was fifty American dollars! I decided to spend the money on a long-distance phone call. Not realizing the difference in time when I called, Paul was not in his office. So I told the operator to call me back when he got there. I waited until midnight. When the phone finally rang, the operator said, "I have Mr. Kohner on the line."

I said, "Hello."

And right away Paul said, "Darling, will you marry me?"

I said, "Will you repeat that?" I wanted to make sure I'd heard him right.

He shouted so I could hear him all the way from Germany, "WILL YOU MARRY ME?"

"Yes!" I said, and hung up the phone.

I ran to grandma's room and said, "Grandma, I'm getting married! Paul just proposed to me!"

We hugged and cried and she said, "Here is the ring he left for you."

I was so happy and much too excited to sleep. In the morning I sent Paul a cable, with no mention of Ernst; it just read, "I love only you."

The next day I went to Columbia to see Harry Cohn.

I told him, "I'm sorry. Something has come up and I can't do the film. I'm going to Europe."

He got angry: "Wait a minute. We made tests of many actors. Yours was the best, and we chose you. And now you have the nerve to tell me you're not going to do the film?"

"That's right," I said. "I'm going to Europe."

"Then that's it for you. You'll never work at this studio as long as I live!"

"That's all right with me," I said. And I quickly left his office.

As it turns out, I could have done the film. It was just a twenty-seven day schedule. I could have made some money and arranged things calmly, but no, I was only thinking of Paul and how quickly I could get to Europe.

I got a long letter from Paul, in which he asked me to keep our marriage plans a secret. He didn't want Carl Laemmle to think that his mind wasn't on his job. Paul was in charge of all production in Germany. I was to tell everybody I was going to Europe to make a film. There really was a picture for me, and he was getting the script. The title of the film was *Ecstasy*. It was going to be shot in Prague, Czechoslovakia.

I wanted to shout to the world that I was getting married to the man I was madly in love with, but I did as he asked.

I decided to call my father because I wanted his blessing.

"I'm going to get married," I announced as soon as he was on the phone. I wanted him to understand that I was not asking for his permission. I told him what kind of a man Paul was, and that he was not a Catholic, but that he was a wonderful man.

After a moment, my father asked, "Is he a good son?"

I answered, "I don't think there is any son as good as this man because his family and his mother are so important to him."

My father said he respected my decision and I had his blessing. Then he said, "Just know that if you get a divorce, you cannot enter this house again, ever!" What else could I expect from my father?

So, I left to get married.

CINE-MUNDIAL

FEBRERO 1931

pita
var

23

"THE MEXICAN ROSE"

I wrote a long letter to Pepe. It was very difficult for me, but I owed him an honest explanation. He had been my only boyfriend, and I always had feelings for him, but they were not serious feelings on my part. If I had never come to Hollywood we might have gotten married by default, but I had left Mexico. And my grand adventure had led to meeting Paul. In my letter to Pepe, I told him that I was in love with Paul and I was going to Europe to be married to him.

Pepe was devastated by the news. He neglected his studies and had to repeat a year of medical school.

I arranged for my grandma to go back to Mexico with friends; then I booked passage from New York to Germany on the S.S. *Deutschland*, as Paul had instructed. I couldn't get to Europe and to Paul soon enough!

There was a girl, Lita Friede, from Poland. She was an extra in crowd scenes. A writer by the name of Emil Forst looked after her. He came to me and said, "Lupita, I hear you are going to Europe. Look, this girl has no future here; she needs to go back to her family in Poland. I cannot afford to pay the whole fare but I can give her some money, if you would help her."

I said, "Mr. Forst, I'd like to help, but my trip already costs so much, and I cannot spend all the money I have in case I have to come back, you know." Paul had arranged for my train ticket to New York and boat passage from New York to Cuxhaven, Germany, but I had other expenses.

Nevertheless, I met Lita and I felt very sorry for her; she had no clothes, no money, nothing. So I said to Mr. Forst, "Instead of first class, I will go tourist and the difference I will give to Lita, and you can match that." So Lita went with me, and we shared a cabin.

I returned my little Ford to the dealer to keep in storage and, on August 20, 1932, Dr. Weitzfelder and his wife took me to the station to board the train for New York.

The Santa Fe Grand Canyon Limited left at noon for the East Coast. I had goose bumps, I was so excited. Mrs. Fry and Ernst were there to see me off. Ernst looked like I must have looked when I had said good-bye to Paul, six months earlier. Emil Forst was there to say good-bye to Lita. The Olympic Games had just taken place in Los Angeles, and the Argentine team was making so much noise while waiting to board, it was hard for us to even hear each other. Finally, the train started to move and we waved out a window until we couldn't see the station anymore. It was September, and it was hot! Lita and I were practically broke, so we didn't go to the dining car. Instead, we ate the fruit and candy that our friends had given us.

The beginning of every journey is full of mixed emotions. When I left Mexico for the first time three years earlier, I was eager to leave home and my father's bad temper. But I was also leaving behind all that I knew and loved; especially my sisters and my brother. I was leaving a familiar life of school and family. Now I was heading out again on a great unknown adventure; this time with no thought of what I was leaving. I was only thinking of the future. I should have had some trepidation. I couldn't even be sure I would find Paul when I arrived—and what then? And if he was there waiting for me, what did it mean to be married? If my parents were any example, I didn't want any part of marriage. And to tell the truth, I was still a little scared of getting pregnant, married or not.

* * *

I kept a diary, a record of that long-ago trip, in a little book that I still have. In it I wrote the following:

At 5 o'clock the first day we stopped in Barstow for half an hour. We got off and ate at a nice diner for 50 cents each. We went to bed early but couldn't sleep. It was too hot. Through Needles, California, it was 120 degrees!

The next day we got up at 7:00 a.m. No breakfast, it was still very hot and we were drinking ice water all the time. At one stop I received a telegram from Willy Wyler, wishing me a safe trip. We had a sandwich and fruit and looked at the lovely scenery.

In Albuquerque we saw an Indian parade and, while walking on the station platform, we met a family with their little boy, Jackie. Lita and I were just as fascinated with the Indians in the parade as Jackie was.

We had dinner for a dollar each in a charming place at a stop in New Mexico. We lost track of time and had to run to catch the train.

The Argentine athletes came to visit us, and we talked until 9:00 p.m.

The next day we were back on our diet of fruit and candy. What we did have was too many boxes and packages, so when we stopped in Kansas City, we took a taxi to a pawn shop and bought a suitcase for a dollar and 25 cents. Back at the station, we had dinner and a manicure. The train left at 6:30, and we went to bed early.

We arrived in Chicago at 7:20 in the morning. Frank Iltes, from Universal Pictures, and Eddy Kohner, Paul's cousin, met us and took us out to breakfast. Chicago is a very charming city. Eddy and Mr. Iltes, who was also from Teplitz, took us to the central depot, where we boarded the Twentieth Century Limited, which left at 10:20. The train was very nice and clean, and for a change we had lunch in the dining car. We were traveling in style now.

We met two gentlemen on the train who bought us ice cream. After so many miles of desert and plains, the scenery between Chicago and New York was green and beautiful. We went to bed early and slept very well.

* * *

When we arrived in New York, a friend of Paul's met us and took us to the boat on Pier 84 at 42nd Street. The S.S. *Deutschland* was huge. We left our baggage on board and took a taxi to a five-and-ten-cent store to buy a belt. In the excitement, somehow, I had lost mine. Then we rode on a two-level bus and sat in the top section. The buildings were so tall and the streets so noisy! I was overwhelmed by New York.

We were taken to the Universal Pictures office, where we met lots of people. I autographed photos for Mr. Manheim of the publicity department, and he gave me letters of introduction to the Universal offices in Paris, London, and Spain.

I met a film distributor from South America who wanted me to change my plans and go with him to Argentina! He promised me all kinds of things.

"I'm on my way to make a picture—perhaps some other time," I said.

They all thought I was going to Europe to make *Ecstasy*; they didn't know I was going to see my sweetheart. Since Paul didn't want Mr. Laemmle to know why I was going to Europe, I never let on about our plans to marry. And since Paul had told me about the picture in Prague, I was very convincing.

The man from South America had seen my movies and he was crazy about me. From that moment, he stuck to us like glue. He took us to dinner, to a speakeasy, and then back to the boat, which was sailing at midnight.

was having a wonderful time with all the German athletes. They called me "*Die Mexikanische Rose*" (the Mexican Rose). They thought I was beautiful.

I said, "*Shush*."

I never thought I was so pretty.

Lupita, with the German Olympic team on the S.S. *Deutschland*

Our departure was terribly exciting, with a band playing, flowers, paper streamers, and so many people saying good-bye. We stayed on deck as tugboats pulled us out into the harbor and shivers went down my neck when the ship sounded its horn as we passed by the Statue of Liberty. It was two in the morning when we finally went to sleep.

Lita and I had a wonderful time. The German Olympic Team was on board and most nights we stayed up dancing and having fun with them.

The trip was almost over when I was called to the captain's office. The wife of Eddie Knopf, a writer working for Paul in Berlin, was traveling in first class. When Mrs. Knopf couldn't find me, she cabled her husband that I was not on board. That's how Paul found out I was traveling tourist. He wanted me transferred to first class immediately. I wouldn't bother changing cabins now; besides, I

"To my sweetheart with all my love—Lupita," 1932

PART TWO

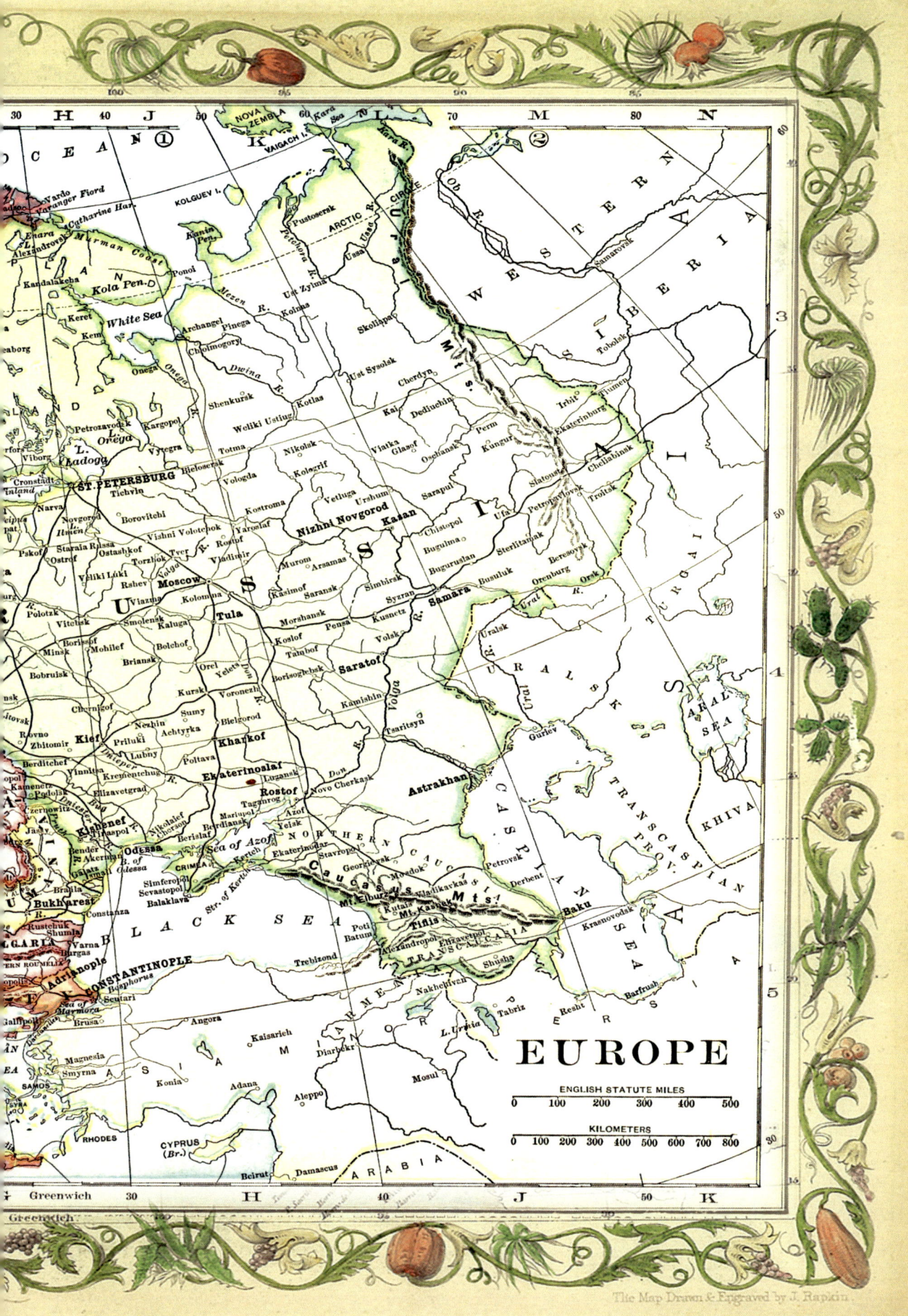

¿Ha comprado el segundo número de **FOTOGÉNICAS?** Pues hágalo antes no se agote la edición

Está de venta en todos los kioscos y librerías; si no lo encuentra pídalo a esta Administración: Mallorca 235

TALLERES GRÁFICOS IRÁNDEZ. — ARAGÓN, 197. — TELÉFONO 71872. — BARCELONA

24

BERLIN—1932

Paul was waiting for me on the dock when we arrived at Cuxhaven, Germany. I hadn't seen him for six long months! As I walked down the steps from the ship, my heart was pounding. I looked at him, unsure of what to say. His arms were full of flowers, but he opened them for me and hugged me. I wanted to kiss him but there were people all around; that would have to wait for later. Instead, I found myself saying, "You didn't want *me* to get fat—how about *you*?"

He wasn't really fat, but he hadn't been starving himself, either. Paul was the handsomest man I had ever seen; better looking even than Ronald Colman.

Lita's sister and brother-in-law were there to meet her. We hugged and said our good-byes. We saw each other one more time the following year when Paul invited Lita to meet us for a weekend in Vienna. I often wondered what happened to her after that.

Paul took care of my suitcase and my steamer trunk, and we boarded a train to Hamburg. We sat alone in a compartment and in my poor English I tried to tell him all about my trip across America, the day in New York, and the boat crossing. Paul was tired; he had been up all night traveling. As he lay down with his head on my lap, the boys of the Olympic team kept passing by our compartment, curious to see the man with me.

I knew then that I had made the right decision. I loved Paul with all my heart, and I knew he loved me. Ursula Blanke's sister, Crystal, hadn't been a threat. I was silly to have doubted him while we were apart. Nevertheless, that long-distance phone call was the smartest investment I ever made.

We changed trains in Hamburg and late that night we arrived in Berlin. Paul's friends, Joe and Margie Pasternak, were there at the Bahnhof am Zoo station to welcome us, along with a man playing "*La Paloma*" on a concertina. It was quite late, so we went straight to the Villa Majestic Hotel, where Paul had reserved a room for me. He left me there and said he would call for me the next day at noon. Paul was staying at the villa of Dr. Arnold Fanck, who was in Greenland directing *S.O.S. Iceberg*.

The next morning, Paul phoned to say he had ordered breakfast for me in the room, and he would come to the hotel to take me to lunch. I waited anxiously until he called again, this time from the lobby. He was waiting for me by the elevator. As we crossed the lobby, two young men got up and tipped their hats, expecting to be introduced, but Paul just tipped his hat, and we kept on walking.

"That's Billy Wilder and Franz Shultz," Paul said. "I expect I'll get a call at the office asking, 'Who's the beautiful new girl in town?'"

I couldn't help feeling a sense of pride when Paul said that. I didn't so much care what other people thought, but to hear Paul say that I was beautiful made me feel warm all over. Of course, I was dressed nicely, just as I had been taught at the studio. I wore high heels and silk stockings, gloves and a hat. By comparison, the German women I saw dressed very badly.

We had lunch at Café Josty on the Potsdamer Platz where five major streets converged. There, at the Haus Vaterland—an enormous building with a domed roof—you could go to a movie, go shopping, or eat in restaurants from every corner of the world. I was lost with the language, so Paul wrote the name of my hotel on a piece of paper for me to memorize: Hotel Majestic, Brandenburgische Strasse 47. After lunch, we walked, sightseeing. The city with its linden trees was overwhelmingly beautiful and, just as in New York, crowds of people streamed in and out of the U-Bahn entrances, the subways.

Paul's brother, Frederick, lived in Berlin; we called him Fritz. Paul had sent money home for Fritz to study, first in Vienna, and then at the Sorbonne in Paris. When Paul brought his brother to Hollywood in 1926, Fritz was surprised to discover that his brother lived in a boarding house and not in a grand villa. He thought his older brother was rich. Fritz worked in Hollywood, writing screenplays. But when he wanted to marry his childhood sweetheart, Mimi Klein, the daughter of their family doctor, his own mother had gone to the American Embassy in Prague to ask them not to give Mimi a visa to go to America. If they were going to get married, they would have to do it in Teplitz! So he had returned to Europe. Fritz and Mimi now lived in Berlin, and they had a three-month-old daughter, Ruthie.

Paul's youngest brother, Walter, wanted to be an actor. He was studying at the Max Reinhardt Seminar in Vienna.

In the evenings we often went out with Joe and Margie Pasternak. Margie was American and Joe was a charming Hungarian. He had been a production manager and producer at Universal Pictures in Hollywood and had been sent by Carl Laemmle to work with Paul. It is difficult to describe what it was like for me at twenty-two to arrive in this European city. In Los Angeles, rich people still rode beautiful horses on bridal paths down the middle of Sunset Boulevard, just as they did on the tree-lined Paseo de la Reforma in Mexico City. There, life was slower. Berlin was more like New York, big and crowded, full of automobiles and streetcars. To add to the confusion, the city was still recovering from what they called the "War to End All Wars." In the streets there were beggars in tattered uniforms and people who looked poor and hungry. But in hotels, restaurants, and nightclubs, Berliners were sophisticated and elegantly dressed.

American Jazz was popular; the Lindy Hop and the Charleston were all the rage. At one club—the El Dorado—there were telephones at all the tables with little flags that had the number of that table. There were lots of calls to our table. Paul would answer, "The lady is not available!" I couldn't believe that the beautiful girls performing on stage were all female impersonators!

I was having a wonderful time. It was late September, with crisp fall weather. Soon I was going to be married to the man of my dreams; life couldn't get any better!

Lupita and Paul, Berlin, 1932

25

PAPA JULIUS

Paul's father, Julius Kohner, came to Berlin from Teplitz. Margie picked me up at the Majestic Hotel to go to Paul's house for coffee and to meet his father. I was very nervous. Margie had told me that a month before, when Paul went home to tell his family that he was going to be married and that his bride was already on the way, his mother got very upset. I was Mexican, I was not Jewish, and, on top of that, I was an actress! Paul's mother had already picked a girl for him to marry from a rich Jewish family in Teplitz.

There had been a terrible argument between Paul and his mother. Paul had walked out and stayed at a hotel that night. Then his mother threatened to divorce her husband if Paul went through with his plans, and his father stayed away all night, too. I had asked Paul about his family when I arrived, but all he said was that they were in Czechoslovakia.

Margie and I arrived late. We had walked around the block several times because I was scared to go in the house. When we finally did go in, I was shaking like a leaf. Paul and his father were already having coffee. Paul got up, kissed my hand, and said to his father, "Papa, this is Lupita." The old gentleman looked me up and down and asked in English, "Do you love my son?"

I answered, "Yes, Mr. Kohner, I do, very much. I wouldn't be here if I didn't love him."

"Come here," he said, pointing to his cheek for me to kiss him. "I never had a daughter. Call me Papa." He put his arms around me and held me. My own father had never done that.

We had coffee and all kinds of delicious pastries, and then Paul's father got up and went to the telephone. He called his wife. They talked a long time. Then he called Paul to the phone: "Talk to your mother." I noticed that Paul was very cold to his mother. Then Papa Kohner got back on the phone and Margie translated for me: "Papa Kohner just said, 'Then I am going to London with the children. They will be married there! I will go with the girl first and Paul will go when everything is ready.'"

I never understood why Papa chose London. But Paul had a good friend, Dave Bader, at the Universal London office; Dave could make all the arrangements. I would have to go first to establish residence.

Papa stayed a couple more days in Berlin. In the mornings he would pick me up at the hotel and we would go walking—*spazieren gehen*, he called it. After lunch he went home to rest. He was still recuperating from his gallbladder surgery.

Then I'd wait at the hotel for Paul to take me to his house in the evening and we would have dinner with his father. Papa Julius was a very sweet man, charming and witty with a wonderful sense of humor. It was very easy to love him. He adored Paul. He had visited Paul in Los Angeles in 1921, and he spoke a little English. When we were alone together he taught me words in German, some I should not have learned.

Paul was busy with several productions. In the

evenings, he had to look at thousands of feet of film coming from *S.O.S. Iceberg* in Greenland and from his other movies being filmed in Berlin.

Papa Julius left; apparently, his wife had relented. She said she couldn't face her friends if Paul did not come home to get married.

The next weekend Paul and I took the train to Teplitz. Paul said, "You don't have to worry, darling, I'm sure my mother will be very nice to you. But if she is not, you don't have to be nice to her." The thought of meeting his mother terrified me. When we crossed the border at Bodenbach, people came to the window, yelling in Czech, "*Pivo, horké párky.*" I looked at Paul and he translated, "Beer and hot dogs."

I couldn't help thinking, without Paul at my side, I couldn't even order lunch.

When we arrived late in the afternoon, there was a welcoming committee at the station: Grandmother Caroline Béamt, a very regal lady wearing all her jewels, her son Rudolph (Uncle Rudy), Aunt Clara Fischer (Tante Clara), Helene (my mother-in-law-to-be), and Papa Julius Kohner. Papa was the first to come forward. He greeted me with a big smile and introduced me to the family. Helene shook hands with me and handed me a small bunch of flowers. Then she examined me from head to toe, as though I had come from another planet. She was less than five feet tall, shorter than me and with no waist at all.

Papa and Paul took me first to the Hotel Dietrich to register, and then we walked to the family house on Hauptstrasse for dinner. The beautiful stone house had two stories and was in the middle of a garden with large trees. That evening Paul's mother had changed into a pink dress with flowers. She said to me, coquettishly, "Did you think I was going to be so young?" Someone translated for me. I didn't know how to respond, so I just smiled politely.

I thought Mexican women were uninformed, but I learned that when Helene became pregnant with her first child, Paul, she had no idea what was happening to her, or why. She had an *amme* (wet-nurse) come from the country to nurse her babies. That was the custom. Helene belonged to the class of women who didn't actually do anything. Each afternoon, she would meet the ladies for needlepoint at a café in the park. She always wore a hat and furs. The serving girls in the cafés, who carried trays of pastries, wore uniforms with white head caps. Helene always ate rich pastries with her coffee. It was a miracle she didn't get fat.

The house was lovely, full of antiques and old furniture. There were tile stoves that burned charcoal for heat in each room. There was a formal dining room and a music room with a piano; all the Kohner children played the piano. Fräulein Maria was their housekeeper and cook. She didn't wear a uniform, just an apron over her long skirt. The serving girl wore starched white. Berlin was even more formal. In Berlin, after I was married, I never went in the kitchen.

At dinner that evening, they had a guest from Holland, a Miss Pilgrimage. Tante Clara did not come; her husband, Heinrich, was sick in bed. At the dinner table everybody stared at me and talked in German. I felt like I was under a microscope.

Just as we were finishing dessert, the phone rang, and the housekeeper approached Paul and whispered, "*Herr DireKtor, es ist für Sie.*" Paul got up to take the call and came back very pale and said something in German. Immediately, everybody got up, put on their coats, and left without saying a word. The lady from Holland sat across from me. We looked at each other for the longest time, not knowing what was going on. Finally, Paul and his father came back. They handed me my coat and took me to the hotel without saying a word. I went to my room, baffled. Paul was staying with his family.

I didn't get much sleep that night. The next morning I dressed and waited. Eventually, Papa knocked at the door and handed me a little bunch of violets. He took me to breakfast at a nearby café, where he drank a beer and made a motion for me not to tell.

Then we walked back to the house. On the way, people stopped to talk to him, sympathetically, and I realized that somebody had died. It was late in the afternoon when Paul came and said I should go with him to visit Tante Clara.

At her house she was sitting in a corner with a candle next to her. She told me that she had been telling her husband what a beautiful girl Paul's bride was, when his head dropped and he died. She was too upset to go to her own husband's funeral.

On the train back to Berlin, Paul said, "Darling, the family would like us to get married in the house, with just family and very close friends. But we would have to postpone our wedding a month, if that is all right with you. And you would have to spend some time in Teplitz because there are certain formalities—meeting the rabbi and things like that. It's up to you."

"If it means keeping peace in the family, and if that's what you'd like, all right."

"I'm not asking for me," he said. "Arrangements can be made for us to marry right away in London."

"No," I said. "If it means so much, then Teplitz it is."

A couple of weeks later, on a weekend, we went back. When Paul left to return to Berlin, I stayed with the family in his old room. The next day I was taken to a Jewish service at the orthodox synagogue. The women sat upstairs, men downstairs. When they announced the impending marriage, my mother-in-law told me, "You must stand up so the congregation can look at you." I stood up so the whole congregation could look at me, but when I sat down the chair had folded up, so I plopped down on the floor. There was silence. I could feel my face burning. When everyone started leaving, I went with my mother-in-law-to-be, her sister, Tante Clara, and my future mother-in-law's stepmother, Caroline Béamt, to stand by the door. They told me, "You must say, '*Friede sei mit Euch*,' which means, 'Peace be with you.'" I stood there on exhibition as everyone passed by and looked at me.

The next morning Papa said, mysteriously, "We have to go someplace." I walked with Papa and my mother-in-law-to-be to a building in the old ghetto. Papa left me there with her; I had no idea what was going on.

Nobody told me what was going to happen. I walked into a very dark place, where there were two old women and a pool of what looked like dirty water. They made me undress, take the pins from my long hair, and climb into the tank of very cold water. I sat there, shivering. One woman had a book in her hand; the other grabbed me by the head and said what sounded like, "*Ikas mihas*," and she dunked me into the water three times. I must have screamed when I came up for air. I can't stand having my head under water, even when I swim, so I got out in a hurry. They handed me a towel. I quickly dried myself, got dressed, and ran out.

Papa was outside with a package, a present, which I later found was a red knit dress. I was terribly upset. We walked back to the house, and there was a Catholic nun. This nun had nursed Papa during his illness. She couldn't understand why my hair was all wet, and I couldn't explain it to her. I was still very upset. I found out this was called a *mikvah*, a cleansing ritual. I wished someone had told me what was going to happen beforehand.

That evening Paul called from Berlin and Papa talked to him in German, then he handed me the phone. He said, "Papa is going to take you to the train depot in the morning. I will pick you up in Berlin." Then he talked to his father again.

In the morning, after my mother-in-law-to-be had gone, Papa took me to the station and gave me a paper bag with cheese and a roll and put me on the train. I slept the whole way. A Chinese man shared my compartment. He'd been looking at me closely. At the border, he woke me to say they needed to check my passport. I must have looked terrible, because when we arrived in Berlin, the Chinese man asked, "Can I be of help?"

I said, "Thank you, sir. Somebody is going to meet me."

Paul came and took me to the hotel, but he couldn't stay; he had to go back to work. I felt so alone. I cried my heart out. I was so far away from Mexico and my grandma. I had no choice but to accept the situation and trust in Paul.

* * *

The next few weeks Paul and I spent every evening together. But 1932 was a very different time from today. There was a sense of propriety, a degree of formality that does not exist now. Our lack of a common language and our innocence kept us from expressing our love and from sharing the intimacy of couples about to be married. Instead, we shared long silences together, just holding hands.

In other words, I was a virgin bride.

26

THE WEDDING CEREMONY

I waited until just a few days prior to my wedding before I returned to Teplitz. Margie Pasternak traveled with me on the train and stayed with me in Paul's old bedroom.

It was the end of October and cold outside, but Margie and I took long walks just to get out of the house. Teplitz was a resort town, a spa with thermal springs that people soaked in to cure all sorts of aliments. There was a medieval castle in a large park and a pond to skate on in winter. Margie and I talked and talked. Her father was German but they had lived in America and he had become a citizen. He managed the two movie theaters that Universal owned in Berlin. Margie had worked as Joe's secretary until they married the year before.

On Saturday night Paul arrived with Margot and Fred Keller from his office, and young Eddie Wallach, the son of a prominent banker, who was to be Paul's best man. That evening the men went out to celebrate; the next day—Sunday—would be the wedding. I couldn't sleep; Margie and I talked all night long.

First thing in the morning my mother-in-law-to-be knocked on the door.

Margie told her, "You can't come in! You have to wait."

Fräulein Maria brought us some breakfast and then Margie helped me dress. I had bought my wedding gown in Hollywood for fifteen dollars. It was white and had a veil with flowers.

Just before noon, Papa came in and asked me,

"My child, are you ready?

"Yes, Papa," I answered.

"Uncle Rudy will give you away," he said with a hint of tears in his eyes.

The living room had been cleared and family and guests were all standing. Paul was standing with the rabbi at his side. He was white as ashes. There was a big mirror on the wall behind them and I wanted to laugh, because I could see Paul's big ears sticking out from under his derby hat. Uncle Rudy led me to them and I stood next to Paul under a white *chuppah* (cloth), held by Eddie Wallach and three other men.

Then the rabbi took a paper out of his robe and started to read, carefully, in Spanish. He said that my name should be Ruth from the Hebrew Bible since I had come from so far away for love. When I heard these words in my language, I thought about home and how there was nobody from my family here with me. I glanced in the mirror and saw big black tears streaming down my face. I had on a lot of mascara and I didn't have a handkerchief. The ceremony ended with Paul lifting up my veil to kiss me. Then Paul smashed a porcelain cup wrapped in a napkin with his foot. He saved a piece of that cup and had it made into a heart-shaped charm for a bracelet with the date of our wedding engraved on it.

After the ceremony, we placed a call to my parents in Mexico. Papa Julius spoke to my mother in his few words of English, telling her how happy he was to have a new daughter in his family; then he spoke to my father. I'm sure they didn't understand each other, but that wasn't so important. They heard each other's voices.

There was a big luncheon at the house, and then we had to go back to Berlin. Papa told Paul as we were leaving, "You take good care of my girl. If you don't make her happy, you'll have to answer to me!" Papa was a wonderful man.

We drove back to Berlin, Paul sitting in front next to the driver, and I in back between Margot and Fred Keller. I was exhausted and quickly fell asleep. When I woke up, I thought I was dead. Everything was white! I had never seen snow before; it was beautiful and peaceful. We stopped at Potsdam outside of Berlin, where Paul's friends gave us a dinner in a fancy restaurant.

It was very late when we finally arrived home. Paul gallantly carried me upstairs to the bedroom of a villa his assistant had rented for us. I was so exhausted I fell asleep again immediately. Paul left early the next morning without waking me. He phoned me during the day, but he came home again very late that night. He was producing two pictures at the Ufa studio, in Neubabelsberg, outside of the city. All that week he left early each morning and came back late. I stayed there in the house with our housekeeper, Frieda, who didn't speak English or Spanish. It wasn't until the next Sunday morning that I woke and found Paul still in bed with me. We were awkward at first; this was new to both of us.

Much later at breakfast, Paul asked, "Do you get bored all day, waiting for me?"

I told him, "No, not at all. I sit by the window doing needlework and listen to the concert."

"Concert?" he asked.

"Yes, every afternoon they play music. People come very elegantly dressed in black, the men in tails and top hats, and the music is very nice."

He called the maid: "Frieda, my wife has said there is a concert every day?"

"Yes, Mr. Kohner," she said, pointing across the street. "There is a crematorium there. They play the music."

Paul was shocked. No wonder this villa was so cheap. His assistant had found it, beautifully furnished. Soon after that we moved to a very nice *pension* on the Kurfürstendamm. The Ku'Damm, as it was also called, was the Champs-Élysées of Berlin. It was where all the best shops and restaurants were, and it was closer to Paul's office.

I knew two ladies in Berlin, Margie Pasternak and a young actress by the name of Fay Wall, who was twenty-one, a year younger than I. The three of us became close friends. We would get together to shop at the large KaDeWe department store or have coffee in the afternoon and then, later, go to meet our husbands. We had a grand time.

One day as I walked to meet the girls, I noticed a car following me. It stopped and the man rolled down his window and spoke to me in German.

"I don't speak German," I said, walking faster. In English, he said he wanted me to get in the car.

"No," I said, and kept on walking. So he got out of the car and chased after me. He said he had a wonderful job for me; I could make lots of money.

I said, "I'm not interested."

He said, "Think about it. Here's my card."

When I met the girls, I told them what had happened.

Margie said, "Let me see the card."

That evening when we met our husbands, Margie said, "Why don't you let Paulie take a look at the card of the person who offered you a job?"

I innocently said, "Oh, yes," and I handed it to him.

I didn't know what it said, but it probably had something to do with a brothel because Paul immediately said, "From now on, you are not going to go out alone!"

After that, the maid went with me whenever I left the house.

27

A TERRIBLE EVENING

When I first arrived in Berlin, Paul had just received the script for *Ecstasy*, the film he had told me about that was going to be shot in Prague. But when he read it, he said, "You're not going to run naked in the woods! You're going to be my wife!"

A month after our wedding, we went to Prague, where we stayed with Paul's friends, Olga and Josef Auerbach. Joe was a very nice man, but not much to look at. He had visited us one Sunday in Berlin and we had gone to the Tiergarten Zoo. When a gorilla came over and stared at Joe, Paul whispered to me in English, "That gorilla must be thinking, 'How can you be so ugly?'" Just then, Joe said to the gorilla, "*Wie Kannst du nur so hässlich sein?*," which means, "How can you be so ugly?" I had to bite my tongue to keep from laughing.

The Auerbachs had a son, Norbert, and two daughters, Dasha and Helga. They were several years younger than me, but I looked their age. The girls were fascinated with American music and insisted that I teach them how to dance the Charleston. One afternoon Olga Auerbach took me to Café Tepna on Wenceslas Square for coffee and *Apfelkuchen*. As we were leaving, I saw Paul sitting in a dark corner and talking with a very pretty girl. I said to the waiter, "*Herr Ober*, please tell the gentleman in the far corner to look this way." I waved to Paul as we left, a smile plastered across my face. That evening he told me the girl, Emmi Reinwald, was an old friend from Teplitz. Paul had a lot of girlfriends before he met me. Emmi was now married and had a two-year-old daughter, Hanna, whom she had said she wished was his. Many years later Hanna sent Paul all the old letters he had written to her mother. Of course, I read them. They were harmless.[6]

* * *

Prague was lovely. We walked to the impressive Charles Bridge over the Moldau. On the other side, the Hradshin castle, built by the Habsburgs, overlooks the city with its charming narrow streets and baroque architecture.

Paul and I visited the Barrandov studio, where Gustav Machatý was directing *Ecstasy*. Joe Auerbach had arranged the film's financing. Gustav had replaced me with beautiful Hedwig Maria Kiesler, also known as Hedy Lamarr.

Hedy Lamarr, Gustav Machatý, and Paul Kohner

When Gustav saw me he said, "So, *now* you come. Kohner shows me pictures of this wonderful, lovely girl, and I said, 'This is the girl for my picture!'

---

6   Paul did everything he could to try to save Emmi. He sent affidavits but in 1938 Emmi Reinwald was taken with her husband, to Theresienstadt, and from there to Auschwitz, where they were executed. Emmi's daughter, Hanna, was saved by a family named Budinski who raised her as their own child in Prague.

And then the girl is not interested?"

I told him Paul had offered me a better contract.

"What?" he said.

"Yes," I said, "a contract *for life*."

Paul laughed. He was handsome, and sure of himself, and I loved him. I had no regrets.

Hedy was beautiful, and her nude lovemaking scenes in *Ecstasy*, including a very expressive close-up of her face in orgasm, made her famous all over the world. She was three years younger than me, born in Austria to a Jewish family. Her first husband was much older, a very rich businessman friend of Adolf Hitler and other high-ranking Nazis. There were rumors that Hedy had to drug her husband with sleeping pills to escape to London, taking just her jewelry with her. There she met Louis B. Mayer, who took her to America and changed her name from Kiesler to Lamarr. Hedy, who co-starred in Cecil B. DeMille's *Samson and Delilah*, once said, "Any girl can be glamorous. All she has to do is stand still and look stupid." But Hedy wasn't stupid; she was brilliant. She invented and patented a radio frequency torpedo guidance system, based on a mathematical theory that was ahead of its time.[7]

After the war, we saw Olga and Joe Auerbach every year at the Cannes Film Festival where Joe swam in the ocean daily, regardless of the weather. He was very rotund and yet he always had beautiful girls around him. He was that charming.

* * *

We had been married two months when Paul took me to a very fancy party given by Erich Pommer, head of Ufa, Germany's most important studio. In 1919 Pommer had personally produced *The Cabinet of Dr. Caligari*, which had been a huge financial success as well as an influential example of German Expressionism. Pommer was celebrating his latest production, Josef von Sternberg's *The Blue Angel*, starring Emil Jannings and Marlene Dietrich. The party was also in honor of Ernst Lubitsch, who was visiting from Hollywood. Paul had taken me to Lubitsch's house in Hollywood many Sunday afternoons before we were married.

This was to be a grand party attended by all of the most important people of the film business in Berlin. I wore my white fifteen-dollar wedding dress, from which I had removed the sleeves. Paul was in tails.

Lupita and Paul, 1932

The party turned into a terrible evening. I was a very innocent, twenty-two-year-old Catholic girl from a small town halfway around the world. I had barely finished high school. In other words, I lacked the sophistication to deal with these people. The party was at a very elegant three-story villa, a mansion. Everyone wore evening dress. I got off on the wrong foot, and then things got worse. After the first introductions, an older gentleman came over to me. He took my hand and kissed

---

7   Hedy Lamarr married six times, but she died alone in 2000, at age eighty-five.

it, as was the custom, and said, "*Küss die Hand, gnädige Frau*," meaning, "Kissing your hand, my lady." In return, I said what I had been taught by Papa Julius, "*Küss mein Tuchas*," which I *didn't* know meant, "Kiss my fanny." Paul turned white. The older gentleman couldn't believe what he and the others around him had just heard. He smiled and said, "Very charming."

Paul took me aside and demanded, "Where did you learn that?"

"From Papa," I said innocently.

"Don't *ever* repeat anything my father teaches you!"

There were a lot of people at this party and Paul knew most of them. He left me for a moment to say hello to somebody and Ernst Lubitsch, who had been watching me from across the room, came over and said, "Lupita, I give this marriage six months. Here is my card—call me when it's over."

"I don't want your card," I said. "Here, take it back!" I threw the card back at him and turned away, very upset. And if that wasn't enough, moments later Mrs. Pommer (one of the dowagers and also our hostess) came over, and with her two hands, lifted my bare bosom out of my dress! Showing it to the others, she said, "*Schau was für eine schöne Brust, so appetitlich*!" which meant, "Look what a beautiful bosom—delicious!"

I was horrified, beyond embarrassed! I swatted at her hands, trying to cover myself again and ran to Paul crying, "Take me home! Please take me home!" He didn't understand.

"We can't go home. We just got here," he said. A young man, Lucien Mandelik, had been standing nearby with his parents. He introduced himself and took Paul aside to explain what he had seen. Then Lucien drove us home. I cried the whole way.

* * *

Many years later, at a party for our fifteenth wedding anniversary in Los Angeles, Ernst Lubitsch apologized to me for what he had said that evening in Berlin about my marriage lasting only six months. I asked what made him say that when Paul and I had just recently married.

"It was very obvious," he said. "You were from different religions, different upbringing, born in two different parts of the world. And you were so beautiful! I really believed that you wouldn't make it. I was very wrong. I apologize."

Ernst died of a heart attack later that year (1947), shortly after receiving a special Academy Award for "Distinguished Contribution to the Art of the Motion Picture." He directed, acted in, wrote, or produced more than seventy-five films. Nicola, his daughter, has been a very good friend to me.

ROTOGRÁFICO
El Semanario de Actualidad

Lupe Tovar
MÉXICO 29 DE MAYO de 1929

28

"IT TOOK A LOT OF COURAGE"

It took a lot of courage to go on my own to Germany in 1932. I gave up my acting career and left my grandma (who had been with me ever since I left my parents' home). I barely spoke English and I didn't know German at all. During our courtship in Hollywood, Paul and I always laughed at the misunderstandings that occurred from our speaking two different languages. I learned some English and Paul learned a little Spanish. German sounded very strange to me. In Berlin the movies were in German and Paul's friends all spoke in German. I tried to learn by reading the *Berliner Tageblatt*; mostly they wrote about the political problems. The Communists were against the National Socialists, and vice versa. Everyone talked about Adolf Hitler and the Nazis. No one took Hitler seriously yet, but everyone talked about him. They called him Schickelgruber, which was his father's name, but he preferred Hitler, his mother's maiden name. I guess he thought Hitler sounded more serious.

We had been married two months when we went to Vienna to celebrate New Year's Eve at the elegant Hotel Bristol. I had always made my own clothes or had a seamstress copy something from a magazine picture. But Paul liked to dress me in the finest European styles. He had given me a full-length white ermine coat made in Berlin by the famous furrier, Penizek und Rainer. I wore it that night over a lavender gown, cut very low.

I made a grand entrance from the top of the stairs. Paul was waiting for me below, handsome as ever. He kissed my hand and took me into the ballroom. We danced all night long. Paul loved to waltz. I was a long way from Mexico—I was in heaven.

When the Prince of Wales entered the ballroom, the music stopped, and he bowed to me! After that, everybody thought I was royalty. I don't think my feet touched the floor all evening! The next day everyone called me "Countess."

A few days later I was sitting in the hotel lobby, having coffee and pastries with Jack Ross, Carl Laemmle's personal secretary, when a man came over and offered to read my palm and tell me my future. He opened my hand and stared at it. Then, after a long while, he told me that I would die before I was thirty and that I would have a very big funeral! When Paul came, I told him what the fortune teller had said. He got so mad he found the man and had him thrown out of the hotel. A year later, what that man foretold *almost* came true.

* * *

Paul was handsome, slim, and always well dressed. And he loved to show me off—this young, lively, foreign girl at his side. We went to many elegant parties, Paul in full evening dress and white gloves, and me in designer clothes. We were an unusually good-looking couple.

German men made a big fuss over me. They were used to frumpy, overweight, badly dressed *Hausfrauen* who only talked about their children.

There were no women my age at parties, at least not at the parties we went to. It was a very strict time for most women. Upper-class young girls were never even taken out to dinner. Married women would go out in the afternoon for coffee or tea at hotels or restaurants, where gigolos were paid by the house to ask them to dance. (Billy Wilder was one of those men who was paid to dance with matronly ladies.) Young girls from nice families didn't go to these tea dances, just bored married women.

We had a large circle of friends and business acquaintances in Berlin. We would meet at the Romanische Café on the Ku'Damm, where actors, artists, writers, and movie people went to gossip. It was the place to see and be seen. Then we went window shopping at Wertheim's, a block-long department store. Evenings we went to dinner parties or entertained at our home; our housekeeper, Frieda, was an excellent cook. Often we had dinner at the Hotel Kempinski, Hotel Eden, or the Adlon on Unter den Linden, and then went to a movie. We saw a lot of movies.

Rudi Fehr was one of Paul's friends. Rudi, a film editor, worked nights at the Adlon Hotel as their pianist. The first night we went to the Adlon Hotel for dinner, Rudi began playing the Mexican National Anthem and tears ran down my cheeks. In 1936 he immigrated to Los Angeles and started a long career at Warner Bros.[8]

We quickly settled into a routine, but I missed my family. I was unable to describe to them in my letters what my life was like; it was so different from life in Mexico. And being married to Paul was different from anything I had imagined. We were both still innocents where sex was concerned, but we enjoyed each other and our privacy. In Mexico one didn't have privacy. There were always too many people living together and your family always knew exactly what you were doing and even, it seemed, of what you were thinking. Sunday mornings with Paul were indescribable.

Looking back, this was our last idyllic time, the calm before the storm.

---

8 He edited *Key Largo* and *Dial M for Murder* and became Jack Warner's trusted advisor.

29

"COULD I HAVE A DANCE WITH YOUR NIECE?"

S.O.S. Iceberg was a big, expensive, outdoor adventure movie. Filming had begun in Greenland, with wide shots of ice floes and many Eskimos in kayaks. The stars were Leni Riefenstahl and World War I flying ace Ernst Udet. Dr. Arnold Fanck wrote the original story, and Tom Reed wrote the screenplay. Dr. Fanck had been directing the film in Greenland; it was shot in German and English. Now, Edwin Knopf arrived to write additional dialogue and Tay Garnett came from Hollywood to direct the English-language version with a different leading man, Rod La Rocque. Rod was married to a Hungarian actress, Vilma Bánky, who had co-starred in Paul's film *The Rebel* with Luis Trenker.

Andrew "Bandi" Marton was the editor of both versions.

Prof. Karl Lorenz, an explorer played in the German version by Gustav Diessl, is stranded on the ice in the North Atlantic. His rescuers also become stranded. The professor's wife, played by Leni Riefenstahl, crashes her sea plane while trying to land in the icy water. Surrounded by polar bears on their shrinking iceberg, the professor, his wife, and their crew of explorers battle the elements and each other.

Paul decided it was too dangerous to film dramatic scenes and close-ups on the real ice so he moved the company to Switzerland. High in the Italian Alps above the village of Pontresina, the crew built a movie set of wood scaffolding. They hosed it down with water every night to turn it into an iceberg.

We stayed with the crew at the Bernina Hofspitz, the only hotel on the mountain. The crew (all men) drank heavily in the evenings, and one night Hans Schneeberger, the cameraman, got roaring drunk. He had a steel plate in his head from World War I, and when he was drunk he got very nasty. That night he went crazy. He started breaking things, smashing things with his fists. Paul tried to reason with him, but finally we locked ourselves in our room. Very early the next morning we were lowered in a gondola to the town below.

The production manager, Alfred Stern, and assistant director, Werner Klingler, could handle the shooting, so Paul decided we should get away for a few days. We took the train to Milan, which was close by. The weather there was warmer, and the Italians were very friendly. We went sightseeing in a horse-drawn buggy to the opera house and to the beautiful Duomo Cathedral.

When we went back up the mountain a few days later, Hans was very embarrassed and apologetic. He knelt and kissed my hand and begged forgiveness for scaring me on that drunken night. Of course I forgave him: Hans was a very good cameraman. He had worked on Josef von Sternberg's *Der Blaue Engel* (*The Blue Angel*) and Paul had worked with him on *Die Weisse Hölle vom Piz Palü*, (*The White Hell of Pitz Palu*). Bandi Marton and his wife, Jarmela, were in Pontresina at that time, too. Bandi had started as an editor and then became a director.[9]

---

9 Later, in Hollywood, he was one of the best action directors. He was one of the three directors of Darryl F. Zanuck's *The Longest Day*, along with Ken Annikin and Bernhard Wicki. Bandi co-directed (with Yakima Canutt) the chariot race between Charlton Heston and Stephen Boyd in William Wyler's *Ben-Hur* (1959).

Max Laemmle came to visit us in Pontresina from Paris, where he was in charge of Universal Pictures Distribution. Max was a cousin of Carl Laemmle. Joe and Margie Pasternak came, too. Ever since Margie had stayed with me the night before my wedding we had been best friends. Pontresina was a nice place to have a winter vacation, especially if you were a skier. I tried, but I didn't do well. It made me nervous to see skiers carried off the mountain on stretchers. One evening we went to the casino in nearby St. Moritz. I'd forgotten to bring my passport and they wouldn't let me in because I was wearing my sailor outfit and I looked too young.

New Year's Eve at the elegant Badrutt's Palace Hotel, a man with a small goatee came by our table and asked Paul, "Could I have a dance with your niece?" Paul took offense and quickly said, "This is my wife! And she only dances with me!" I was having a grand time; Paul and all his friends were so attentive, and even strangers were attracted to me.

* * *

Berlin was a beautiful, sophisticated city, but very decadent. Prostitutes brazenly walked up and down the Kurfürstendamm; you could tell what they were by the high, military-style boots they all wore. They were also the only women who wore too much makeup. On the Ku'Damm you could see men in women's clothes, women in men's clothes, beggars, and elegant people all in one place. The beggars were often men missing an arm or a leg, still wearing tattered bits of uniforms with medals from the last war.

Filming a close-up of Rod La Rocque—*S.O.S. Iceberg*— Paul at far right

My German was getting better. Paul didn't want me to read the newspapers, but I read them anyway. He didn't want me to worry about the political situation; there was obvious trouble. There were strikes by transportation workers and constant demonstrations. There was marching in the streets day and night and there were stories of Nazis attacking Communists and the police. Things got so bad in June of 1932 that Martial Law and a nighttime curfew were declared.

When new elections were held, the Nazis won a large share of the vote and I began to see Nazi swastika buttons on men's lapels.

Die Weisse Hölle vom Piz Palü German Poster

AUTHOR'S NOTE:

THE END OF THE WEIMAR REPUBLIC

Named for the city where a new constitution was written after Germany's defeat in World War I, the Weimar Republic was an attempt to establish a liberal democracy in Germany. It lasted from November 1918 until March 1933, when it was replaced by Adolf Hitler's Third Reich. In the twenties, Weimar Berlin rivaled Paris and London as cultural centers.

In November 1923, one American dollar was worth a mind-boggling 4.2 *trillion* German marks! A glass of beer cost 150 *billion* marks! Paper money was reprinted by stamping additional zeros on existing notes, fueling a period of hyperinflation.

Employees were paid daily and rushed out to buy anything—a necktie or a loaf of bread, just to get rid of their worthless cash before it lost even more value. It was cheaper to burn money than to buy firewood. Banks suffered huge losses. Debts, mortgages, and taxes were paid off at a fraction of their value.

During and immediately after the inflation of the twenties, the arts flourished. Berlin had three major opera companies and twenty classical orchestras. American Jazz was very popular. Josephine Baker, the black American dancer, was accompanied in her show *La Revue Nègre* by Sam Wooding's all-black eleven-piece jazz band. Bertolt Brecht wrote *Mother Courage and her Children*. Brecht and Kurt Weill collaborated on *Mahagonny Songspiel*, *The Seven Deadly Sins*, and their version of *The Beggar's Opera* (*The Three Penny Opera*), with a score based on American Jazz. Fritz Lang made his seminal film *Metropolis*. Josef von Sternberg directed Marlene Dietrich and Emil Jannings in *The Blue Angel*, a story by Heinrich Mann and Carl Zuckmayer. In the twenties, Thomas Mann wrote *The Magic Mountain* and Alfred Döblin wrote *Berlin Alexanderplatz*. This was also the heyday of Berlin's modern art movements led by such artists as Jean Arp, Wassily Kandinsky, and Gustav Klimt. Ludwig Mies van der Rohe was the director of the innovative Bauhaus Design School, which had been founded by Walter Gropius.

The inflation and the harshness of the Versailles Treaty at the end of World War I, with heavy reparation payments imposed on the Germans, created an atmosphere ripe for revolt. There was widespread unemployment and food became scarce in the cities. Although anyone with foreign currency could still live in luxury, and many lived an extravagant lifestyle, there was dire poverty in most of Germany. In ten years, Germany's economy went from hyperinflation to The Great Depression of 1930–1933. This was the end of the halcyon days for Berliners.

By 1932, one-third of the work force was unemployed. There were mass demonstrations by fascist storm troopers aimed at Jewish businesses. At night, unemployed men ran through the streets yelling: "Heil Hitler!" and "Death to the Jews!" The police were useless: only the Communists and Socialists were willing to face up to the Nazis. Berlin was on the brink of civil war.

On January 30, 1933, Adolf Hitler was appointed chancellor by President Hindenburg. That night SA and SS troops marched through the crowded streets of Berlin. The SA or Storm Troopers was a paramilitary organization of the Nazi Party—often called Brown-Shirts for the color of their uniforms—brown tunics and trousers, and caps with chin straps. The SS, Hitler's personal bodyguards, wore black uniforms with lightning-flash insignia. The SS Death's Head Units were those put in charge of concentration camps.

In March 1933, Hitler's National Socialist Party came to full power, marking the end of the Weimar Republic. The official party platform banned modern art and art produced by artists considered of racially inferior strain in favor of "Heroic Art," which was meant to exemplify the pure German Aryan race. Joseph Goebbels became propaganda minister with power over all radio, press, and cinema.

As a result of anti-Semitism in the arts, Max Ernst immigrated to America with the help of art patron Peggy Guggenheim. Because of his status as a "degenerate" artist, Paul Klee fled to Switzerland. A flood of talented people in all the arts began to emigrate; many came to America.

Unemployment reached 35 percent. Berlin now had over 600,000 unemployed workers. Conditions for these individuals were so bad that many lived in tent-camps outside the city.

That April of 1933, Lupita and Paul had been married and living in Berlin just five months. With Lupita's Mexican passport, Paul's American passport, and salary paid in dollars, they still enjoyed an elite status.

30

"FRÄULEIN, HALT!"

On April 1, 1933, the *Judenboykott* (the boycott of Jewish businesses) began. Jewish-owned stores had to be marked as such in big letters. Jewish workers were fired from non-Jewish businesses. Jews could no longer work for the government, even as mail carriers. Paul was nervous over how this would affect his film productions. We were all conscious of the change in official attitude, and yet I was still cocky.

An important producer in Berlin, a Mr. Robert Neppach, sent Paul a script for me; it was called *La Paloma*. I read it and I liked it. It had been almost a year since I had worked and I was eager to get back in front of a camera.

Paul said, "Would you like to do it?"

"Yes, if it's all right with you."

Paul said, "Yes. Go ahead and meet with Mr. Neppach."

I went to the producer's office with the script. They were very pleased to see me and, after talking for a while, Mr. Neppach said he liked me very much and that I could have the role on one condition: "During the filming, you would have to live in a hotel as Fräulein Tovar. You could not live with your husband." I clearly did not understand, so he went on, "He is Jewish, yes?"

I looked at him, tossed the script on his desk, and said, "In that case, you know what you can do with this." And I walked out.

When I told Paul what had happened, he had a good laugh.

The next day they called Paul and apologized, saying I had misunderstood. Would I reconsider? There was nothing to misunderstand. So I said, "No, they can go to the devil."

We were extremely naive. We didn't realize how dangerous and how far-reaching this anti-Semitism had become. In the *U-Bahn* (the subway), there were always men trying to collect money. On one side would be a Nazi in a brown uniform, with a cap in his outstretched hand and, on the other side, was the gray, the Communist.

The evening of May 10, 1933, I went to meet Paul. He had phoned and told our housekeeper to walk with me as far as the Underground. From there I had just two stations to go before getting off at Mauerstrasse. When I came out across from the Universal Pictures office, the whole street was filled with Nazis, marching and singing, carrying red and black flags and torches. Their stamping boots were like thunder on the cobblestone street. I was afraid, but I didn't want to stay where I was. I said to myself, "If I don't risk it, I won't get there, so here I go!"

I crossed the street, pushing between the Nazis to get to the other side. A policeman yelled at me, "*Fräulein!*" He blew a whistle and shouted, "*Fräulein—Halt!*" I kept going, ignoring his orders. Paul and Mr. Keller came running to pull me into the building. They had been watching from an upstairs window.

We stayed late in the office that night and watched the Nazis burn books in a bonfire on the street below us. It had happened overnight!

Yesterday had been normal, and today there were Nazis in uniforms and men in brown shirts everywhere. That was scary!

The next day, like magic, there were red and black Nazi flags flying from every window—every window but ours. When I went to my dressmaker, even he was wearing the Nazi uniform! Papa Julius, naughty as ever, had told me what to say to any stranger who bothered me in the street. I was chased one day because I told a Nazi something I shouldn't have. I said, "*Leck mich am arsch*," a *Berliner Schnauze* (a common expression in Berlin), which I didn't know meant "Kiss my ass." I didn't realize the danger; I needed to keep my mouth shut. Luckily, a taxi driver rescued me. He appeared out of nowhere.

"*Fräulein!*" he shouted. He reached over and opened his door for me to get in, and quickly drove me away. He peered at me through his rear view mirror and said, "Fräulein, do be careful. Next time there might not be one of us around." He was a Communist. They hated the Nazis and the Brown-Shirt Storm Troopers. They were all hoodlums as far as I was concerned.

I got out, thanked him, and walked home, looking over my shoulder at every street corner. When I told Paul about it, he said, "Darling, please don't leave the house anymore, except with me, all right?"

Still upset, he called his father and said, "Papa, do me a big favor and do not teach Lupi any German!" Papa must have asked, what happened? because Paul explained and I could hear Papa laughing like the dickens at his end. Papa took great pleasure in teaching me bad words. He was naughty, naughty, naughty. From then on, it was too dangerous for me to go out alone, most of all because I was too outspoken. So I stayed home and listened to the radio, but there was nothing to listen to but political speeches. It seemed that all day long, Joseph Goebbels was on the radio, giving speeches.

Then I received a notice to appear at the local police station. Paul read it and decided to go himself with Walter Klingler, who was not Jewish.

At the station the clerk said they had a report that Lupita Tovar (that's what my passport still read) was living with a Jew, and that was *Rassenschande* (a disgrace for the race) and not permitted. Paul was furious. He pulled out his American passport and said, "I am a journalist. I write for seventy American newspapers and in half an hour what is going on here in Germany will be all over America!" He took out a card (it was his membership from the Beverly Hills Breakfast Club), and said, "Here is my press credential!"

Luckily, the man could not read English. He examined it and said, "Please, do not say anything. I am only doing my job. How long does the lady expect to stay?"

"She will leave just as soon as possible," Paul answered.

When Paul came back to the apartment, he tried to hide his concern, but after dinner he said, "We have to move from here."

Nobody believed this could happen. People thought this Austrian, Adolf Hitler, was a joke. They called him "The Little Corporal," a crazy person who would vanish in three months. But he didn't, and we began to hear of arrests and disappearances. The disappearances, especially, had a devastating effect on friends and families. On the streets, we frequently saw *Grosser* Mercedes-Benzes speeding by, Swastika pennants on their front bumpers.

I went to see our friend, Dr. Castillo Nájera, the Mexican ambassador. He said to me, "If you ever have trouble, call me at any hour." He gave me his private phone number and again said, "Any trouble at all, call me, even in the middle of the night." He was very serious. It was the first time I realized there was real danger.

AUTHOR'S NOTE:

A VERY DANGEROUS TIME

The danger was greater than Lupita and Paul could have imagined. The escalation of Nazism was happening overnight.

When the *Reichstag* building (the seat of the German Parliament) was set on fire on February 27, 1933, Adolf Hitler, the new chancellor of Germany, blamed it on the Communists and used the incident to introduce the Enabling Act, which gave him dictatorial powers.

On April 1, 1933, all Jewish businesses were boycotted, which led to the introduction of the law that barred Jews from government positions and all other prominent posts.

On May 10 of that same year, the infamous book burnings took place in cities across Germany. In Berlin's Opernplatz alone, storm troopers burned a pile of twenty-thousand books. Books by authors such as Erich Maria Remarque, Berthold Brecht, Sigmund Freud, André Gide, Marcel Proust, Upton Sinclair, H. G. Wells, Jack London, and Ernest Hemingway were publicly burned.

Hitler and Goebbels gave daily propaganda speeches over the radio. Soon the beautiful trees that ran down the center of the famed Unter den Linden were removed to make room for military parades.

In June of 1933, the SA Brown-Shirts committed the infamous Kopenick Blood Week. Avenging an anti-Nazi demonstration, Brown-Shirt gangs rounded up over five hundred Communists and Socialists and threw them into SA prisons, where many were tortured and shot.

The SA rivals, the SS and Gestapo, then took control of all the German police forces. As a step toward systemizing their campaign of terror, the Gestapo began establishing concentration camps around the country.

By July 14, 1933, all political parties except Hitler's NSDAP were abolished.

In October, Hitler withdrew Germany from the League of Nations. Next, he renounced the Treaty of Versailles, in which Germany had accepted full responsibility for World War I, the obligation to pay reparations, the loss of territories such as Alsace-Lorraine to France, and the loss of all of its overseas territories.

Communist and Socialist newspapers were immediately banned and the remaining papers were forced to dismiss their Jewish staff members.

On June 28, 1934, Adolf Hitler decided to purge the SA, which, under its leader Ernst Roehm, was competing for control and was rumored to be a bastion of homosexuality. Hitler ordered the top SA Brown-Shirt officials to gather at Bad Weissee, a resort town south of Munich. When he arrived with a unit of SS guards, Hitler placed all of the

Brown-Shirts leaders under arrest, charged with gathering to plot a *Putsch*, an attempt to overthrow his government. Some were killed on the spot; the rest were transported to Munich's Stadelheim Prison, where more executions took place. That same night, local leaders of the SA in Berlin were killed in a wave of brazen murders known as the "Night of the Long Knives."

President Hindenburg, who had been little more than a puppet for Hitler, died on August 2, 1934, giving Adolf Hitler totalitarian control as he merged both the office of president and chancellor into one. On August 19, 1934, some thirty-eight million Germans voted to approve this action.

Taking advantage of the anti-Semitic sentiment, the Nazis launched successful propaganda campaigns, blaming the Jews for the loss of World War I, high unemployment, and poverty.

Starting in May 1935, Jews were forbidden to join the *Wehrmacht* (army), and by 1936, Jews were banned from *all* professional jobs.

31

"LET HER DIE IN PEACE"

The opening night of *S.O.S. Eisberg,* as it was spelled in German, was held on August 30, 1933, at the Ufa-Palast am Zoo, the grandest movie house in Berlin.

The actress Leni Riefenstahl had played the part of a pilot who attempts to rescue her husband, Dr. Carl Lawrence, an explorer. Just before the film began, Leni arrived outside the theater with a motorcade and made a grand entrance with an escort of uniformed SS men. She marched proudly to the stage, faced the audience, and shouted, "Heil Hitler," giving the raised-hand Nazi salute. Many in the audience stood up. Then Joseph Goebbels, head of the propaganda ministry, joined her on stage, and now the whole audience stood up and gave the stiff-armed salute, shouting, "Heil Hitler!" I did not stand up, not until two strong hands from the row behind lifted me to my feet, whether I wanted to or not.

I said to Paul, in English, "I wish I had a bomb in my hands."

S.O.S. Eisberg German poster

There were a lot of Jews in the audience and, as soon as the lights went out, they started to leave the theater. When the film was over, SS men cleared the way for Leni. Leni had become a favorite of Adolf Hitler. He wanted her to direct Nazi propaganda films and she took advantage of the opportunity. There was a rumor that she had seduced him, which was contrary to another rumor that he was impotent. We were still discussing with our friends whether this bad Austrian joke, who stood just five feet tall and walked with a limp, was to be taken seriously. We should have been smarter. I should have been more worried about Paul's status as a Jew, even though he was an important man with an American passport. We were still pretending that things were normal.

* * *

In the fall of 1933, we were invited to dinner at the home of the director Alfred Zeisler. He was married to Lien Deyers, a Dutch actress. We accepted the invitation, taking the train through the forest of Grünwald to Neubabelsberg, where they lived.

There were ten important guests for dinner that evening; the guest of honor was Prince Wilhelm, a grandson of Kaiser Wilhelm II. The moment the prince entered and surveyed the room, he made a beeline for me. He kissed my hand, and this time I was careful to say the right thing. The whole afternoon I had been rehearsing how to say, "*Königliche Hoheit*," (Royal Highness). He was very stiff at first, but soon he loosened up and

Lupita, 1933

was chatting away. He gave instructions that place cards at the dinner table be changed so we would sit together. Paul was seated at the other end of the table with a scowl on his face.

The dinner courses came and went and the prince kept on talking to me. I was hungry, but I didn't want to be rude so I didn't eat. Then, as the last course was served, I said, "*Herr Prinz, jetzt werde ich essen!*" (Mr. Prince, now I'm going to eat.) Everybody was shocked, but he laughed, and so did I. After dinner the prince wanted to dance with me. A rumba record was playing, so the two of us danced, and then he sat at my feet and talked to me some more. He asked me what my favorite flower was, and I told him it was lilac.

The custom was that no one could leave until the prince left, and it got later and later. He didn't leave until six in the morning. Everybody made the *Knicks* (curtsy), but when I was about to, he held me up and said, "Not you, my queen."

It was dawn when he finally left. We gathered in the kitchen, where everyone laughed hysterically at the prince's behavior. "Boy, he sure fell hook, line, and sinker for you," Alfred said. We fixed some breakfast and took the train back to Berlin.

The next day, so many lilacs arrived they filled every corner of our apartment. Then a letter came, an invitation for me to come to the prince's estate for the weekend. Paul answered it, saying that he and his wife would be delighted to spend the weekend at the Kaiser's estate. We didn't hear back; he only wanted me. Sadly, I heard that the prince died at the very beginning of World War II.

* * *

In October, we moved again, this time to the Pension Imperial on the Kurfürstendamm. One Sunday we went to Wannsee, a nearby lake with a lovely beach, to meet people for lunch. I had to go to the bathroom constantly and noticed blood even though I had just had my period. I didn't tell Paul; I knew he had to go to Marseille the next day to see the French writer Marcel Pagnol. He would have stayed with me if he knew I wasn't feeling well.

I was very pale most days, but when Frau Lustig at the pension saw me the next day, she knew something was wrong. She had nursed her sister, who had just died. She immediately called her doctor, Hugo Weinberg.

Dr. Weinberg came and examined me. I was hemorrhaging. He wrapped me up in towels, carried me to his car, and drove me to the Kolder Allee Clinic.

When Paul called the apartment that evening, the maid told him I'd been taken to the hospital. He called his brother Fritz and told him to get his wife's doctor, Theodore Cohn, to see me immediately. Dr. Cohn came and was angry that he hadn't been called first. I was very weak from loss of blood.

The next day a Catholic nun came and she sang to me. I was twenty-three years old, but the doctors were not allowed to operate unless my husband first gave permission; they waited and waited. Paul arrived late that night, and they explained everything to him. I had a tubal pregnancy that was about to burst. He wanted Dr. Cohn to take care of me, but Dr. Cohn said—in front of me—"*Armes Kaninchen, lass sie in Ruhe sterben.*" (Poor little rabbit. Let her die in peace.)

Dr. Weinberg spoke up vehemently: "*No!* Let me operate, but I must do it now, in the next five minutes!" In my poor German, I said, "*Herr Doktor Weinberg, worauf warten Sie? Bitte operieren Sie sofort!*" (Dr. Weinberg, what are you waiting for? Please operate right away!)

They gave me anesthesia there in the room, and the surgery was done immediately. For three days, I didn't know if I was dead or alive. The whole time Paul stayed on a cot by my bed. When Dr. Weinberg came to see me, he said, "You gave us quite a scare." Paul looked worse than I did; he hadn't slept in days. He tried to make a joke of it, saying, "Several times I had to chase the funeral people away." I was worried that I may not be able to have children in the future, but Dr. Weinberg assured me that I could.

Papa Julius called from Teplitz; he wanted to comfort me. He wanted to come to Berlin, but he was not well either. He once told me that he would rob a bank to get me the biggest diamond if I gave him a grandson. Papa gave me the warmth and love I never had from my own father.

Paul was about to start a film in Vienna.[10] He didn't want to leave me behind, so even though I was weak, a few weeks later, he took me with him. That night on the train, the bandages around my middle were too tight and Paul undid them so I could sleep. But in the morning he couldn't put them back on me and he had to take me to our hotel on a stretcher. The Park Hotel Schönbrunn was very elegant, a lovely place to recuperate. Paul had a nurse come and stay with me during the day until I could take care of myself again.

I recovered quickly from my operation and soon I was able to sightsee in an old-fashioned horse-drawn carriage. Vienna is a beautiful city with elegant buildings and cafés on every street corner. The people were genuinely warm; they had charm and a softer accent than Berliners. Even the weather was more pleasant; a warm *Föhn* was blowing. At the Drei Husaren, Paul's favorite restaurant, I met the popular Jewish-Hungarian actress Gitta Alpar. She had a fantastic singing voice. Gitta was living with Gustav Fröhlich, an important actor who was not Jewish. We were all becoming more conscious of who was Jewish and who was not. The anti-Semitism in Vienna was just as bad as in Berlin.

In 1938, when I was safely back in Los Angeles, I wrote an affidavit and put all the money I had in a bank account in the name of that doctor, Hugo Weinberg, who saved my life in Berlin. He was then able to get a visa to get out of Nazi Germany. Hugo was so grateful that when he saw me again he vowed, "As long as I live, I will take care of you and never charge a penny." We got him a job with Dr. Tiber, our obstetrician, while he went back to school to get his American medical license.

When I had to have my appendix taken out a few years later, Hugo performed the operation. Some friends came to visit me in the hospital the night before and brought me a bell pepper as a joke. The next morning I hid it under my nightgown and when we were already in the operating room I took it out and told Hugo, "You can put this in, in place of my appendix, Doctor." Everyone had a good laugh, but after they passed it around, they had to scrub up again.[11]

---

10   Paul's film was *Leise flehen Miene Lieder*, also called, *Unfinished Symphony*. Pretty twenty-one year old Mártha Eggerth starred in the film, along with Luise Ullrich. The film was shot in two languages with Helen Chandler playing Luise's role in the English version. Helen had been Eva in the English version of *Dracula*. Hans Jaray played the composer Franz Schubert, upon whose life the story was based. Willi Forst directed, Walter Reisch wrote the German screenplay with Forst while Benn Levy wrote the English dialogue.

Mártha had a beautiful singing voice. She married opera star Jan Kiepura and in 1938 they escaped to America, where Mártha and Jan had a big success starring in *The Merry Widow* on Broadway.

Walter Reisch married Elisabeth (Liesl) Handle, a young Viennese actress and ballerina. Liesl had a part in the Schubert film, too, and she and Walter also emigrated and were our neighbors in Los Angeles. Walter wrote *Ninotchka* with Billy Wilder.

---

11   Hugo, a tall handsome man, married his German girlfriend, Edna, in the living room of our home in Bel-Air.

… 32 …

ADVENTURES IN FILMING

On one of our first trips to London, Paul had a surprise for me. We stopped for lunch at the Connaught Hotel and there was Robert Flaherty. I was so happy to see him. I hugged him, and I think I cried. We talked about our first meeting in Mexico, just four years earlier, when he chose me (over sixty-five other contestants) to go to Hollywood.

Robert told us of the years he spent filming in the South Pacific. In 1926 he had taken his wife, Frances, and their three young daughters to a remote island, where they lived for a year with Samoan natives on a small island and filmed their daily lives for a documentary he called *Moana*. It was, he said, a very primitive existence. After that, he left his family in Connecticut while he went back to Tahiti with director W.S. Van Dyke to film *White Shadows* for Irving Thalberg. Next he teamed with the respected German director F.W. Murnau and again returned to the South Pacific. Now, Robert was in London filming yet another documentary.

Robert Flaherty and Paul were my guardian angels; they made my dreams come true.

* * *

We went back to London for the opening of *The Doomed Battalion*, a film Paul made with Luis Trenker and Tala Birell. As we entered the lobby of the Dorchester Hotel, there was Sam Spiegel with Adrian Brunel and Buster Keaton. I already knew Sam from Berlin. He came over and said, "Paul, I'm going to borrow your wife for a moment."

When we approached the other two men, Buster Keaton looked at me and said, "That's my girl!" His comment meant nothing to me at the time.

That night we went to the premiere, and the next morning Sam came to our suite. He told us he was going to make a film with Buster Keaton, *The Invader*, which was later called *An Old Spanish Custom*.

Sam said, "Paul, I need your wife for Buster's film."

"*What?* You're *crazy!*" Paul brushed him off with, "We're leaving in an hour and I don't want to miss our train."

Sam was originally from Poland, but he was at home everywhere. He came to see us the next week in Berlin; he really wanted me for this British film. At first Paul said no, but Sam was very persuasive. He explained to Paul that, as an actress, I was used to being busy working at a studio; that it was no fun for me to sit alone all day waiting for him to come home at night. He said that after the *Flitterwochen* (the honeymoon), I would get very bored. "If you're smart, Paul, you'll let her do the film. That way she'll be occupied for a while."

So Paul asked me if I'd like to do this comedy in London. It was just for a few weeks, so I said, "Yes, if you don't mind. I'd love to work in a studio again."

I went back to London, to the Dorchester Hotel, where Sam sent me flowers every day. He was a very charming man. After a rocky start in his early career, when he often produced pictures using the name S. P. Eagle, he went on to produce many award-winning films such as *On the Waterfront*, *The Bridge on the River Kwai*, and *Lawrence of Arabia*.

Buster Keaton was drinking a lot while we were making *The Invader*. In one scene he almost drowned me. We were filming on a stage with a very large water tank. The scene took place on a yacht; the railing breaks and I fall into the water. Buster was supposed to jump in to save me, but, instead, he jumped in and had trouble swimming. He almost drowned himself and he kept pushing me under. Finally, several members of the crew saw that I was really in trouble and jumped in to save me.

The next day, all Buster said—in his serious, deadpan way—was, "Sorry, kid."

"That's all right, Buster," I replied. What else could I say? After that incident he was very sweet to me. I liked him. Lyn Harding was in the film, too, as well as Esme Percy, Andreas Malandrinos, Clifford Heatherley, Hilda Moreno, and Webster Booth. Adrian Brunel was the director and Edwin Greenfield wrote the script.

Before we finished *The Invader*, I got an offer to go to Madrid to star in a film for Erich Darmstaedter and his Hungarian partner, Géza Pollatschik. They had produced the very successful *Eight Girls in a Boat*, in Berlin. Géza, who later changed his name to Polaty, had been the editor on Arnold Pressburger's *Berlin Alexanderplatz*, based on Alfred Döblin's famous novel. Paul knew all of these people, so when I asked him if he would mind, he agreed that I should go to Spain.

* * *

Vidas Rotas, or *Broken Lives*, had already begun filming in Madrid with a girl the producers had brought from Mexico. Through the Mexican consul in London, I talked on the phone to the consul in Madrid. I told him I did not want to take a job away from another actress. He told me that I would be doing everyone a favor, because the girl was going to be replaced regardless; she

Buster Keaton and Lupita in *The Invader*, 1933

couldn't remember her lines, and all she did was cry all the time.

I left London by train and took the night boat across the English Channel. The train ride through France was beautiful. I changed trains at the Spanish border. Then everything was easier; everyone spoke my language.

The book *Vidas Rotas* was written by Concha Espina, a very well-known writer. It was about a famous pianist. He has a girlfriend in Madrid, but when he goes to Mexico for a performance, he falls in love with this Mexican lady. They get married and return to Madrid. He plays in a concert and his new wife is there, but his old girlfriend is in the audience, too, and she's pregnant! One morning, somebody brings a baby to the door of the pianist's home and his wife adopts the child, not knowing the baby is her husband's with the former girlfriend. Soon after, the wife also gives birth and she takes the babies to the park. The real mother of the adopted baby comes to the park, and the two women become friends. Of course, the Mexican woman knows nothing about this woman's previous relationship with her husband. Eventually, the truth comes out. The marriage is finished, but a bond has formed between the two women.

When I went to London to film *The Invader*, I was only going to be gone for a month, during which time Paul came to see me twice. That was a long trip from Berlin. But now I was in Spain and that was a lot farther. Luckily, Francisco (Pancho) Cabrera, one of the producers of *Santa*, and now a co-producer of *Vidas Rotas*, was in Madrid. He escorted me around town, and when Paul came from Germany the three of us had dinner almost every evening. Paul, Pancho, and I became such good friends in Spain, and later in Mexico, that we told him if we had a son we would call him Pancho.

Vidas Rotas, Miguel Pereira, Maruchi Fresno, Enrigue Zabala, G.Pollatschik, Lupita, Francisco de P. Cabrera, and director Eusevio F. Ardavin

The Spanish Civil War was just beginning. Mexico supported the Republicans while Germany was supporting General Francisco Franco and the Nationalists. Actual fighting had not yet started in 1934, but the country was splitting up and everybody was taking sides. Paul would often call from Germany and ask how the situation was, but then we would be cut off. I think somebody was listening to long-distance phone calls, especially from Germany.

The last day, I sat with the crew at lunch. We were all sad that the filming was over. I missed Paul terribly, but living in Spain and working again in my own language was a pleasure.

My producer, Eddie Darmstetter, drove me through the night to Barcelona. From there I would take the train across France to Germany. Because of the political unrest, everyone was very nervous about traveling. As I got into Eddie's car, he showed me a pistol and asked, "Do you know how to shoot one of these?" I laughed and told him that my father had taught me how to fire a gun when I was just eight years old. He handed

Lupita and Enrigue Zabala— Vidas Rotas

Vidas Rotas—Lupita

had been arranged with several newspaper people. I had just told everyone how sweet and wonderful my husband was when Paul got through to me on the phone; he was loud and furious. "Where the hell are you?" he shouted over the phone for everyone to hear. "I want you out of there immediately!" The news about the situation in Spain was bad, and he was very worried.

The only train I could board right away was a freight train to Paris. That night, a woman was having a baby right there on the train, without a doctor! As the eldest of nine in our family, giving birth was familiar to me. Another woman and I helped the mother as best we could. And after much sweating, panting, and screaming, she gave birth to a healthy baby boy.

Paul met me at the station in Paris and right away said, "We're leaving for St. Moritz, immediately!" He was starting *The Rebel* with Luis Trenker. We rushed through the station and caught the next train for Switzerland, but somehow my luggage didn't make it. There we were, at the elegant Palace Hotel in St. Moritz, and I didn't have anything to wear but my traveling clothes.

me the pistol and told me that if we were stopped for any reason, that I was not to hesitate to shoot. I held that gun in my lap the whole way.

I had phoned Paul and told him where I thought I would be staying in Barcelona, but I was taken to a different hotel. Paul reached me the next evening at the Universal office, where a cocktail party

"This is the last time I'll let you go away for work!" Paul said. I remained quiet as he put on his evening clothes and went down to meet our friends for dinner while I stayed in the room, where I was happy to catch up on some sleep.

ARTISTAS HISPANAS
LUPITA TOVAR
protagonista de la película española «Vidas rotas»

Paul made several films with Luis Trenker, who was an actor, film director, champion skier, and mountain climber. Together they made *The Doomed Battalion*, *The Rebel*, and *The Prodigal Son*. These were called "Mountain" or "Alpine" films.

Walter Klinger, Paul Kohner, Marian Marsh, and Luis Trenker

They were very popular in Europe, and the actors, like Luis Trenker, were real athletes who performed their own stunts.

An awful thing happened while making *The Rebel*. Paul had a Swiss friend, a very rich film financier, by the name of Weissman. This man had a villa in St. Moritz, where he lived with his mistress, Frau DoKtor Neumann, and her young son. We had dinner with them often at the Palace Hotel, where we were staying. When Paul had to go for a few days to the filming location—a rugged place far up in the mountains—I had planned to stay behind. The Swiss couple invited me to stay with them at their villa, and I accepted their invitation.

I slept well, but awoke to find the Swiss financier on top of me! He was trying to pull up my nightgown, feeling for my underwear! I screamed and pounded on his chest. I fought him off. He stopped and pleaded with me not to tell anyone. His mistress had gone to the village with her child and there were no servants in the house.

He offered me anything if I would keep quiet. I grabbed my clothes and ran. At the station, I got the next train up the mountain to the movie location.

Werner Klingler, the assistant director, saw me and immediately took me to Paul. I was still shaking as I told how his friend had tried to rape me! Paul went white. He couldn't believe what I said; he was in shock. Paul had a lot of respect for this older man, and now he didn't know what to say. We returned immediately to St. Moritz, where I insisted we have a face-to-face confrontation with Herr Weissman. Paul called him and he came to the hotel with his mistress.

"I want my husband to know exactly what you did!" I said. The color drained from his face. He didn't expect me to tell. I repeated what I had told Paul. "Is this not what you did?" I shouted at Herr Weissman.

The mistress cried, "Say it isn't so. Say it isn't so!" She moved a few steps away. But he just hung his head and said nothing.

Paul was terribly upset. He blamed himself for leaving me while he went to the film location. He promised never to do that again.

After the war, when we were in Cannes for the film festival, we were invited to the British film party. When we walked in, there was the Swiss financier, Herr Weissman, with the same mistress still at his side. When they saw us, they quickly left.

The Prodigal Son, French poster

33

ARRESTED AT THE BORDER

Paul's final film production in Berlin was *Der verlorene Sohn* (*The Prodigal Son*). The lead was again Luis Trenker, who also directed the film and co-wrote the story. Maria Andergast was his co-star. This was Paul's biggest production. They filmed in the Swiss Alps, the Italian Dolomites, and in New York City. This was 1934, and America was in the middle of the Great Depression. The story revolved around a rich American woman who invites her Swiss mountain guide to visit her. When he arrives in Manhattan

Maria Andergast, Luis Trenker, Marian Marsh, Lupita, and Paul

unannounced, she is away on vacation and he has to fend for himself in the big and often cruel city.

The Propaganda Ministry, led by Joseph Goebbels, had now taken charge of all film distribution and publicity, and they were not going to let a Jew—even one with an American passport like Paul—take credit for this important movie. The day of the premiere (November 6, 1934) film posters all over the city omitted Paul's production credit. He let the Propaganda Ministry know on behalf of Universal Pictures that a print of the film would not be available for that evening's premiere unless his credit was restored.

By the end of the day, a crew had pasted a separate banner across each movie poster in the city announcing: "A Paul Kohner Production."

Max Laemmle and Alfred Stern, both nephews of Carl Laemmle, had come from Paris for the premiere that night. When the lights went out the first projection on the screen was a newsreel showing Hitler's entry to a huge hall in Nuremberg decorated with brightly colored flags. He was followed by his aides, Göring, Goebbels, Hess, and Himmler as thousands in the hall raised their hands in stiff-arm salute. Then Hitler gave a speech about Germany's desire for peace for the next thousand years. At the end of the newsreel our audience stood and applauded.

When the picture was over and we left the

theater, there were Hitler Youths and Brown-Shirts outside. They were pulling people out of their cars and beating them up. It was horrible, and there was nothing we could do. We quickly got in a taxi. Alfred tried to hide his face with a handkerchief. Paul held up his American passport to the closed window and we made our escape. Max and Alfred were too afraid to go to their hotel, so we went back to our apartment. None of us slept that night. In the morning we took them straight to the train station.

Under the new racial laws, Universal Pictures could no longer be owned by Carl Laemmle, a Jew. Paul stayed because, even though he was a Jew, he felt safe with his American passport; he was the only one who could arrange the transfer of the company to a German business group, headed by Herr von Etzdorf. Von Etzdorf was an elegant man who spoke English very well. I hated him; I was absolutely sure he was a Nazi. To our surprise, after the war, we discovered that Herr von Etzdorf had actually been an English spy!

So we stayed, while everyone else was getting out. All the relatives of Carl Laemmle at the Universal office left. One by one, they all left Berlin. They knew that at any time of the night there could be the dreaded knock on the door. People all around disappeared and were never heard from again.

* * *

We had become close friends with many of the directors, writers, producers, and actors with whom Paul worked. By the summer of 1935, there was a mass exodus of these talented people. Among those who left were Curtis Bernhardt, William Dieterle, Billy Wilder, Walter Reich, Rudi Fehr, and Henry (Bobby) Koster. Directors Robert and Curt Siodmak left, too, with their uncle, Seymour Nebenzal, who had produced the classic film *Mayerling,* with Charles Boyer and Danielle Darrieux, and directed by Anatole Litvak. Seymour continued producing films in America.[12]

---

12   His son, Harold Nebenzal, a successful writer who speaks several languages including fluent Spanish, wrote the story and screenplay for one of my son's films, *Kinjite.* The film community was, and is, a very small family.

* * *

At least once a month we traveled by train to Paris, London, or to Czechoslovakia. It was forbidden for Jews to take valuables or more than thirty Deutsch marks in currency out of Germany. Again, Paul thought his American passport would protect him, so he was helping a lot of friends. He used to come to me with rolls of bills and say, "Darling, can you hide this?" I would take a Max Factor jar of cold cream, remove the thick cream, put the money in waxed paper, and replace the cream on top. Then, when we got to our hotel in Paris, he would say, "Darling, we have to empty the jar."

One time I was knitting a sweater when Paul came and gave me a thick roll of bills. I kept knitting as we crossed the border. I had hidden the money in the ball of yarn. When we got to Paris, he said, "Darling—the money I gave you?"

I said, "Oh, God. Can't it wait?" It was Sam Spiegel who had come for the money, and I had to unroll all the yarn. It was a game for me; I felt like Mata Hari. With our foreign passports, we were able to make many trips to help people get their valuables out of Germany.

Then, either the border guards got suspicious or somebody betrayed us.

* * *

We were on our way to Teplitz for a weekend visit with the family when we were arrested at the border between Germany and Czechoslovakia. The train stopped at Bodenbach and we gave our passports to the police who had entered our compartment. When they saw our names, they asked us to go with them and to bring our suitcases. We were taken off the train to the customs building. Just as Paul was taken one way and I the other, Paul said he had forgotten one suitcase and would go get it. He rushed back into the train, away from the guards. He told me later that before the guards caught up with him, he had taken ten thousand Deutsch Marks from his pocket and had thrown the money under the seat of an empty compartment. He hadn't told me what he was carrying. He had decided he would carry it himself instead of exposing me to the risk. If they had found that money we would have been in serious trouble.

I was taken to a cold, bare room without even a chair to sit on, and left there. A fat, nasty woman came in and ripped the lining of my fur hat and coat and told me to get undressed to my panties. My long hair was tied in a bun—she made me take it down. I was stupid and said in German, "Do you want to look in my ass, too?"

I was shivering in the cold, and I may have called her a few names that I had learned in German. After a thorough search, she threw my clothes at me and told me to put them back on. Next, my small suitcase was ripped through and my clothes emptied on the floor.

When I was taken back to their office, Paul said, "My wife doesn't speak German."

The fat woman said, "Oh, yes, she does, and she has a dirty mouth."

Outside, we could hear our train departing.

I said I wanted to call the Mexican ambassador in Berlin. They laughed and said that was not possible. Instead, they said I might just disappear and no one would know what had happened to me.

I insisted, saying, "Ambassador Nájera is a personal friend of mine. I have his home phone number!" Just then, one of the men going through Paul's briefcase found a photo of Paul shaking hands with the minister of defense, Colonel Werner von Blomberg. The photo had been taken in front of the Graf Zeppelin when the great dirigible had briefly visited Los Angeles on its round-the-world flight. There was also a personal note from Colonel von Blomberg, thanking Paul for an invitation to a screening in Berlin. The guards changed their tone: "Why did you not say you knew the minister of defense?"

Paul, bluffing, offered to call his good friend to vouch for him, saying, "I have his private home number."

"No no no, that will not be necessary," the guard said. But he insisted that we both sign a statement that we had been treated well. I refused.

"Make your wife sign," the guard said.

Paul said, "Lupi, please sign."

I was frightened for Paul. So I signed the paper, but I added, "Under protest."

When they finally released us, our train had left. So we hired a taxi to take us over the mountains to Teplitz. When we got in the taxi, I was going to say something to Paul, but he told me in English not to talk because of the driver. We drove for the next two hours in silence.

You were only allowed to take thirty marks out of Germany. And our thirty marks went to pay a fine for not declaring an English five-pound note they had found in my makeup case.

Paul's penchant for being photographed with important people had served us well. We had escaped what could have been a very dangerous situation. Colonel von Blomberg was promoted to general field marshal, minister of war, and commander-in-chief of the armed forces, until he was forced to resign in 1938, when he married a prostitute half his age. The Nazis had a strange code of ethics.

Der Reichswehrminister.

Berlin W 10, den 4. Februar 1933.
Königin-Augusta-Straße 38/42.

Sehr geehrter Herr Kohner!

Für Jhre freundlichen Glückwünsche und die Einladung zu einer Filmvorführung sage ich Jhnen meinen verbindlichsten Dank. Leider ist es mir wegen starker Jnanspruchnahme z. Zt. nicht möglich, einer solchen Vorführung beizuwohnen. Jch möchte mir aber vorbehalten, später einmal bei passender Gelegenheit von Jhrer liebenswürdigen Einladung Gebrauch zu machen.

Jhr sehr ergebener

v Blomberg

COLONEL von BLOMBERG'S LETTER
English translation:

Dear Mr. Kohner

For your kind congratulations and the invitation to a film screening, I extend to you my sincere thanks. Unfortunately, due to strong demands made on me at this time, it is not possible to attend such an event. I would ask you however that later at some fitting opportunity, I will be able to make use of your amiable invitation.

Yours very truly
v Blomberg

When we arrived in Teplitz, instead of going to our hotel, we stopped at the house to get money from Papa to pay the taxi driver. Paul said not to mention what had happened, but everyone asked why we hadn't arrived on the train. As usual, they had all been waiting for us at the station.

"What happened?" they asked. "Why didn't you call?"

Paul said, "We missed the train. We were taking a walk." They didn't believe us.

Papa peered at me closely and asked, "And you, *Kleine*, you were *spazieren*?"

"*Ja, Papa*, we were taking a walk," I answered, unable to meet his gaze.

"Now tell me the truth," he said. So Paul started talking and explained everything.

Papa warned us, "You can't go back. You can't, because you are going to get in serious trouble."

We agreed. We called Frieda and told her to pack up the apartment and ship everything to Teplitz. I had stomachaches for days. We decided to go to Paris to wait out the situation in Germany. We felt certain the German people would wake up to the mistake of supporting Adolf Hitler and his Nazis.

When we left Teplitz, all the family accompanied us to the station—everyone, that is, except Grandmother Caroline Béamt. They hadn't had the heart to tell her we were leaving. But she found out, and she came (as always) carrying her cane. She looked sad. In front of the family she took off her emerald earrings and gave them to me, saying, "I want Lupita to have these." Then she said, "This is the last time I am going to see you."

I said, "Oh no, *Tante* Clara, we're coming back."

"No," she said, shaking her head.

To avoid passing through Germany, we took the train through Switzerland to Paris. Paul had been on the phone to his office for hours. He was terribly upset not to be able to go back one more time, but Papa was right; we didn't dare go back to Germany.

* * *

Looking back, I can't believe how naive and foolish I was. Perhaps I was not afraid because I had experienced danger growing up in Mexico during a time of revolution. I certainly didn't know anything about European or Jewish history. I had never heard of anti-Semitism or pogroms.

I told Paul when we first met, "We are all God's children, no matter how we worship Him." That is how I felt then and that is how I feel now.

It is still impossible for me to understand whatever it was—fear, hatred, jealousy—that caused a people to persecute their Jewish neighbors, often children and the elderly. And denying knowledge of what was going on around them as so many Germans did after the war was over—is a lie that I cannot accept. The Nazis were incomprehensively proud of their plan to exterminate millions of souls—their "Final Solution to the Jewish Question."

Paul and I were fortunate to escape. We only found out later the depth of the horror that transpired under Nazi rule. By then, we were safely away, but for many of our friends and many of Paul's family, there was no escape.

Paul, Helene, Julius, and Lupita

ALLO
PARIS

4 F.   FÉVRIER

34

LUCKY TO ESCAPE

The Lord Byron Hotel in Paris was the gathering place for Berlin refugees. It was cheap and depressing. Our first stop was to Les Galeries Lafayette department store to buy a change of clothes. We had arrived in Paris with just the few clothes we had taken with us for the weekend in Teplitz.

There was a lot of confusion among the many refugees: "Is it really unsafe to go back?" they asked.

"How long do you think Hitler and the Nazis will be in power?"

"Where are my family members and neighbors who disappeared?"

"Where can I sell this gold watch?"

Paul was getting paid in dollars by Universal, so when our housekeeper, Frieda, arrived from Berlin, we moved to a very nice apartment near the Arc de Triomphe at 1 Square Villaret Joyeuse. There, we were able to invite everyone over to dinner. Frieda had closed our apartment in Berlin and shipped our clothes and personal things to the family in Teplitz. Papa Julius now sent them on to us in France.

We waited, hoping for the situation in Germany to get better. None of our friends thought Hitler could stay in power very long; it was against reason. Paul went to the Universal office every day; mostly, he was trying to help refugee friends get settled. There was nothing else for him to do. I spent a lot of time with the wives, and my German was improving. But one day I got out of the Metro and I didn't recognize where I was. I asked a gendarme for directions—in German, English, and Spanish. I kept repeating the name of our street and finally he understood what I was asking. He took me by the shoulders and turned me like a child in the direction I should go and said, "*Voilà*." After that, I got serious about learning French.

* * *

Even though we were safely away from Berlin, there were Nazis in Paris, too. Richard Eichberg was a successful director and producer in Berlin. When Paul and I got married, Richard had given us a gift of a Rosenthal china service. His girlfriend was the actress Tilla Garden. I got a phone call in Paris from Tilla inviting us to dinner. They were staying at the elegant Hôtel de Crillon on the Place de la Concorde. Could we meet them there, and then we would go to Chez Korniloff (a well-known Russian restaurant on the rue d'Armaille)? I called Paul; he said yes, but I should go on ahead and he would meet me at the Crillon.

When I got to the hotel, I used the house phone in the lobby to call Tilla. She told me to come up to their suite. As I entered the room, the first thing I saw was a loud, awful Nazi in uniform! Richard introduced me as Fräulein Tovar, not Mrs. Paul Kohner. Well, this Nazi immediately made a play for me, asking me where I lived, if I spoke German—and other personal things about my life. When Paul called from the lobby, Richard motioned for me to take the call in the bedroom. There, he pointed to another door that led out to the hall corridor. I told Paul on the phone, "Don't come up!"

I escaped out to the hall and the elevator. Paul and I ended up having dinner by ourselves at Little Hungary, one of our favorite restaurants. When I called Richard to apologize, he said the Nazi had been furious that I left. Incidentally, the Hôtel de Crillon became the headquarters of the Nazi High Command after Paris was occupied.

Richard was not Jewish. He stayed on in Berlin until 1938, where he directed a German film of the Jules Verne story, *Michael Strogoff*.[13] Somehow, Richard managed to get money out of Germany; when we met again after the war, he had bought a villa in the south of France.

Max Laemmle was busy managing Universal Pictures' distribution for all of Europe. He was engaged to lovely Bobbie Schulman who was taking classes at the Cordon Bleu Cooking School. Many evenings she would make delicious dinners for us in the tiny kitchen of their apartment. Max and Bobbie were married in Paris and their son, Robert, was born there. They didn't leave for America until late in 1938, just before the start of World War II.

The upheavals in our lives created a strong bond between us. In Los Angeles, Max started a chain of movie theaters that showed mostly European films. Paul and Max were part of a "*Kränzchen*," a circle of friends who met every month for dinner and discussion of world affairs.[14]

* * *

It was spring; I was learning to speak French, and Paris was lovely. But the stories we heard from refugees arriving daily from Germany were unbelievably horrible. They told of arrests and beatings and dreaded concentration camps.

Paul was reluctant to go back to America. He had established himself as an important man in Berlin, where he had made twenty-six films. In Berlin, he had the power to finance films of his choice. In Hollywood, he would have to start over again; he would be one of several producers at the studio competing for financing.

Paul said, "You know, going back means starting at the bottom. Here, I'm a producer, an important man."

I told him I loved him no matter who he was.

Six months later, the news from Germany was even worse. The Nazis were solidly in power and no one was challenging them. More and more refugees were fleeing Hitler's Germany and all who could were leaving for America. Film production had slowed all over Europe and Paul was restless; he was not happy doing nothing. I finally convinced him that we, too, should leave for America by saying, "We can always come back."

We boarded the S.S. *Ile de France* at the port of Cherbourg. That evening, when we crossed the English Channel to take on passengers at Southampton, Paul wanted to get off the boat. He argued that our bags weren't even unpacked.

He said, "Darling, this thing with Hitler won't last. Let's get off the ship." I again told him that we could always come back. He was not convinced.

Finally, I said, "Paul, I've never said no to you, but I am not getting off this ship!"

I knew deep inside that the trouble in Europe would get worse and that we had been very lucky to escape.

---

13 I was in a Mexican version, *Miguel Strogoff*, a few years later.

14 Max's son Bob and grandson Gregory now manage the very well-respected Laemmle theaters. Every year they invite me to their Seder dinner at Passover. This retelling of the story of the exodus of the Jews from Egypt carries on the tradition of teaching children who they are and the value of remembering the trials and tribulations their ancestors endured for them.

PART THREE

35

STARTING OVER IN AMERICA

We arrived in New York on the first of April 1935. The city was bustling and cheerful. Prohibition was over and that night John Auer took us to a nightclub. Paul loved to play the piano and he played very well. He went over and sat down at the piano, and a very drunk man came over and asked, "Can you play something about Texas?" When Paul started playing, the man brought Paul a drink and gave him a tip. I laughed and told Paul that, just in case things didn't go well in Hollywood, he could always have another career. The next day we took the train west. This time we traveled first class and we ate our meals in the dining car.

I never thought I could be so happy to see Los Angeles. The sun was shining (as it always seems to in California) and there was no talk of beatings, arrests, or Nazis. Paul was busy again at the studio and that made our lives easier. I got my little Ford out of storage and Paul bought a LaSalle.

Our apartment on Franklin Avenue near Highland had a small kitchenette. One hot summer afternoon, Paul called to say that he had met an old friend from Czechoslovakia, Francis Lederer, and wanted to bring him home for dinner. Francis was a leading man, a matinee idol.[15]

I had been terribly spoiled by Frieda, our housekeeper in Europe, and I really didn't know what to do in the kitchen. I went to the market and bought a raw, plucked chicken. Back at the apartment, it was so hot and, as I was alone, I took off all of my clothes except for my bra and panties. I heated cooking oil in a large pot and, when the oil started sizzling, I dropped the chicken in. A big mistake! The hot oil splashed on my bare stomach and I screamed in pain! The woman who managed the apartments came running. She was helping me with cold compresses and tea leaves when Francis Lederer and Paul walked in.

Francis started dating a young girl named Margo, from Mexico City. Her full name was María Margarita Guadalupe Teresa Bolado Castilla y O'Donnell. I knew María Margarita from Eduardo Cansino's dance class, when I first arrived in Hollywood. She used to come with her grandmother, just as I did. That seemed like a lifetime ago, even though I had only been gone three years.

It was not easy for Paul to get back to a position of producing at Universal. He had to deal with Junior Laemmle's jealousy. Junior considered Paul a rival for his father's affection and trust.

As a producer, Paul had to find a story that the studio wanted to invest in and one that had good roles that could be cast with popular actors or stars. The first picture Paul made when we returned was *Storm over the Andes*, shot in both English and Spanish. It starred Jack Holt, Antonio Moreno, and Mona Barrie. I was in the Spanish version, called *Alas Sobre el Chaco*, with Antonio Moreno and José Crespo. W. Christy Cabanne directed both versions. It was an unusual story about the fighter pilots on both sides of the war between Bolivia and Paraguay. Both versions were box-office successes and Paul was back on top.

---

15 He had starred in *The Pursuit of Happiness* on Broadway and in the movie version with Joan Bennett. In Europe he was best known for *Die Büchse der Pandora* (*Pandora's Box*), starring Louise Brooks.

José Crespo, Lupita, and Carlos Borcosque—*Alas Sobre el Chaco*

I immediately started a film directed by John Reinhardt. It was a South Seas tale called *Captain Calamity* in the English version with George Houston and Marian Nixon, and *El Capitán Tormenta* in the Spanish-language version starring Fortunio Bonanova and me.

* * *

Juan Torena, Fortunio Bonanova, and Lupita—*El Capitán Tormenta,* 1936

We moved from our small apartment to a two-story house on Toluca Lake in Burbank, which was very close to the studio. It was a lovely neighborhood of movie people: Mary Astor, George Brent, and Mary Bryson lived nearby. We used to row around the small lake to visit one another, and every night we would feed a big white swan named Sebastian. On Sundays, we had coffee on the lawn, and the neighbors would come over. Willy Wyler would arrive on his motorcycle, once driving right through the house!

José Bohr visited us. Although José was born in Germany, he grew up in Argentina and then lived in Mexico, where he directed films. José asked, "Paul, would you allow your wife to go back to Mexico to make a picture with me?"

Paul turned to me, "Would you like to?"

"Yes," I said, "if you wouldn't mind."

So back I went to Mexico and made *Marihuana* for José, with Barry Norton, René Cardona, and José's daughter, Carmelita Bohr. Carmelita was in love with a young actor, Pedro Armendáriz, who was just beginning his career. Against her parents' wishes, she and Pedro married.[16]

José Bohr and Lupita—*Marihuana,* 1936

A month after I returned to Los Angeles, I was in a stage play *Cuando La Vida Florece*

---

16   Pedro Armendáriz went on to become one of Mexico's great actors; their son, Pedro, Jr., carries on the tradition.

(*When Life Blooms*), by the writer Rafael Trujillo. The theater was on Grand Avenue in downtown Los Angeles. In 1936, there was still an audience in the Mexican immigrant community for legitimate stage productions.

On opening night, I was very nervous. Paul had invited great actors like Edward G. Robinson and Walter Huston, and they were sitting in the first row. I had the lead, and they probably wouldn't understand one word of the play, as it was being performed in Spanish. The other actors all had day jobs as waiters and as extras in the movies. There was no money for wardrobe, so I wore a dress I had knitted myself. The review in *La Opinión* was good, and it was thrilling for me to perform live on stage, even though it was just for a few weekends.

Lupita, *Cuando La Vida Florece—When Love Blooms*

36

WITH PAUL IN MEXICO

In 1936, Paul was the supervising producer for Universal Pictures. That year, he made *East of Java* with Charles Bickford and *Next Time We Love* with Margaret Sullavan and Jimmy Stewart. Maggie had been married to Henry Fonda; then she had married Willy Wyler, while he was directing her in *The Good Fairy*, but that marriage was too wild to survive. They fought and broke furniture, and finally Maggie went to Juarez, Mexico, to get a "quickie" divorce. Then Maggie married Leland Hayward, an agent and producer.

I got a phone call one day from Alfonso Pesqueira, the Mexican consul. He was at Universal Studios with General Saturnino Cedillo, who was now the minister of agriculture in Mexico. General Cedillo wanted to see me. "Would you please come, Lupita?" said Alfonso. He sounded a little stressed. This was the same General Cedillo who had pursued me in San Luis Potosí four years earlier. I was hesitant, but I drove to the studio.

The general, with ten tough-looking bodyguards, was waiting for me on Paul's set, where they were filming *Next Time We Love*. Paul loved important people and liked to have his picture taken with them. I couldn't complain; his photo shaking hands with Colonel von Blomberg had gotten us out of trouble on the German border. Paul was very impressed by this large, dark, Indian-looking man and his entourage. I tried to tell Paul that Cedillo was a very dangerous man. I regretted that I hadn't told him about my narrow escape in the middle of the night in San Luis Potosí. I had sworn Mrs. Fry to secrecy for fear that Paul wouldn't let me go back to Mexico. Now, Paul thought I was exaggerating. I couldn't make him understand my concern. Paul arranged to have a picture taken of us, and then he invited the general to our house.

Carl Laemmle, Lupita, and General Saturnino Cedillo

General Cedillo arrived with all of his bodyguards and a German by the name of von Merck, who was an advisor to the general and traveled with him. Cedillo told me that he had looked for me all over Europe; he had gone to our embassies in Paris and Madrid, asking for me. He was obsessed with me. "If I had found you, would I have had a chance?" he asked. In Mexico, this kind of man just took a girl if he wanted her; here, he was being more civilized. Paul served him champagne and then the general wanted to go to Ciro's, a supper club on the Sunset Strip, where all the important movie stars went to see and be seen.

Ciro's was full when we got there, but the general insisted on bringing in his bodyguards. I explained that there was no need for them here, but the general said he had lots of enemies and he couldn't take a chance. He wanted his men close to guard his back, so they stood around our booth like a chorus line. He ordered a bottle of Napoleon Brandy with dinner and drank it all himself.

"Are you happy with this man?" the general asked me. "If not, I will cut off his ears!" He was famous for doing just that. Paul didn't speak enough Spanish to understand.

The next evening, General Cedillo invited us to a dinner in a restaurant downtown. Alfonso Pesqueira was invited, too; he wisely did not bring his wife. It was a very strained evening with lots of drinking. Paul found it exciting, foreign, like being in one of his movies. He wanted to know more about Mexico.

* * *

I wanted Paul to meet my family, so we decided to take a trip. I had my little Ford that we arranged to take with us on a boat of the Panama Pacific Line to Acapulco. I didn't know that Paul had written to General Cedillo, letting him know that we were coming.

When we got off the boat in Acapulco, a representative of the general was waiting for us with a large touring car and bodyguards to take us to Mexico City. One of the guards drove our Ford.

We stopped for lunch at a papaya plantation, where little children were running around naked. I guess I hadn't prepared Paul for this side of Mexico; he was not used to seeing such poverty. He ordered roast chicken. Next thing you know, somebody was chasing a live chicken around our table. When they caught it and had wrung its neck, Paul changed his mind and asked for scrambled eggs instead. When he asked where the bathroom was, he was given a handful of newspaper and a stick and pointed in the direction of an outhouse. He asked what the stick was for, and was told it was to keep the pigs away. You can imagine how this sophisticated European man felt about that!

It was already dark when we got to the charming hill town of Taxco, so Paul insisted that we stop for the night. The best hotel was the Rancho Telva. General Cedillo's men went in to get rooms and were turned away. I couldn't blame the innkeeper; they were a rough-looking bunch. I sent in a note on my card, explaining who I was, and Paul and I were immediately given their best room. We had dinner on the patio and Mariachis serenaded us under our window. There is nothing more Mexican than Mariachi music.

The next day, General Cedillo's men escorted us to the capitol. Paul was very impressed as we drove down Paseo de la Reforma, Maximilian's magnificent boulevard that leads from Chapultepec Castle to downtown (and was first called the Emperor's Avenue). Starting with the Diana fountain, the broad tree-lined avenue is interrupted with *glorietas* (roundabouts), with statues to Cuauhtemoc (the last emperor of the Aztecs), Christopher Columbus, and the winged Angel of Independence (the guardian angel of the city). We drove past Parisian-style mansions that rivaled the old houses of New York's Fifth Avenue. On the bridle path, we saw horse-drawn carriages and elegant men riding thoroughbred horses. Mexico City, in 1936, was a mixture of European elegance and rural simplicity.

At nine-thirty the next morning, I got a call from the lobby. I went downstairs to find both my father and General Cedillo waiting for me. The general seemed to devour me with his eyes. He begged me to ask for anything; was there anything he could do for me? My father was so impressed that afterwards he wanted me to ask the general to arrange a job for him where he would get a government salary without doing any real work. Of course, I refused to ask for such a thing.

We went to my father's house, where Paul kissed my mother's hand in the European manner. She wasn't used to that. Grandma was doing everything she could to make Paul feel comfortable while my sisters and my brother were on their best behavior. My father was so impressed with Paul, or maybe intimidated, that after lunch he very ceremoniously gave Paul a diamond ring that he took off his finger. Paul didn't want to accept it until I told him to take it; it had been paid for by money I had earned and had sent to my father to buy a piece of property. Instead, he had used the money to buy that diamond. Paul had the diamond reset in a ring for me.

It was wonderful to see my family, especially my grandma; I had missed her terribly. Many times in the first years of my marriage, I had wished she had been there to talk to. My sister Lucy was madly in love with her future husband, Jesús Inaraja Aristi, a Spaniard. Sarita was twelve, Guillermo was ten, and my youngest sister Mary was only nine.

General Cedillo had invited us to Sunday lunch at his house in San Ángel and Paul had said yes before I could stop him. The general sent a car for us.

When we arrived, we were shown into a large room with a lot of people we were not introduced to. The general personally served us champagne, warm. Paul tasted it, but when the general tried to refill his glass, Paul said, "No thank you, it's a little too warm."

"You must drink," the general said. "You served me champagne in your house!" Then Cedillo rinsed his mouth with the warm champagne and spit it out!

After lunch, we were taken to the bullfights at Cuatro Caminos where we sat in a front-row box protected by bodyguards from possible assassins' bullets. The general was not taking any chances. This was Paul's first *corrida*, and he was taking pictures.

The atmosphere was charged with excitement as trumpets played "*La Macarena*" and the ceremony began. Two men on horseback—*aguacils*—dressed in sixteenth-century black costume, rode across the bullring to request a symbolic key from the *presidente*. Then they separated and slowly rode left and right around the ring to the *toril*—the gate that would let the bulls in. The gatekeeper swung open the wooden barrier and the trumpeters played "*Cielo Andaluz*," announcing the *paseo* of the *toreros*— three *matadors* and six *bandarilleros,* dressed in their *trajes de luces, picadors* on horseback, mule-drivers and mules to haul away the eventual dead bulls, and finally the *monosabios*, men dressed all in red who help the *picadors* maneuver into position, and who would rake the sand and get rid of traces of blood at the end of each of the six fights. When the parade reached us, the *matadors* saluted the judges seated high above us, and gave their dress capes to friends and dignitaries in the front rows. I had been taught all of this by Antonio Moreno, who had taken me to *corridas* when we were making *Santa*, and by Pancho Cabrera in Madrid. It was all very colorful and Paul was fascinated in spite of the blood and inevitable death of the *toros bravos*.

The following evening, we went to the Palacio de Bellas Artes to see a performance by Marian Anderson, the black American singer who, in her own country in 1936, could not eat in "White Only" restaurants or stay in hotels where white people stayed. She had just completed a concert tour of Europe, during which Arturo Toscanini called her "the voice of the century." In Mexico, she was treated like royalty and, when the audience gave her a standing ovation, tears ran down her face.

We had invited Diego Rivera and Dolores del Río, but Paul made the mistake of also inviting Cedillo to the concert. We were with Diego in the lobby when the general came in with his entourage. Paul introduced the two men and Diego got very serious; they were political opposites. Diego was a Communist while Cedillo was an extreme anti-Communist. I had to sit between them to keep the peace. That was an evening when I could barely breathe.

Paul, Lupita, Marian Anderson, Dolores del Río, and Diego Rivera

We took a day trip to the archaeological site of Teotihuacán. Many cultures have inhabited this ancient city; most recently the Aztecs at the time of Spain's conquest of Mexico in 1521. It was my first time to see the huge Pyramids of the Sun and the Moon, and they took my breath away.

We went to the floating gardens of Xochimilco. These islands were created by the Aztecs to grow corn on the lagoon that surrounded Tenochtitlán, the old Aztec capital which is Mexico City. (Today, small boats take visitors through canals between the islands.)

We had dinner at El Patio with Diego, where handsome young Ricardo Montalban introduced himself and asked me to dance a tango.[17]

We went to Chapultepec Park and visited the castle of Maximilian von Habsburg, who had been placed in power by Napoleon III in 1864. Maximilian ruled Mexico for three years as emperor, but when the French withdrew their support, he was overthrown by Benito Juárez, a Zapotecan Indian from Oaxaca. That was the end of Mexico's War of Independence from the Europeans. Benito Juárez served a total of five terms as president and is still the most beloved of all Mexican leaders.[18]

After ten exhausting days, we traveled back to Los Angeles by train, with my little Ford riding on a flatcar with us. As I had hoped, Paul had fallen in love with Mexico.

---

17   Ricardo starred with Esther Fernández in the 1943 remake of *Santa*.
18   In 1939, *Juárez* was made into a highly regarded film directed by William Dieterle from a screenplay by John Huston and Aeneas MacKenzie, and starred Paul Muni as Benito Juárez.

37

GOOD FRIENDS

One of the many friends Paul helped over the years was a young Norwegian writer by the name of Erling Bergendahl. Back in 1928, when Bergendahl was desperately broke, Paul advanced him money to return to Norway. When asked how he could repay the kindness, Paul suggested an introduction to Bergendahl's friend, the Norwegian Nobel Prize-winning author, Knut Hamsun. On his next trip to Europe, Paul and Erling visited Hamsun on his farm, south of Oslo. Hamsun was grateful for Paul's generosity to his young friend, so when Paul asked if he could buy the film rights to his book *Victoria*, Hamsun said yes. *Victoria* was one of Paul's favorite stories—a classic love story with a tragic ending. Paul wanted to personally produce this film, but that wasn't to be. Paul sold these film rights to M-G-M in order to make the down payment on our house.

We were living in the rented house on Toluca Lake and we wanted to buy it. We wanted to have a baby. We wanted three boys and three girls, but our chances were slim. One fallopian tube and one ovary had been ruined during my ectopic pregnancy operation in Berlin. So, when my doctor called Paul at his office to tell him I was pregnant, Paul was overwhelmed. He came home with a big bouquet of flowers.

We immediately wrote a letter to Papa Julius to tell him the good news, but he never received it. He died the day before of a heart attack; that was in May of 1936. Paul's first thought on hearing the news was, "How will I tell Lupita?" He knew I loved Papa more than my own father. Papa Julius had been a wonderfully supportive man who cared for me from the moment we met. I was a foreigner who didn't speak his language. He didn't know my parents, who were halfway around the world. All he knew was that I loved his son and that Paul loved me. Papa welcomed me and he loved me.

That summer, when I was pregnant, we were already in escrow on our two-story rented house when I slipped and tumbled down the stairs. On top of that, a toddler had just fallen into the lake and drowned!

So I went looking for another house, away from Toluca Lake. A real estate broker took me to an area called Bel-Air, where he showed me a Mexican-style house on Stone Canyon Road. I fell in love with the house immediately. It had a red-tiled roof and white stucco walls. It was surrounded by sycamore and oak trees, and a creek ran through the front garden. The house had been built by an Austrian countess who had died just as she finished building it. Her relatives in New York didn't want the house, so it was put up for sale. That night I told Paul, "I've found our home."

Stone Canyon Road was not even paved in 1936, and there were very few neighbors. When Paul saw the house he said, "It's on the other side of the world!"

"You'll just have to get up a little earlier," I said. I was determined.

The house cost seventeen thousand dollars, a lot of money for us at the time. The property was one and a third acres of land, and it was just a few miles from the University of California and

Westwood Village. Paul brought his friends to get their opinions. Lucien Mandelik, who was a real estate investor, told him the property had lots of possibilities and advised him to buy it. Willy Wyler looked at the house and said, "Paul, if you don't want it, I'll buy it." That, and my determination, convinced Paul, but a writer, Mel Baker, was also interested in the house. Paul spoke to him and explained that his wife wanted the house and that he was going to buy it for me, no matter what. So it didn't make any sense for the two of them to get into a bidding war. We got the house and Mel built a house farther up the canyon. And that's how Paul came to sell his film rights to *Victoria*—to raise the money for the down payment.

Bel-Air was named for Alfonso Bell, an early California oil man and land developer. His own hacienda-style estate was a short walk from our house. It had riding stables, guest houses, and a fire station. In 1946, the Bell property was converted into the beautiful Hotel Bel-Air.

After the war, we went to Oslo to visit Erling Bergendahl, who had indirectly enabled us to buy our house when he introduced Paul to Knut Hamsun and facilitated buying the rights to *Victoria*. Erling had now become a successful businessman in Norway. He represented Columbia Pictures and was president of the Norwegian Film Producers Association. Erling and Paul had kept up with each other's careers through correspondence and they were both looking forward to meeting again after so many years. But when we arrived at Oslo airport, Paul was paged by Erling's wife. Her husband had died suddenly of a heart attack. Paul and I went to pay our respects and we left Oslo the next morning.

* * *

Paul was thought of as part of Carl Laemmle's family, if not Carl's favorite "son." But the fact was that Carl already had a son, Carl Junior, and a daughter, Rosabelle. Carl had always hoped that Paul would marry Rosabelle.

Junior, as Carl Laemmle's son was known, was only twenty-one when his father put him in charge of production at Universal Pictures. Carl was concerned that at his advanced age, should anything happen to him, his son would not be prepared to take over the studio. So he decided to hand over the reins while he could still be a guiding influence. Soon, there was friction between Junior and Paul.

Carl spoke to Paul and they agreed that it would be best if Paul moved to another studio. At one time, Irving Thalberg, now in charge of production at M-G-M, and Harry Cohn, head of Columbia, had worked for Carl Laemmle. Carl wrote a letter to Thalberg, and Paul moved to the M-G-M Culver City studio. One year later, due to Junior's budget excesses, Carl Laemmle was forced to sell Universal Pictures.

Paul found it difficult to get a picture made at M-G-M, a studio where he didn't have long-standing relationships. It took a while, but finally Paul was preparing a film of that same Knut Hamsun novel, *Victoria*. Norma Shearer, Irving Thalberg's wife, would play the lead.

In September of 1936, when I was seven months pregnant, we were driving back from a weekend at Lake Arrowhead when we heard on the radio that Irving Thalberg had just died of pneumonia. He had always been frail, with a weak heart and severe allergy problems, but he was only thirty-seven years old! Their house at the Santa Monica Beach, on what was known as "The Golden Strand," had a special air filtering system throughout to help Irving breathe more easily.[19]

Irving Thalberg's death was a tragedy for Hollywood. He was well liked and many owed their careers to him. Women and men wept at his funeral service at the B'nai B'rith Temple. Thalberg was known as the "Boy Wonder" at M-G-M. His talent

---

19 I know this because in 1971, my *consuegra*, my son's then mother-in-law, Mary Bradley, bought the house. It still had a projection booth and a movie screen that rose up from a section of the living room floor, from the days when the Thalbergs watched movies at home.

and good taste had resulted in some of the best motion pictures of their time, including *A Night at the Opera, Grand Hotel,* and *The Good Earth.*

For Paul, the handwriting was on the wall. Without Irving Thalberg to sponsor him, he would have a difficult time getting his pictures made.

By chance, Paul bumped into Harry Cohn at the Brown Derby Restaurant. Harry, president of Columbia Pictures, asked Paul to come work for him; so Paul left M-G-M, intending to produce *Victoria* for Harry. Part of Paul's deal with Columbia was a writing job for his brother Fritz, who was in London struggling to make a living.

Fritz and Mimi and their daughter Ruthie came to Los Angeles but Fritz had a rude awakening when he found out that he had been hired solely at Paul's request and not on his own merit. The whole relationship at Columbia was unworkable. Harry was too abrasive a character; he and Paul argued over the merits of *Victoria* and Paul quit, giving up the security of his studio contract. We had saved some money, so we were not immediately worried, and Paul was in no rush to jump into another bad situation.

* * *

We were invited by John Huston to spend a weekend at Nan and Walter Huston's house at Running Springs, near Lake Arrowhead, a two-hour drive from Los Angeles. Nan, John's stepmother, preferred New York, where she and Walter had met and acted together on the stage; but Walter was now working in movies, and that meant living in California. Since neither of them liked Hollywood, they had built a large house, more like a hunting lodge in the woods, with several guest rooms and a swimming pool. John and his English wife, Lesley Black, were our hosts that weekend. In spite of being seven months pregnant, it was Lesley who had driven them to Running Springs. In 1933 John, who had had several drunk-driving arrests, had a very bad accident on Sunset Boulevard. A woman, Tosca Roulien, stepped out from between two parked cars and he hit her. She was the wife of a Brazilian actor who, coincidentally, was working in dual-language films just as I was. When Tosca died, John was devastated. The whole thing was hushed up, but he moved to England for a while. Now, John was back and writing the screenplay for *Sergeant York,* which led to the opportunity to write and direct his first movie, *The Maltese Falcon.* Both films received nominations for Best Screenplay.

Ernst Laemmle was there at Running Springs with his bright English girlfriend, Nina Jean Fraser. Willy brought his new girlfriend, Margaret Tallichet; we called her Talli. Then, Willy's brother, Bob, and his parents, Leopold and Melanie, arrived.

Ernst, Nina, Talli, Lupita, and Paul

David Selznick, who had a house nearby, stopped in and said he had heard a rumor that there was going to be a wedding. "Who's getting married?" he asked.

"I am!" I answered. That got a big laugh; I was eight months pregnant. It was a very happy time. We were all close friends. Love was in the air and two of us were pregnant. That afternoon, Talli and Willy surprised us by getting married, there in Walter's house. They had known each other a very short time, but their marriage lasted as long as ours.

Ernst and Nina were the next to get married. Ernst had been a film director at Universal. Ernst's father, Siegfried, was Carl Laemmle's brother. Ernst then worked with writer/director/producer Preston Sturges. But Preston's film career slowed down; he opened a popular restaurant called The Players, and when Universal Studios was sold, Ernst found himself out of work. By then, he and Nina had three children. They moved to Lake Elsinore to manage a ceramics factory; that's when Ernst became ill. At first he thought it was just an ulcer, but it turned out to be cancer. We found this out on a New Year's Eve, and it hit us all hard. Toward the end, I helped Nina take care of Ernst, giving him injections for the pain. Ernst was the first of our friends in Los Angeles to die.[20]

Talli and Willy had four children. Sundays we were often at their house. The men would play long games of gin rummy while the children had swimming lessons, and later, we watched movies in their screening room.

---

20   To support her children, Nina went to work in television writing for *Zane Grey Theater*, *Peyton Place*, and many other popular shows.

38

BECOMING AN AGENT AND A FATHER

Frank Orsatti, a talent agent, married actress Lien Deyers in 1936 and they, too, bought a house on Stone Canyon Road. Lien had moved here from Berlin after divorcing Alfred Zeisler. It was at the Zeislers' dinner party in Neubabelsberg that Prince Wilhelm had made such a fuss over me. Frank Orsatti had been a successful "importer" of liquor during Prohibition—I was told he brought it in by boat from Mexico. Somehow he became a close friend of Louis B. Mayer and it was Mayer who helped him become a talent agent. Frank had been helping Paul cast his films, and maybe that's where he got the idea of becoming an agent himself. After all, Paul was always getting jobs for people. And without a strong alliance with one of the studios, it was going to be difficult to continue producing films. Paul was accustomed to being in charge and did not like working for someone else. We had discussed the pros and cons of his starting his own business; I reassured him that I would go along with whatever he wanted to do.

Paul was walking on Sunset Boulevard in Beverly Hills, deep in thought, when he ran into his friend Oscar Cummins, a lawyer. Oscar was watching workmen paint a small, elegant two-story building.

"What are you doing now, Paul?" Oscar asked.

"You know," Paul answered, "I'm thinking of opening a talent agency."

"Well, I own this building," Oscar said. "Take a look. You could have an office here." That settled it; Paul borrowed five thousand dollars each from both Willy Wyler and Joe Pasternak and started his agency at 9169 Sunset Boulevard. That was the address of the Paul Kohner Agency for the next fifty years.

Several times, Paul could have bought the building for very little money, especially after the attack on Pearl Harbor on December 7, 1941, when there was fear that Japan would attack California. But Paul always had one foot in Europe; he never expected to stay in Hollywood forever. If I hadn't insisted, we would never have bought our house on Stone Canyon Road.

Paul's first deal as an agent happened after a meeting at Universal, where the executives and Joe Pasternak were discussing their new contract player, Deanna Durbin. The problem was they didn't have a story for her. After the meeting, Paul ran into Konrad Bercovici, a writer, and invited him to lunch in the commissary. Konrad was broke; he hadn't eaten in days. Over lunch, Paul asked if he had a story suitable for Deanna Durbin. Konrad told Paul a story, Paul liked it and asked if he had an agent. He didn't.

"Then I'm your agent," Paul said.

Paul went back to the executives and sold them Konrad's story for $25,000. Konrad nearly fainted when Paul told him the good news. Now, Paul really *was* an agent. Over the years, Paul represented Konrad, his brother, Leonardo, and Leonardo's son, Eric—all very successful writers and producers.

Walter Huston came to Paul for representation. Then John Huston asked Paul to represent him (he would do so for more than fifty years). Aeneas MacKenzie was only a script reader at Warner Bros. when Paul sold his talents as a writer, getting him a job with John Huston, writing the screenplay for *Juárez*. Several years later, a William Morris agent asked Aeneas why he didn't leave Paul's small agency. "Because I like his wife," he answered. Writers, directors, and actors who had known Paul as a knowledgeable producer came to him, confident that he would guide their careers with wisdom and integrity.

* * *

I was eight months pregnant in October when we moved into the house on Stone Canyon Road. At first, we slept on a mattress on the floor with only boxes of books to sit on. With my big belly, Paul had to help me up in the morning.

Our house has a Mexican red-tiled roof, but the inside was very European. There were only two bedrooms with a bath between them. Paul had a Hungarian designer, Paul László, build modern furniture for the house. I didn't like the style, but Paul was so happy. Little by little, over the years the house became more Mexican. I didn't fight for it; it just gradually happened.

* * *

Maggie Sullavan had become pregnant about the same time that I did. One evening over dinner, she and Leland offered us a bet; one thousand dollars to whichever of us would give birth first. Paul said, "I'll take that bet." I won on November 11, 1936, when our Susanna Guadalupe was born at Cedars of Lebanon Hospital.

My mother was staying with us at the time and she had brought my little sisters, Sarita and Mary, with her from Mexico. When I first started feeling contractions, my mother said, "Oh, no, that's nothing; it's way too early." But I said to Paul, "Call my doctor!" Paul called Dr. Leon Tiber and also called all of his friends.

Willy Wyler and Preston Sturges met us at the hospital, where they kept Paul busy playing gin rummy in the corridor while I was delivering Susan. My mother was with me; she kept telling me to keep quiet, not to scream so much. I had to tell the doctor to get my mother out of there!

We took Susan home with a nurse from the hospital, and every day at five, Paul would come home to help give Susan her bath. He was so excited about being a father. It was as though Susan was the first baby ever to be born.

When the hospital nurse had to leave us, we called an employment agency and hired a young German woman, Josephine Gumbert, and she would stay with us for the next ten years. Josephine had come here from Munich. At first, she could not speak English, so our children began life speaking German. We didn't switch to English at home until Hitler declared war on the United States in December 1941.

* * *

The news from Europe continued to get worse. Starting in 1937, a Jew could no longer own a business in Hitler's Germany. So many people we knew, and friends of people we knew, were desperate to leave their homeland. Friends wrote to us, begging for help. Many had managed to leave with just the clothes on their backs, and now needed money to survive while waiting for visas in neutral countries like Switzerland and Portugal. We tried everything we could to get Paul's family out of Czechoslovakia. We wrote to everyone we knew, mostly under my maiden name, Tovar, which seemed safer for them than Kohner.

In Berlin we had known the Egyptian consul general, Alex Bhabi; I think he was a little bit in love with me. Whenever he saw me, he would ask if Paul was still the man for me. I wrote to him, asking for help in getting visas for the family. He wrote back that he would do everything he could.

To enter America, you needed not only a visa but also an affidavit, which was a guarantee that you had a job waiting for you, or at least sufficient money in a bank account in your name to show that you could survive here.

Paul was spending most of his time trying to help these refugees. That's how he got the idea to start the European Film Fund.

AUTHOR'S NOTE:

THE EUROPEAN FILM FUND

In the 1930s, America had very strict rules governing immigration. Embassies and consulates in each country had a quota for émigrés.

In 1937, Paul Kohner started the European Film Fund, which later became the European Relief Fund. Its purpose was to collect money from the better-off members of the émigré community and deposit these monies into a fund from which it would be disbursed to those in need on the basis of a loan or, in certain cases, as a grant.

Members of the fund were also asked to find work for these refugees. Columbia's Harry Cohn was not to be outdone by the other studios. Legend has it that when confronted by Paul Kohner, he agreed: "What Jack Warner and L. B. Mayer can do, I can do better. I'll take ten of those scribblers." Paul had convinced Jack Warner to take four writers and L.B. Mayer to take six writers. Twenty lives were saved that day.

In 1938, the fund was incorporated, making it a non-profit organization. Donations made by the members were tax-deductible.

In 1940, it became even more difficult to emigrate, with the additional requirement of a character reference or political affidavit. Members had to plead with fellow émigrés to secure all refugees, some of them stranded at a European port and desperate to get out, with affidavits, which would enable them to come to the United States. An affidavit was a guarantee by an American citizen that the person in question would not become a financial burden to the United States government, and required the sponsor to vouch with their bank account. However, an affidavit did not replace the still-necessary visa. Paul Kohner himself supplied more than sixty refugees with affidavits.

Although the name European Film Fund suggests European co-productions, it was an organization whose aim was to rescue and financially support mainly, although not exclusively, German Jews.

Founding members included Paul Kohner, Ernst Lubitsch, William Wyler, William and Charlotte Dieterle, Liesl Frank, Joe Pasternak, Henry Blanke, Henry Koster, Billy Wilder, Heinz Herald, and many more.

By the end of World War II, more than fifteen hundred German and Austrian émigrés worked in the Hollywood studios. The list of German-speaking film directors and writers is impressive and includes Max Reinhardt, Billy Wilder, Fred Zinnemann, Curtis Bernhardt, Otto Preminger, Fritz Lang, Ernst Lubitsch, Edgar Ulmer, Max Ophuls, Hans Kraly, Thomas Mann, Erich Maria Remarque, Emil Ludwig, Heinrich Mann, Bertolt Brecht, Vicky Baum, Franz Werfel, Joe May, Alfred Döblin, Walter Reisch, and Leonhard Frank, to name just a few. Actors included Albert Basserman, Sigi Arno, Alexander Granach, Carl Esmond, Fritz

Kortner, Fritzi Massary, and dozens more.

The German government bestowed several honors on Paul Kohner in recognition of his help to so many of its citizens. The Deutsche Kinemathek in Berlin has devoted a room of its film museum to a permanent exhibit of Paul's papers and has published a book of his correspondence called *I am an Incurable European – Letters from Exile*.

39

"*KAFFEEKLATSCH*" AT THE KOHNERS

The following year, 1938, Paul and I made another trip to Mexico. It was wonderful to see my family again, especially my grandma. She loved Paul, so when he asked her, "How about visiting us for a couple of months?" she agreed, and we took her back with us.

Two months later at breakfast, grandma said, "Paul, the two months are up."

He said, "Grandma, where are you happier, here or there?"

"Here, of course," she said.

"Then we won't talk about it anymore."

My grandma lived with us for nineteen years, until she passed away at the age of eighty-six. She adored Paul. Sometimes she said he was too good for me.

Grandma Sullivan was a pioneer woman. She had large, capable hands; she had helped build her own house in Salina Cruz. Grandma helped me plant fruit trees on our property and taught me how to take care of them. Grandma was a quiet woman, firm but tranquil—valuable traits in the volatile daily life of Hollywood. And whenever I went to Mexico to work on a film, I always knew my children were safe with her in charge.

* * *

The news from Europe came via personal letters and newspapers, as well as newsreels that were shown before every movie. Pathé Newsreels, Fox Movietone News, and Universal Newsreels kept us informed. The news was all bad. Japan invaded China in July of 1937. In September 1938, the Sudetenland, which included Teplitz, was annexed by Nazi Germany; thousands of Jews left for Prague, which was still unoccupied. War was imminent and we were desperate to get the family out of Europe.

We were finally able to get two visas, one for Paul's mother and another for his brother, Walter. But Walter was unable to convince his mother to leave. It would have meant leaving behind her stepmother, Caroline Béamt, her sister, Tante Clara, and her half-brother, Rudy. They were a close family and Helene simply could not leave them.

Walter was especially reluctant to leave his girlfriend, Hanna Bloch. When Hanna's father was no longer allowed to work in Teplitz, he moved with his family to a one-room apartment in Prague. Walter reluctantly said good-bye to Hanna, and on October 28, 1938, he flew to London. From there he sailed on the S.S. *Roosevelt* for New York and then took a Greyhound bus to Los Angeles. He hoped to arrange for Hanna to join him in Los Angeles. Walter was able to get her an affidavit, but she still needed an American visa.

Hanna did manage to get a visa to go to Amsterdam, where she had distant relatives. At the American Consulate in Amsterdam, Hanna was told that, because of the quota, she should not expect a visa to enter America for another three years!

On November 10, 1938, the newspapers were full of the "*Kristallnacht,*" the night of broken glass.

169

On that night, all over Germany, Austria, and the Sudetenland, synagogues were burned and Jewish-owned businesses and shops were destroyed, their windows smashed. The streets were littered with shards of broken glass. No Jew was safe that night. Thousands were arrested and sent to concentration camps, their houses broken into and ransacked. Four months later, German troops occupied all of Czechoslovakia, then on September 1, 1939, Hitler invaded Poland. After that, all of Europe was at war.

The Germans invaded Holland on May 10, 1940. The Dutch surrendered after just five days. On that same date, France was invaded.

Hanna was still living in what was now German-occupied Amsterdam. She worked as a typist for the Refugee Committee, which kept a file on every Jew in Amsterdam. This job entitled her to a special stamp in her identity papers, stating that her work was essential to the war effort. She met and fell in love with Carl Benjamin, the brother of a girlfriend of hers. In July 1942, Carl's name appeared on a list of men to be deported to a labor camp. Hanna and Carl immediately married in the hope that their marriage would protect both of them from the dreaded camps. But the Nazi SS and Dutch police arrested them anyway, and they were sent to Camp Westerbork.

* * *

In March of 1941, President Franklin D. Roosevelt and Congress repealed the Neutrality Act of 1935 that was intended to keep America out of another European war. Now, America could support her allies with war material. All of these events we discussed in detail with our friends.

After the attack on Pearl Harbor, December 7, 1941, Japanese-Americans were sent to internment camps. There already was a curfew imposed for noncitizen "enemy aliens." Germans and Italians, who had not been processed for American citizenship, had to be indoors or in their homes by 8:00 p.m.

Sunday afternoons, many Europeans came to our house, where there was always coffee and pastries and the feeling was always *gemütlich* (cozy). Our home became their meeting place, and a home away from home. These displaced artists and intellectuals would talk about the news from Europe; who was working and who was not, and who was sleeping with whom. Inevitably there would be a game of gin rummy that had to end before curfew when many had to scurry home to their temporary quarters. Germans tend to comply with rules.

Some of these émigrés became successful actors, writers, directors, and producers. Others were not so fortunate. A few went back to Europe after the war because they could not adjust to life here, especially the women. They had never done housework in their previous lives. Here they lived in tiny apartments and had to do their own cooking and cleaning, a hard adjustment for many of them.

But on Sundays, it was always open house, a "*Kaffeeklatsch*" at the Kohner's.

Lupita and Paul, 1941

40

"SHOT WITH HIS BOOTS ON"

Early in 1938, I had been happy to go back to Mexico to make the comedy *El Rosario de Amozoc*. The producer was Vicente Saisó Piquer, a Spaniard. José Bohr directed, and I had the lead with Emilio Tuero and Carlos Orellana.

On the last day of filming, the persistent General Saturnino Cedillo sent one of his bodyguards to my father's house with instructions to bring me to him.

The newspapers were calling the general "The Bull of San Luis Potosí" and a "fascist." President Cardenas turned against him and kicked him out of his cabinet. My father knew all this, and he knew how dangerous General Cedillo was. He told Cedillo's man that I was no longer in Mexico.

That night, my father put me on a train for Los Angeles and told the porter not to unlock my compartment for anyone. When the train stopped in San Luis Potosí, on the way north, it seemed to me as if we were in that station forever. It wasn't until we were moving again that I felt safe.

* * *

Later that year, I had a small part in a film called *Blockade* that we shot in Los Angeles. It was a romance set during the Spanish Civil War, directed by William Dieterle, starring Henry Fonda, Leo Carrillo, and Madeleine Carroll. The Motion Picture Academy nominated John Howard Lawson's script for Best Story. John was a member of the American Communist Party, and *Blockade,* did have political undertones.

Walter Wanger was the producer for United Artists. Walter was married to Joan Bennett and was one of the busiest producers in Hollywood. He won the National Peace Conference Award for *Blockade*, but the film was also picketed by the Catholic Church, which was pro-Franco.

Next, I had the lead with George O'Brien in *The Fighting Gringo*, for director David Howard at RKO. George was a sweetheart. Paul and I became very good friends with George and his wife, Marguerite O'Brien; we often went to their ranch for the weekend.[21]

* * *

I never got tired of going to Mexico—it was always home to me. In the fall of 1938, when I was five months pregnant with Pancho, I went back to make *María*, which was adapted by José López Rubio and Chano Urueta, from a novel by Jorge Isaac. Our cameraman, Alex Phillips, had to work hard to avoid showing that I was about to have a child. Rodolfo Landa, Miguel Arenas, and Josefina Escobedo were my co-stars.

---

21   Their daughter, Orin, and our daughter, Susan, are still close friends in New York, where Orin plays the double bass with the New York Philharmonic.

The Fighting Gringo poster

While I was filming *María*, Sam Spiegel was also in Mexico; I think he didn't have a visa to enter the United States. When I had first met Sam in the lobby of the Majestic Hotel in Berlin in 1933, he had taken Paul aside to talk to him privately. Later, there was a knock on the door and a bellboy delivered a beautiful orchid for me. It was from Sam. I was very impressed—that is, until Paul told me that Sam had just borrowed the money from him to pay for that corsage. Sam was a fascinating man; he was very kind and generous to me when I worked for him in London. But in his early years as a producer Sam had difficult times, too.

Sam called and asked me to be his guest of honor at a dinner party he was giving at El Patio, one of the best restaurants in Mexico City. That evening there were twelve of us, including the French and German ambassadors and many important people from the Mexican film industry. The table was set with beautiful flowers and the menu was magnificent. Sam had outdone himself; it was a scintillating and elegant dinner party. Two days later, I got a call from the restaurant owner; Sam had not paid the bill and could not be found! I ended up paying that bill. That was typical of Sam. When he showed up in Los Angeles a few months later, speculation was that Sam had had to swim across the Rio Grande, like so many "wetbacks."

Sam's exploits in the film business are legendary; he was larger than life. He had talent and guts and, eventually, he became very successful. He saved Columbia Pictures when, after the success of his production of *Lawrence of Arabia*, he allowed the studio to delay paying him large sums of money they owed to him.

LUPITA TOVAR en "MARIA" de JORGE ISACS.

PROXIMO ESTRENO EN EL CINE "ALAMEDA"

OCTUBRE 30 DE 1938

Nº 2

cinegramas

Lupita and Josefina Escobedo in *María*, 1938

Talli Wyler, Lupita, and Sam Spiegel on the *Malahne*, 1960

Sam's yacht *Malahne*

Years later, Sam entertained us on his yacht, *Malahne*, anchored in the harbor of Monte Carlo. By then he had produced many award-winning films, including *The African Queen* and *On the Waterfront*. Now he lived on Grosvenor Square, in the heart of London; he kept an elegant apartment in New York and a house in Beverly Hills.

We had almost finished filming *María*, when one morning I found a woman waiting for me outside the studio. She was desperate to talk to me. She said General Cedillo had sent her to get me—to bring me to him. Cedillo had started his own revolution in the state of San Luis Potosí, with his ten-thousand-man army. President Lázaro Cárdenas had just sent federal troops north to put down this rebellion. I knew Cedillo was dangerous when he didn't get what he wanted, and he still wanted me. I explained to the woman that I had to work; that a lot of people depended on my being on the set that day.

"But what will I tell my general?" she pleaded. She was frightened and I couldn't blame her.

"Give the general my very best regards," I said, "but tell him that I can't leave my work, and to please forgive me."

Two days later, I read in the newspaper that General Saturnino Cedillo had been shot dead. "*LO MATARON CON SUS BOTAS PUESTAS*" was the headline ("SHOT WITH HIS BOOTS ON"). I was lucky *not* to have been there with him at the time.

Lupita and General Saturnino Cedillo

AUTHOR'S NOTE:

GENERAL SATURNINO CEDILLO

In truth, I never gave much credence to my mother's stories about this dangerous General Cedillo. Then I came across this 1937 *Time* magazine article and I gained a new respect for what my mother had told me.

Two months ago the Mayor of Valles, State of *San Luis Potosí*, was murdered. General Saturnino Cedillo, boss of San Luis Potosí, appointed another Mayor, but the townspeople resented the dictation, and called for a regular election. A fortnight ago, they arranged a meeting to agitate for their rights, and invited several hundred Labor sympathizers from Mexico City to attend. Boss Cedillo's men opened fire on the gathering from hotel windows and doors. Throwing up street barricades, the two groups potshot at each other for eight hours; they were stopped by the arrival of Federal troops. Four lay dead, several wounded.

This first sharp clash between Cedillo, former Minister of Agriculture who split with pudgy-cheeked President Lázaro Cárdenas over the Government agrarian policy (TIME, Aug. 30, 1937), and Leftist Laborites, Mexican observers last week interpreted as the opening volley of a Mexican Right v. Left struggle. Unorganized, Mexican Rightists have been unable to present any formidable opposition to the 42-year-old "social revolution" of President Lázaro Cárdenas. But last week, news-wise correspondents saw the Rightists rallying around swarthy-skinned General Cedillo, predicted that Mexico contained the makings of a little Spanish civil war.

Leftists, egged on by their most fiery orator, Vicente Lombardo Toledano, Secretary General of the Confederation of Mexican Workers, have barked at Cedillo's heels for months. Their cries of 'Fascist' influenced Cárdenas in dropping the "Bull of Potosí," General Cedillo, from his Cabinet. Since then, President Cárdenas has been trying gingerly to pull Cedillo's political teeth in his home bailiwick. To get the general safely out of Mexico, he offered him the choice of a foreign diplomatic post. "I have no interest in foreign affairs," retorted Cedillo, "I find conditions in Mexico much more interesting."

Next the Cárdenas-dictated congress sent a committee to San Luis Potosí to investigate "refraction against the government and the constitution." The committee returned with a report of Cedillo's sins, which included failure to establish socialist education, ownership of huge haciendas, failure to guarantee privileges to labor unions, permitting Catholic schools. The committee recommended that the Cedillo Government be ousted. One month ago Cárdenas closed the Government aviation school in Potosí, ostensibly for economy, actually to remove a possible weapon from Cedillo. The old general countered with the purchase of six fast planes from the U.S. stored away on his ranch. Afraid to move against Cedillo because of his private army of over 10,000 men, the last in Mexico, Cárdenas has placed encampments of four thousand federal troops on the borders of the State, strung them along the new Pan American highway.

41

SELLING VACUUM CLEANERS

By Christmas of 1938, I was nine months pregnant. When my labor pains began, Paul drove me to Cedars of Lebanon Hospital, where we spent the day and that night, nervously waiting. The next morning the contractions stopped, so Paul went back to work. Ernst Laemmle drove me home. At the end of the week, my doctor examined me again and recommended a Caesarean section; Pancho wasn't coming out on his own. We scheduled the procedure for Saturday when Paul would not be working. Also, William Dieterle's wife, Charlotte, told fortunes, and she recommended being born on a Saturday for good luck.

This time Paul was so nervous and he was driving so badly that I made him pull over to the curb and trade places with me. That's how we arrived at the hospital, with my belly sticking out so far I could hardly turn the steering wheel. Paul Julius was born January 7, 1939. We called him "Pancho" after our very good friend, Francisco (Pancho) Cabrera, who had been one of my producers on *Santa*.

* * *

I did not work again until October, when I was in *Tropic Fury* for W. Christy Cabanne, with Richard Arlen and Andy Devine. The story took place on a rubber plantation in the Amazon rain forest that was recreated on a sound stage at the studio.

Then I had a role in *South of the Border* with Gene Autry, for director George Sherman. Gene was a real cowboy, a lovely person, and a true gentleman. Smiley Burnette was his sidekick and Duncan Renaldo was also in the film. I had a famous near-miss-kiss scene with Gene while riding in a carriage. It was in the script as a kiss, but Gene Autry never kissed a girl; he was very pure for the kids. (Today we would have been doing more than just kissing.)

Lupita and Gene Autry — *South of the Border*

* * *

I had two healthy children, a wonderful husband, and I was working whenever I wanted. But there was another side to our lives beside the war in Europe; there was also the plight of the refugees who had made it to America.

SOUTH OF THE BORDER poster

The European Film Fund was stretched thin, helping the people who were arriving daily. Getting them paying jobs was not easy. First, they had to learn English. Then, they had to accept the fact that no one knew them here. They may have been the biggest stars in film or on the stage in Germany, but they were nobodies here.

Albert Bassermann had been called "Germany's greatest actor," but when he arrived in Los Angeles in 1939 with his wife and daughter, he didn't speak a word of English. He asked Paul to represent him. Paul hired a coach to help Albert memorize scripted lines. He was such an impressive actor that he got away with this ruse, playing small parts in several movies, such as William Dieterle's *Dr. Ehrlich's Magic Bullet*. He had already signed to play another small role in a film at Columbia for Harry Cohn, when Walter Wanger offered him a leading role in *Foreign Correspondent* with a salary of fifty thousand dollars! Paul tried to get Albert out of his previous commitment, but Harry threatened to sue Albert Bassermann and Paul if Albert didn't show up for work.

Albert asked Paul to arrange a meeting with Harry Cohn. Reluctantly, Harry agreed. Albert, who was always beautifully dressed, showed up dressed in rags. Paul said that Albert gave the performance of his life that day as an old man who had lost everything, fleeing with his family from Nazi Germany. He begged Harry to release him from his commitment so he could take the other, better-paying job to support his starving family. He appealed to the humanitarian side of Harry, which most people said didn't exist. Harry

Cohn believed Bassermann and took pity on him. He told Paul to tear up their contract and assured Bassermann that he could always work at Columbia.[22]

One day, the doorbell rang and there was Harry Sokal at the door. I knew Harry from Berlin, where he had been very successful. He had produced *The White Hell of Pitz Palu* with Paul.

Ernst Lubitsch, Albert and Mrs. Bassermann, Charlotte and William Dieterle

Luis Trenker and producer Harry Sokal

Tall and athletic, Harry was always charming and fun to be with. Now, he had a very embarrassed look on his face; he looked as though he had made a mistake and wanted to turn around and run away. He had a vacuum cleaner in one hand and all the attachments in the other. He was selling vacuum cleaners door-to-door. I bought one, of course, but on the installment plan.[23]

---

22   There are many stories about Harry Cohn. When he died, Red Skelton said of the crowd at the producer's funeral, "Give the people what they want and they'll come out in droves." It was also said that Rabbi Edgar Magnin refused to deliver the eulogy at Cohn's funeral, on the grounds that anything complimentary to such an ogre as Cohn would be a lie. "Nonsense!" he was told: "You can always find something nice to say about anybody that's truthful!" Rabbi Magnin finally agreed. He opened his eulogy with the statement, "His brother was worse."

23   Later, in 1970, it being such a small world again, Harry's son, Henry Sokal, went to Mexico as Pancho's assistant director and film editor on *The Bridge in the Jungle*.

42

DESPERATE TO HELP

On September 1, 1939, Hitler invaded Poland, and two days later the Second World War began. We tried desperately to telephone the family in Teplitz. After two days, we finally got through and we heard Paul's mother, sounding very far away, begging us for help! Then she was cut off and we were told the lines to Czechoslovakia were no longer working.

Paul called James (Jimmy) Roosevelt, the son of President Franklin D. Roosevelt. They had met when Jimmy had come to Los Angeles wanting to produce motion pictures. Paul had made introductions for Jimmy who in return had been helpful with the European Film Fund; now he promised to do all he could for us. He may have spoken to his father, and perhaps F.D.R. gave orders to the State Department to intercede.

We never found out who helped Paul's mother get out of Europe. One day, a cable arrived saying Mother was on the S.S. *Conte di Savoia* and would be arriving in New York on a certain date. The cable was not signed. Someone had gone to Teplitz and had gotten her out. Helene still had her Czechoslovakian passport and the American entrance visa from the time when Walter had tried to take her with him. But whoever rescued her had also arranged an exit permit and had sent her by train to Italy, where she boarded the S.S. *Conte di Savoia*. With all the people we had contacted and asked for help, we never were able to thank that person. Helene Kohner arrived in New York with just the clothes she was wearing. Friends of Paul's met her and put her on a train to Los Angeles. The rest of the family, my mother-in-law's sister, Tante Clara, Grandmother Béamt, and her son, Rudy, were still in Teplitz. They could only get out if they, too, had visas and that seemed next to impossible.

Paul said, "There may be a way. Lupi, you must fly to Mexico and get them to transfer visas." That might enable them to get to Mexico via neutral countries like Switzerland or Portugal.

I was on the next flight and I was in President Lázaro Cárdenas's office the next day. Alfonso Pesqueira, who had been the consul general in Los Angeles, was with me. I told our story to President Cárdenas and a group of four or five men; I told them it was a matter of life or death. I told them of the terror I had witnessed in Berlin and the stories refugees had told regarding the horrors of the concentration camps. It was winter in Europe and the cold alone, not to mention malnutrition, would kill the elderly and the children in these camps. I told how Paul's mother had begged him to rescue her and his family but so far only she was safe. I was in tears as I said, "If you don't give them visas, they'll be sent to die in those camps!"

The men were shocked at what I told them about the situation in Germany; they called their embassy in Prague.

The Mexican consul in Prague immediately sent a man to Teplitz with the visas, but he arrived one hour too late. Paul's family had been taken out of their house and sent to Auschwitz, the "death camp."

Ten years later, in 1949, a stranger came to Paul's office. Tante Clara had written to Paul from Auschwitz and had given the letter to this man saying, "If you survive, I have a nephew in Hollywood, California, please see that he gets this."

Paul came directly home; he was terribly upset. I never saw the letter, but it must have been heartbreaking for Paul to read his aunt's final words; he had come so close to saving her.

43

"THE BATTLE OF LOS ANGELES"

Willy Wyler's first big success was his adaptation of Emily Brontë's *Wuthering Heights*. Now he was preparing to shoot *The Westerner*, and he had written a part for me. I was nervous because Willy was known to be very rough on his actors on the set. The girl who was the leading lady, Doris Davenport, had a devil of a time because she was not prepared and Willy was not very kind. In front of everybody he told her, "Get out of here and study your part!"

I was supposed to be an abandoned mother with a child, so I was holding a baby. In the middle of the scene the baby wet his pants. I felt it, and my face showed it.

"*Cut!* What happened, Lupi?"

I said, "Well..." and I held up the wet, dripping baby. Gary Cooper was laughing so hard his face was red. Somebody changed the baby's diaper and we started again. In the scene I watch people walking by; one of them is the father of this baby. Willy yelled, "*Cut!* Let's do it again."

I said, "Willy, what do you *want*?"

He said, "What would you do if the man you loved had betrayed you, abandoned you and your baby, and now you see him?" So in the next "take" when I saw the father coming, I gave the baby to somebody and knocked the father down on the ground. I got on top of him and started slapping him, calling him all sorts of names. The scene went on and on. I finally said, "Please say 'Cut,' Willy." Everybody burst out laughing.

I think that scene was left on the cutting room floor.

In 1941, I again worked for George Sherman at Republic Studio in *Two-Gun Sheriff* with cowboy hero Don "Red" Barry, Lynn Merrick, and Fred Kohler, Jr.

In November I was invited to ride as guest of honor on a float in the Santa Claus Parade down Hollywood Boulevard. Susan sat with me, all bundled up. She was very excited, waving to the crowds that lined the boulevard. Gene Autry was the Grand Marshal, riding his horse, Champion, and a military band played drums and bugles.

* * *

Despite the war in Europe, our lives went on with a false normality. By May of 1940, the German army had overrun the British Expeditionary Force on the continent, forcing their withdrawal from Belgium and France. In the comfort of our movie theaters we watched newsreel footage of the "Miracle at Dunkirk," where more than a thousand boats, some just small fishing boats, braved the English Channel to rescue hundreds of thousands of British, Canadian, and French soldiers from the beaches and harbor of Dunkirk, France. British Prime Minister Winston Churchill gave a speech that we heard on the radio. He called their defeat on the continent a "colossal military disaster." But he went on to rally the spirit of the English people, telling them that the "Battle of Britain" was just beginning: "Let us brace ourselves to our duties, and so bear ourselves that if the British Empire and its Commonwealth last for a thousand years, men will say, 'This was their finest hour.'"

We were all shaken by these words.

***

To most Americans, the war in Europe was still far away. Americans remembered World War I too well, and weren't eager to get involved in Europe's problems again. All that changed on December 7, 1941, when Japan attacked Pearl Harbor. Now we were at war with Japan and, four days later, America entered the war against Germany.

Thousands of men volunteered to join the army. Paul was considered too old to serve at thirty-nine, so he volunteered as an air raid warden. He was issued a gas mask and a special helmet. His main duty was to make sure that none of our neighbors showed light from their windows whenever the sirens wailed. Paul would walk up and down Stone Canyon at night. At that time our neighbors included Greer Garson, Cary Grant, Judy Garland, Clark Gable, and Carole Lombard. Many agents, producers, and directors lived on Stone Canyon. Those walks were social events.

In February, there was a rumor that a submarine had been seen off the coast of Santa Barbara. The next night somebody reported seeing a Japanese airplane flying over our city and searchlights lit up the sky. We could hear heavy guns firing. The next day the newspapers called it "The Battle of Los Angeles." Falling bullets from our own anti-aircraft guns had ended up killing three civilians!

The mood of the country changed overnight. Now, it wasn't just the European immigrants who were concerned. Newspaper headlines were all about the war in Europe and in the Pacific. All the young men we knew were going off to fight.

***

On May 4, 1942, Michael Curtiz tested me for a part in *Casablanca*. One of the screenwriters was Julius Epstein, who lived up the street from us. Will Rogers, Jr. and Helmut Dantine were also tested that day. Helmut did get a small part in the classic film. Unfortunately, I didn't. Madeleine LeBeau played the role I tested for.

***

There was a big demand for European directors and actors to work on the anti-Nazi pictures that were so popular. But there was one time when Paul's office was expecting a big commission check and it didn't arrive. I knew they didn't have enough money for the payroll on Friday, so I went to the bank and withdrew my savings. I took the money to Paul's office and gave it to Mr. Keller, the accountant, and said, "Will this help?"

Later that day, when Paul asked Mr. Keller, "Has the check arrived?"

Mr. Keller said, "You don't have to worry, we'll be all right."

"But, how…?" Paul asked.

"Your rich wife has saved us," he said with a big smile.

Fred Keller had worked with Paul in Berlin. Paul also employed Arthur Robitschek as his bookkeeper. Arthur was from Paul's home town of Teplitz, where he had worked for Papa Julius on the *Filmschau* publication. After the war, Paul's brother Walter joined him as an agent, along with Jack Fife. Carl Forest headed the new Television Department and Ilse Lahn was the head of the Literary Department. Paul's secretary was Jack Ross, who had been Carl Laemmle's secretary when Paul was still working for Universal Pictures. Back then, when production would slow to a halt each winter, Paul would travel to Europe for six weeks to visit his family. He would justify his unpaid vacation by visiting the Universal branch offices and sending cables back to Mr. Laemmle with story suggestions and news from Europe. In 1928 he had been reprimanded via Jack Ross for his "desire to burn money," by using too many words in those cables.

DAILY PRODUCTION AND PROGRESS REPORT

FORM 96 2500 10-41 SF4276C

TESTS: -- "CASABLANCA" #697 Day **Monday** Date **5/4/42**

Name of Production	"WILL ROGERS"	No.	715	Name of Director	MICHAEL CURTIZ

Number of Days Alloted: | Production Started: | Days Elapsed Since Starting: | Status of Schedule:
Estimated Finish Date: | Revised Finish Date (If Ahead or Behind): | Name of Set | Location | Finished?

Company Called	9:30AM		SOUND & PHOTOGRAPHIC TESTS
Lng; Up-Reh. 'til	10:20AM	SCRIPT REPORT	Int. Cafe Set
Started Shooting	10:20AM		Stage 3
Lunch Called	12:00N		
Time Started	1:00PM		
Dinner Called			
Time Started			
Time Finished	3:45PM		

CAST

S-Start W-Worked H-Held F-Finish R-Rehearse

Cast		Time Started	Time Finished	Slate No.	No. of Takes	Time of Ok Takes
"CASABLANCE"				3195	1	
LUPE TOVAR "Yvonne"	T	10AM	10:50A	3196	1	
				3197	3	
				3198	6	
MARIAN HALL "Annina"	T	10AM	10:25A	3199	2	
HELMUTT DANTINE "Jan"	T	11AM	11:45A			
"Will Rogers" #715 WILL ROGERS, JR.	T	1:00PM	3:45PM			
Assisting Tests:						
JOHN RIDGELY	W	9:30A	11:45A			
PETER WHITNEY	W	9:30A	10:50A			
CRAIG STEVENS	W	10AM	10:25A			
RUTH FORD	W	11AM	11:45A			
FRANK WILCOX	W	1PM	3:45PM			

STAFF

		Time Started	Time Finished
Supervisor			
Director	Curtiz	9AM	3:45PM
Dial. Dir.			
Unit Mgr.			
1st Asst.	Page	8AM	"
2nd Asst.			
Extra Asst.			
Script Clerk	Moore	8:45A	"
Cutter			
Music:	Ellfeldt	9:30A	12:00N
Tech. Adv'r.			
CAMERAMEN			
Head	Faudio	9AM	3:45PM
2nd	Joyce	9AM	"
Asst.	Meinardus	8:45A	"
Still Man			
PROP MEN			
Head	Hafley	8:30A	"
Asst.			
Service:	Robinson	8:30A	"
VITAPHONE			
Mixer	Riggs	9:15A	"
Boom	Williams	8:30A	"
Recordr	Ullman	9AM	"
Gaffer	Johnson	8AM	"
Best Boy	Swanner	8AM	"
Grip	Harris	8AM	"
Makeup	Greenway	8AM	"
	Bau	12N	"
Hair Dr.	Burt	8AM	11:45A
Wdrbe.	Roberts	8AM	3:45PM
	Blanchard	8AM	11:45A

Setups Today: 5

EXTRAS	ANIMALS	LUNCHES	Script Scenes Taken
STAND-INS	ANIMAL HANDLERS		
		Stand by	Added Scenes Taken
		In Scenes	

Remarks: SOUND & PHOTOGRAPHIC TESTS

OTR: Kindly indicate above: If any artist delays director starting work or arriving later than time called, state reason, or any mechanical delays

Casablanca Production Report

Universal Pictures Corporation

730 FIFTH AVENUE
NEW YORK

CARL LAEMMLE
PRESIDENT

December 12, 1928.

Mr. Paul Kohner,
c/o Berlin, Germany Office.

Dear Paul:

Mr. Laemmle has turned over to me some of the telegrams which you sent him on December 10th, and he asked me to call your attention to the unnecessary use of words.

In one of your telegrams, you used the phrase "for your information." This phrase is absolutely wasted and with the words costing 12-1/2 cents each, there was an expense of 37-1/2 cents that could be saved. Also, in another telegram when you speak of Mr. Dieterle, the Director, you use his full name Wilhelm Dieterle. Here too, a word could have been saved. Furthermore, you sign your cable with your full name, Paul Kohner, - Kohner would be sufficient. I am sure you have never received a cable from Mr. Laemmle where he used the full name of Carl Laemmle. He always signs his cables "Laemmle."

Needless to say, the use of these unnecessary words, which could have been so easily avoided, has not made any too good an impression on Mr. Laemmle. In fact, he has expressed himself by saying that he can see a desire on your part of just to burn up our money.

I hope you will take this letter in the spirit in which it is written and that you will benefit by this advice in the future and will use more care in wording your messages.

With kindest regards, I remain

Cordially yours,

Jack Ross
Secretary to Mr. Laemmle.

JR:T

Jack Ross letter

44

MORE FILMING IN MEXICO

At the end of 1942, I went to Mexico to film *Recordar es Vivir* (*To Remember is to Live*) for director Fernando A. Rivero, with comedian Mario Moreno "Cantinflas."

Then in January 1943, I was back again to star in a film version of Leo Tolstoy's *Resurrección* for Clasa Films, with Emilio Tuero and Sara García. The script was written by Gilberto Martínez Solares, who was also the director; his brother, Raúl, was the cinematographer, and Mauricio de la Serna was the producer.

Lupita and Sara García in *Resurrección*, 1943

I made the mistake of staying at my father's house. When we shot a sequence that required darkness and rain at a location outside of the city, my sister and I came home well after midnight. My father opened the gate and let Sarita in and then put the chain back on, saying, "Not you, you have no place here!" He turned and walked back in the house. The assistant director, Alfonso Sánchez Tello, who had driven us from the set, couldn't believe what he had just seen and heard. There I was, still with my makeup and costume, with no place to sleep. So Alfonso took me to his sister's house to spend the rest of the night. I was married and had two children, and yet my father still treated me like a child. The next day Alfonso told Mauricio de la Serna what had happened. Mauricio went and talked to my father.

"This is unbelievable," Mauricio said. "How can you do this? We were working in Tlalnepantla, where there was no phone. We had to film another take and then another and it got late. But I've never heard of behavior like this. You are wrong, sir. You must take your daughter back."

As usual, my timid mother was of no help. My father relented and said I could come back. But I knew my father disapproved of my working in films so much that if a newspaperman called, he would behave badly. So I moved to a small hotel.

When the picture was finished, I went to say good-bye to my family. My father wasn't there, even though it was a Sunday. He was probably drinking at a cantina, as usual. For the next eight months, the letters I sent home were all returned unopened and he disconnected the phone so I couldn't call!

* * *

The war in Europe was raging. Movie stars like Jimmy Stewart, Gene Autry, and Robert Montgomery, just to name a few, were in Europe in harm's way. The mood was somber, but the Motion Picture Academy still held their awards ceremony. Paul and I took Talli Wyler with us to the ballroom at the Ambassador Hotel. Willy was in England, filming *The Memphis Belle: A Story of a Flying Fortress*, one of the best documentary films of the war. That evening Willy Wyler won an Oscar for directing *Mrs. Miniver*. Talli graciously accepted the award for him.

* * *

I got an offer to return to Mexico in 1944 to star in *Miguel Strogoff* (from the book by Jules Verne), with Julián Soler, Julio Villarreal, Anita Blanch, Andrés Soler, and Victoria Argota. Miguel M. Delgado was the director and Mauricio de la Serna was again the producer. Mauricio met me at the train station and took me to a furnished apartment he had rented for me. When I called my father, he said, "Come stay at the house."

I said, "No, Father, after three days there will be trouble again; this way we'll remain friends."

* * *

Paul and his brother, Fritz, came to Mexico toward the end of filming *Miguel Strogoff*. Traveling on the same train with them from Los Angeles was a certain General Juan Ascárate, who was an important minister in the government. The general was traveling in his private rail car, but somehow he and Paul met and quickly became friends. They spent much of the trip playing cards. The following week, General Ascárate invited us to his house. It was a pleasant lunch and I didn't think any more of that day. But on our return to Los Angeles—when our train stopped at the border in El Paso, Texas—I saw that we were being closely watched by two men in suits and hats. They looked like actors playing movie detectives; they watched as we got in line to show our passports. At that point they approached us and asked us to accompany them to a small office. For a moment I was reminded of our arrest and strip search at the German Czech border in 1934.

The men were FBI agents and they had files an inch thick on us. They knew exactly where we had been in Mexico and who we had seen every day. When they asked if we had lunch with General Ascárate, I told them, "Yes, we were invited and one does not refuse such an invitation." It seems that this general was a known Nazi sympathizer. He was connected with people who were sending messages to Germany by short-wave transmitter. These FBI men knew that I spoke German. As they kept talking, it became clear that they wanted me to work for them. They wanted me to pose as a waitress in a diner near the border in San Diego, a diner frequented by German-speaking people. They wanted me to be a spy! Paul immediately said, "Unequivocally, no!" He said he would not permit me to be at risk. I was relieved and disappointed at the same time.

* * *

I had many offers to continue making films in Mexico, but the long separations from Paul and the children were becoming very difficult for me. Pancho had asthma and Susan was at the age where she needed her mother's attention. As a child, Pancho would take everything apart, doorknobs, clocks, radios—anything he could get his hands on. My grandma would always defend him, saying, "Let him be. He's learning something useful." Susan was an avid reader and was an A student. I still made trips to see my family in Mexico and often, during their summer vacations, Paul and I would take the children with us. But *Miguel Strogoff* was the last picture I did away from home.

Late in 1944, I had a part in the short film, *Gun to Gun*, for Warner Bros. It was billed as "Blazing Action in Old California!" It was directed by D. Ross Lederman, and co-starred Robert Shayne, Pedro De Cordoba, Harry Woods, and Tom Tyler.

On the adjoining stage, Vincent Sherman was directing *In Our Time* with Paul Henreid and Ida Lupino, and Paul came by to say hello.

Lupita and Paul Henreid

Then in 1945, George Sherman directed me in *The Crime Doctor's Courage* for Columbia, with Warner Baxter, Hillary Brooke, Jerome Cowan, and Robert Scott.

These films were shot at the studio or at ranches in the San Fernando Valley. Each film only took a few weeks to shoot and had low budgets. Never mind; we needed the money.

Warner Baxter, Lupita, and Jerome Cowan in *Crime Doctor's Courage*

* * *

With gas being rationed, it was easier to stay at home and have fun. So summer evenings on our backyard patio, we square danced. We had records for music and a professional "caller" came, dressed in Western costume; we tried to dress the same way. Some evenings we had twenty or thirty guests. Our next-door neighbors, Jane and Herbert Sturdy, were teetotalers, so when the dance was at their house, guests would drift back and forth to our back door for something stronger to drink. It was great fun, and even the Europeans square danced with enthusiasm.

Susan, Paul, Lupita, and Pancho, 1944

45

LIBERATION IN EUROPE

As soon as Walter, Paul's youngest brother, became an American citizen, he joined the army. He was trained as a translator and interrogator and was sent to Europe to work in psychological warfare. France had been liberated and the Allies had pushed the German army back to their homeland. Walter was sent to the Duchy of Luxembourg. As he had studied to be an actor and had a good speaking voice, he was given the job to broadcast news to Germany over Radio Luxembourg. Part of his message was to encourage German soldiers to surrender. That finally occurred on May 8, 1945.

The war in Europe was over. Concentration camps were being liberated. Walter began searching for Hanna Bloch, his girlfriend from Teplitz. He had no idea where Hanna had been held or even if she had survived. It had been seven years since Walter had seen her.

Two weeks later, a letter arrived at Paul's office addressed simply to "Walter Kohner, Sunset Boulevard, Los Angeles, California." The letter was from two American soldiers who had liberated the camp where Hanna was last held:

May 10, 1945
Dear Sir

We are happy to inform you that we have found your friend Hanna Benjamin Bloch while liberating a concentration camp. She is well and safe.

Cpl. Herbert Shuckart

Sgt. W. Lohmann

Paul sent the letter on to Walter, but it did not say which camp Hanna had been liberated from or where she was now. Walter borrowed a Jeep and drove first to Karlsbad, where Hanna had once lived and worked, and then he drove to Teplitz. Along the way he overturned the Jeep and had to requisition a civilian car.

Miraculously, Hanna's brother, Gottfried (Friedl) Bloch, had also survived the camps. Walter found Friedl by chance on a crowded sidewalk in Prague. They embraced and Walter told the tearful Friedl that his sister was alive!

Hanna had survived several concentration camps—first Westerbork, in Holland, then Theresienstadt, near Teplitz. From there she was sent to Auschwitz, in Poland, and finally to Camp Lenzing, a sub-camp of the infamous Mauthausen "Death Camp" in Austria, where Heinrich Himmler, Chief of the SS, instigated a policy of "death through work." Inmates there were forced to work with their bare hands in tunnels and rock quarries until they died.

Walter found Hanna, in June of 1945, through the repatriation center in Amsterdam, where she had gone after her camp was liberated. They were married in Luxembourg on October 24, 1945. Walter had a dog, a German shepherd named Lux, that they smuggled onto the boat to America in a duffle bag. Then, by wearing dark glasses and pretending Lux was Walter's seeing-eye dog, they brought him to California and started life over again.

* * *

Hanna's brother, Friedl, had been a medical student. After the war, he completed his studies in Prague. His interest was psychiatry, an unpopular subject under Communist rule in Czechoslovakia. With the creation of Israel in 1948, Friedl took advantage of the last emigration permitted by the U.S.S.R. and settled in Tel Aviv.

In May 1953, Hanna and Friedl were united on a popular American television show, Ralph Edwards' *This is Your Life*. It was a total surprise for Hanna. She thought the evening was going to be about Jeffrey Hunter (one of Walter's clients), who was sitting next to her in the theater.

When Ralph Edwards came to them, and said, "This is *your* life, Hanna Bloch Kohner," she almost fainted. Hanna was led to the stage, where Ralph introduced her to the theater and television audience. The show was live, not recorded, and that heightened the drama.

They had found Corporal Shuckart, who had rescued Hanna and had written the letter to "Walter Kohner, Sunset Boulevard." With special dispensation from the State Department, Ralph Edwards had also brought her brother, Friedl, from Israel. The last time Hanna and Friedl had seen each other was through a Barbed-wire fence fifteen years earlier. At the end of the evening there wasn't a single dry eye in the audience[24].

---

24   Hanna and Walter's daughter, Julie Kohner Greenberg, has kept her parents' story alive by telling audiences across America about her mother's personal Holocaust experience. She calls her talks "Voices of the Generations."

46

BULLFIGHTS AND OLD BOYFRIENDS

The Mexican border is only a three-hour drive from Los Angeles, so a lot of movie people used to go to Tijuana for the weekend to watch the bullfights and to gamble. (This was before Las Vegas became popular.) People gambled at the *frontón* courts, where players wore a *cesta*, a long narrow wicker basket strapped to their hand like a glove, that they used to catch and throw a hard cork ball over ninety miles an hour. The game is called Jai-alai. Rosarito Beach, only half an hour from Tijuana, had a resort hotel and a regular casino for gamblers.

A group of us loved to go to the bullfights. Antonio Moreno, my director on *Santa*, was an aficionado, as were John Huston and film star Gilbert Roland. Gilbert was one of the few actors who made the successful transition from silent films to talkies. He was born in Ciudad Juárez, Mexico, and was "Latin-lover" handsome. Early on, he had had an affair with Norma Talmadge, which had caused her divorce from Joe Schenck, chairman of Twentieth Century-Fox and one of the most powerful men in Hollywood. Joe Schenck then became a "friend" of Marilyn Monroe, who was just starting her career. (There are lots of stories I could tell about the game of musical chairs, or beds, that was part of Hollywood.)

The celebrity crowd that came across the border on weekends made it possible for promoters to afford the best bullfighters and the best bulls. On Sundays in Tijuana we would have lunch at the Foreign Club, where Caesar salad was prepared at our table by Chef Caesar Cardini. In the rooms upstairs, the bullfighters would dress and make their preparations for their four o'clock date in the bullring. After the fight, it was time for celebrating.

Carlos Arruza was one of the best bullfighters at the time, and he was exceptionally handsome, too. He had earned millions fighting in Mexico and Spain; only Arruza could guarantee a sold-out Plaza de Toros. One Sunday, Carlos was appearing in Tijuana with Silverio Pérez and Juan Silveti, also excellent bullfighters. The bulls were coming from the La Punta ranch, known for breeding the bravest bulls. We took Pancho and met up with Tony Moreno and Gilbert Roland.

Antonio Moreno, Lupita, Carlos and Mrs. Arruza.

That afternoon, Carlos dedicated a bull to me. He took off his hat, his *montera*, and said, "This one is for you, Lupita." As part of the ritual, he stepped on the little board rail that circles the inside of the bullring, the *estrivo*, and with his back to me, he tossed me his hat over his shoulder. It is customary to return the honor by giving a gift to the *torero*, so I took off a ring I was wearing and put it in the hat and passed it back to him. (Gilbert Roland used to take off his gold watch to give to a *torero*.) It was a magnificent afternoon.

Carlos visited us in Los Angeles on a warm summer day. We were swimming and we loaned Carlos a bathing suit. The children were fascinated with his terrible scars from afternoons in the bullring.

When Carlos retired, he got restless and decided to go back to fighting bulls, this time in the Portuguese style as a *rejoneador*. The capework and the placing of the *banderillas* is done from horseback. The matador wears a simple black outfit, leather chaps, and a *sombrero cordobes*, a wide-brimmed hat. The horse is high-schooled and unafraid. Only at the end of the ritual, the final *tercio*, does the matador face the bull on foot with a *muletta* and sword for the kill.

Another weekend in Tijuana, we bumped into Pepe Ocaranza, who had been very much in love with me in my high school days. Pepe had become a doctor. I had told Paul all about my childhood boyfriend. Paul immediately asked Pepe a lot of questions: "Are you married? Do you have children?" He was, and he had a five-month-old daughter. Paul said, "I'd like to meet your wife. Can I invite you to dinner?"

We had dinner in a place that had music and Paul asked Pepe's wife to dance with him. That left Pepe and me alone. We didn't dance; but we got a chance to talk. Paul was very smart that way.

47

FRIDA AND DIEGO

When I first arrived in Hollywood, Ernesto Romero from the Mexican consul's office introduced me to a young law student from Mexico, Arturo García Formentí. Arturo had come to Los Angeles for a debate. The following year when I went back to Mexico for the opening of *La Voluntad del Muerto*, Arturo called. He wanted to introduce me to Frida Kahlo; they had been at the university together. He took me to meet Frida at the house and studio she shared with her husband, Diego Rivera, who was in San Francisco for an exhibition of his paintings. I had met Diego in Los Angeles; he was the opposite of handsome, but for some reason women were crazy about him. During his lifetime, he had four wives and many love affairs. Perhaps it was because Diego loved women so much.

As a child, Frida had polio, which had deformed one of her legs. Then, at eighteen, she was in a terrible streetcar accident and nearly lost her life. A piece of steel, a hand rail, had penetrated her back. After that her life was filled with many operations and constant pain.

The day Arturo and I visited her, she had just had another operation and couldn't get out of bed; so that's where we sat and talked. Although obviously in pain, Frida was very curious. She wanted to know what my impressions were of Hollywood and what stars I had met. I told her about my producer, Paul Kohner; I hadn't even told my family about Paul. I told her about the night of our first screening of *La Voluntad del Muerto*, that President Ortiz Rubio's sons had attended. I got the impression that she didn't like Mexican politicians.

* * *

I met Diego again in 1946, at Dolores del Río's house. Diego liked to paint women and had just finished Dolores' portrait. That evening Diego told me, "I would like to paint you."

I said, "I'd like that, but I live in California."

"Well," he said, "the next time you come, would you get in touch with me?"

I said, "Yes, definitely."

The following summer I was in Mexico with Susan and Pancho. We rented a house in the Lomas de Chapultepec. Paul stayed for a few weeks, but then he had to go back to work. One day the children and I visited Frida and Diego at their *casa azul* (blue house). Diego was working in his studio next door; it was pink on the exterior and had a high ceiling, skylights, and many windows. Along the walls were tall papier-mâché figures—the type that would be festooned with fireworks during village fiestas. Pancho was fascinated with these giants. A man would stand inside each figure and, with rockets and pinwheels lit—he would run around the plaza scaring and delighting children. We had seen that spectacle one night in the plaza in Taxco. There was also a litter of Mexican hairless *ixcuintle* puppies that Susan fell in love with. Diego asked, "When can we begin your portrait?"

I said, "Diego, what I would really like is a painting of my children."

Diego watched Susan and Pancho as they moved about the studio. "Yes," he said. "I would like to paint them. But on one condition—that I paint you next."

Susan and Pancho were nine and seven that summer. Every day we would go to Diego's studio in San Ángel. As he sketched them and then painted, we talked and became great friends. Diego was a very interesting man, and very charming. We talked about his travels in Europe and the political situation in Mexico. Miguel Alemán had just won the presidential election, succeeding Manuel Ávila Camacho. Diego said he hoped Alemán would carry out his promise to give women the right to vote; that did not happen for another seven years.

Diego Rivera painting Susan and Pancho, 1946

Frida often could not get up from her bed so we would go across to their house and have tea and sandwiches. When she could not sit up, Frida painted lying in bed with a mirror propped up above her.

Later that summer, Raymond and Robert Hakim called. They were visiting from Paris and they wanted to meet Diego. The Hakim brothers were Egyptians who made pictures in Hollywood and Europe. They had produced *The Southerner*, which was directed by Jean Renoir, and was nominated for three Academy Awards.

I took Raymond and Robert to the Palacio de Bellas Artes, where Diego was working. He had started this large mural at Rockefeller Center in New York. But Nelson Rockefeller had objected that Diego included the likeness of one of his heroes, Vladimir Lenin. Diego had offered to add Lincoln to the mural, but Mr. Rockefeller turned that down. Diego was paid, but his mural was destroyed. The following year, Diego repainted the same mural in the atrium of the Palacio de Bellas Artes, but now it needed some repairs. Diego came down from his scaffolding and I introduced everyone. While Raymond and Robert were admiring the huge mural, I asked Diego how much I owed him for the children's portrait; we had never discussed that. When I started to write him a check, he stopped me. He said the painting was a gift to the children. He had grown very fond of Susan and Pancho and had even given them the hairless *ixcuintle* dog that is in the painting.

He said, "I only wish I had made two separate paintings so there would not be trouble later." I was overwhelmed; I didn't know what to say. Then Diego reminded me of my promise to let him paint my portrait. I promised him I would be back soon.

When the crate with the painting arrived in Los Angeles, Josephine helped me unpack it, and we stood the painting in the dining room. It was magnificent. I called Paul at his office and asked him to come home right away. I told him I was having trouble with a worker who was digging in the garden from a recent mud slide.

"Can't you handle it?" Paul asked.

"No," I said. "It needs a man."

So Paul came home and asked, "Where's the worker?"

I led him into the dining room, and when he saw the painting he was speechless. I told him that Diego had refused payment; that the painting was a gift to the children. Paul immediately called Diego to thank him.

* * *

When I went back to Mexico, Frida, who always dressed in colorful Mexican dresses and exotic jewelry, loaned me the earrings I wore as I posed for Diego.

* * *

When Frida died in 1954, Diego was devastated. She was a very vocal Communist, but in spite of her controversial politics her coffin lay in state, in the huge lobby of the Palacio de Bellas Artes, as her friends and adoring public paid tribute. Ex-president Lázaro Cárdenas took his turn standing guard over her through the night, along with many artists, including José Chávez Morado, David Alfaro Siqueiros, and Miguel Covarrubias.

When Diego became ill with cancer and needed cobalt radiation treatment, which was not available in Mexico, the American government refused to let him come here. Paul tried to intercede but was unsuccessful. I was in Mexico at the time, so I went to visit Diego. He said he was leaving for Russia the next day; that was the only place he could get treated. He was already very weak.

I said, "I'll go with you to the airport to say good-bye."

He said, "No, darling, don't. There will be cameras and if they see you there, you won't be able to go back to the United States either, because they will say you are a Communist."

"*Me*—a *Communist*? I don't even know what a Communist *is*!"

"No, darling, we say good-bye right here at the studio."

A year later, when Diego returned from Russia, he had an exhibition of the paintings he had done there and in Poland. John Huston was in Mexico, and we went together to see the exhibit.

John said, "Lupita, you know Diego, don't you?"

"Yes, we're friends."

Diego Rivera painting Lupita's portrait

"I'd like to meet him," John said. "I'd like to see his studio." So I took John to meet Diego and they got along like old friends.

* * *

After Frida died, Diego married Emma Hurtado; they had known each other many years. But three years after Frida's death, at the age of seventy, Diego died. I felt very sad. He had so much charisma; when you were with him, you felt as if you had known him forever. He was so polite and he had such lovely manners; he was such a romantic man. Today, Diego Rivera is considered the greatest Mexican painter of the twentieth century.

Portrait of Lupita by Diego Rivera

48

THE MYSTERIOUS B. TRAVEN

After the war, Paul and I often traveled to Europe to meet with his clients. One time, Paul said, "We will have to go to Zurich to see a publisher by the name of Joseph Wieder. He represents a German writer, B. Traven, who lives somewhere in Mexico; he's a mystery man, his books are well known, but no one knows who he is. I have to get the rights for his story, *The Treasure of the Sierra Madre*. John Huston wants to make it into a film."

Paul showed me the letter from the Zurich publisher.

"He writes that Traven lives in Petatlan, in the state of Guerrerro, and goes by the name of Martínez. This man lives just a few miles from Acapulco," I said.

Paul wrote to B. Traven who signed his letters B. T. or just T, via his publisher in Zurich, saying that he wanted to meet him. A month later, he heard back from Traven that he was only interested in meeting me; that I should come to Acapulco.

Paul sent me by boat with a copy of Traven's book. Once there, I was to arrange a future meeting between Traven and Paul. I invited my family to come to Acapulco to spend a few days together. And for a few days we behaved like every other family on vacation. Even my father was pleasant.

The press always printed stories about me

```
                            Febr.27.


Querida Lupita:
            Received your message. You know I am not living
in the port but rather far outside. Strange I had a feeling
that you were here and that's why I came in yesterday. My first
impulse was to rush to the Hamacas,though on second thought I
realized that you might not be alone and it would be embarrass-
ing somehow for both. It seems incredible that you are here
beneath the same sky,beneath the same moon. I still cannot and
won't believe it until I see you with my own eyes. Will,you,
please,come to the Playa de Caleta for a swim or just sitting
there and look at the ocean,dreaming of islands far away. Come
alone or else I might get frightened,and I think I have so very
much to tell you which is all meant only for you and for you
only. Tell nobody of this meeting for reasons which I shall
explain to you later and which you will understand. Be there,
if you please,today,Saturday,between 4:30 and 5:30 in the after-
noon. If you cannot make it today or I am unable to come,we
will change the date to tomorrow,Sunday,same place,same time.
Te espero con el corazon en mis manos.          T.
```

B. Traven letter Febr. 27.

whenever I was in Mexico. Right away the Acapulco newspapers announced that I was there and staying at the Las Hamacas Hotel. The next day I received a note from B. Traven, asking me to meet him the following day. The custom in Acapulco was to go to one beach in the morning, and in the afternoon everyone went to the other beach. I was to go to the morning beach, Caleta, in the afternoon.

Alejandro Galindo, a director, and his brother Marco Aurelio Galindo, a writer (both friends of mine), were also staying at our hotel. They told me that Caleta Beach would be deserted at that time in the afternoon and it might be dangerous. They insisted on driving me. Alejandro and Marco waited in the car while I went and sat on the beach alone with a copy of Traven's book. There were three people in the water, but no one else on the beach.

Soon somebody was throwing pebbles at me from a distance—the scariest native you ever saw in your life. He was very dark and wore only a tiny G-string; he came and sat next to me. I got frightened and ran back to the car. My friends were disappointed not to have seen the mysterious B. Traven. We were sitting, talking in the lobby later, when a boy brought me another message that said: "Did you think I was going to steal your diamonds? Why didn't you come alone? I asked you to come alone!"

I looked around. "Wait a minute," I said to the

```
                    Febr. 28.

Dear Lupita:
            Por aparencia Dios no lo quiere. Everything goes
wrong so it seems. I was at the beach, yesterday, from four to
seven. In vain I waited for you. Perhaps you had another date
somewhere else and very important and likely in connection with
your work.
            Shortly after five I knew that you could not make
it and so I took a swim. I had just gone in when I noticed a
car of a greenish color coming up and parking right at the
beach where the chairs are rented. Out of that car a lady stepped
which at first sight I thought might be you. But then I realized
it couldn't be you in spite that she looked like a movie actress.
It simply couldn't be you because that lady was entirely Hollywood
going Santa Barbara, stunningly dressed in a white flowing bath-
robe latest design and a very cute and becoming Hong-Kong hat.
She glanced around and then walked up the beach to where the
restaurants are. As the lady was accompanied by a heavy body-
guard to protect her from being kidnapped I knew it couldn't
be you because I think you wouldn't take three tough guys along
when going for a swim or to meet somebody of whom you know that
he is not thinking of robbing you of your diamonds. So I discarded
the idea that it might be you and kept on waiting for Lupita
Tovar. In the water I had met another American who was there with
his wife, and later we sat on the rocks near the Caletilla Bar.
I went back to port in the car of this couple. Late in the evening
we were sitting in the Colonial, where there was a kind of a barn-
dance. I thought I could stay over Sunday, but this morning I got
an opportunity to go back to Petatlan, and as those opportunities
are rare I will take it. I am sure I'll see you some time in Mexico
City because I hope you took my advice going into Mexican pictures
and stay there for a long and successful time.     Regards      T.
```

B. Traven letter Febr. 28.

boy, "who gave this to you?"

"He's gone," the boy said, holding out his hand for a coin. I gave him some money and sent him on his way. The next day I got another letter:

I called Paul and told him what had happened. The next day my father hired a car and we all crowded in for the drive back to Mexico City.

I stayed at the elegant new Hotel Reforma, the first twelve-story building in the city and very controversial as it sat on the Paseo de la Reforma, a boulevard of private mansions. Diego had painted the panels for the hotel's popular Ciro's bar. A few days later Paul met me and I got another note. This time Traven wrote that he would meet me at five o'clock in the lobby of my hotel. I waited, but Paul insisted on waiting with me. Traven didn't come at five o'clock. That evening he sent a box of candy and a message that he had been there but that I was supposed to meet him alone! He obviously liked to play games and enjoyed being mysterious.

We returned to Los Angeles, but Paul was still determined to meet this mysterious B. Traven. There was more correspondence, always through the Büchergilde Gutenberg, Traven's publisher in Zurich. Finally, I got a letter from Traven's translator, who arranged a meeting at her house in Mexico City.

The translator was Esperanza López Mateos, the sister of a future Mexican president, Adolfo López Mateos; she was also related to cameraman Gabriel Figueroa. When we got to the house all the windows were covered with paper so you couldn't see in. We were ushered into the parlor where she sat me so that somebody in the dark room behind me could see me.

After waiting a while Paul said, "Now, look here, where is he?"

"Well, he's been delayed," she said. She left and when she came back she turned me around a bit more and said to Paul, "You know, Mr. Traven would be so happy if he could have a picture of your wife."

I said, "Well, I don't know..."

Paul said, "I have one here in my portfolio."

He took it out and wrote on the back: "This is ridiculous. What is wrong with you? Are you so deformed that you cannot show yourself?"

We never did meet Traven on that trip.

I didn't realize it at the time, but I had met B. Traven many years earlier. It was in Guadalajara when I was doing publicity for a Universal film. Mr. Alarcón was with me at a press conference in the hotel. There was a very tall, skinny man with very blond hair and very sharp blue eyes, standing in the back. He was constantly eyeing me, staring at me while I was talking with the press.

He came forward and said, "Will you dance with me?" Musicians were playing a waltz in the lobby.

I looked at him and said, "No. I'm sorry, I'm busy."

He was stubborn. "I will not move until you dance with me."

I said to the reporter who was interviewing me, "You know, it really bothers me that this man keeps staring at me."

"Well, dance with him and then we'll get rid of him."

So I got up and said, "All right," to the tall, skinny man.

We danced for a few moments, and I said, "Thank you."

When I finished my interview, he had disappeared. I remember he had on white shoes, which was more common in the tropics but very unusual here, and he wore an ill-fitting suit. His Spanish was fluent.

Traven always sent me little scraps of paper, items from local newspapers of the towns and villages where my pictures were shown. Apparently, he was in love with me. He wrote a story, a screenplay, just for me, called *Mercedes Ortega Lozano*. It was never made as a film and never published; I may have the only copy.

MERCEDES ORTEGA LOZANO

- The story of a flipped woman -

Screen Play

By B. Traven

Time: Today

Location: San Antonio, Texas, and environments for correct local color.

The Author's recommendation is for the Leading Lady:
Lupita Tovar, for the English and for the Spanish version. Miss Tovar will unconsciously speak English exactly as one would expect from the character. In the Spanish version she should speak with a distinctly pronounced Pocho accent. (Miss Tovar knows what is meant by that.) Apart from that Miss Tovar seems, in the author's opinion, to have all the qualities and combine all the conducements written into the character.

for the Leading man:
George Raft or La Rue, or somebody between these two types of character.
By no means Arturo Cordova or a similar type as this would, indirectly, alter the basic quality and true nature of the heroine.

Mercedes Ortega Lozano screenplay

AUTHOR'S NOTE:

THE ENIGMA OF B. TRAVEN

B. Traven is one of the most mysterious figures of twentieth-century literature. Although he claimed to be American, his books were initially published in German. His novels have been translated into more than thirty languages and have sold more than thirty-five million copies. They are required reading in Mexican schools.

There are many theories about the true identity of B. Traven. He was probably born in Germany in 1882; he died in Mexico in 1969. At various times, his aliases included: Ret Marut, Hal Croves, Traven Torsvan, Bruno Traven, Arnold, Barker, Feige, Kraus, Lainger, Wienecke, and Ziegelbrenner. Some believed he was the illegitimate son of Kaiser Wilhelm II.

He was said to have been one of the leaders of the post-World War I revolution in Bavaria—a radical named Ret Marut, an actor, writer, and editor of a revolutionary magazine. In the bloody suppression of that revolt, Ret Marut was found guilty and sentenced to death. He escaped and disappeared without a trace.

When John Huston was filming *The Treasure of the Sierra Madre*, he asked that Traven come to the location to help with the screenplay. A man who called himself Hal Croves, a representative of B. Traven, arrived and signed on as a technical consultant. At first Huston thought this man was Traven himself, and that was what Croves was implying. But afterwards, Huston said that Traven's personality as expressed in his writing did not match that of Hal Croves in the least.

Traven's publishers never met him. No one even knew in what language he wrote his stories—they often seemed to emerge simultaneously in Spanish, English, and German. His manuscripts invariably came from someplace in Mexico, usually with a post office box number as the only return address.

Traven claimed to have entered Mexico in 1914. He settled first in the oil town of Tampico. From there, he published stories in German periodicals under the name of B. Traven. In 1926 he published his first successful novel, *Das Totenschiff* (*The Death Ship*).

Traven wrote stories of social injustices, of cruelty and greed. His early books dealt with men either looking for work or having found it, being caught in a worldwide exploitative system. His philosophy was that of a "Wobbly," a term for followers of the Industrial Workers of the World, the I.W.W. This was a union movement that started in Chicago in 1905 at a convention of socialists, anarchists, and radical trade unionists, who were opposed to the American Federation of Labor (AFL), which divided groups of workers by crafts. The goal of the I.W.W. was to promote worker solidarity in the revolutionary struggle to overthrow the employing class. Wobblies believed that all workers should organize as a class—industrial unionism as opposed to craft unionism. Their slogan was, "An injury to one is an injury to all."

Esperanza López Mateos, whose brother Adolfo López Mateos later became president of Mexico, was Traven's translator and secretary until she committed suicide in 1951. Whatever she knew about Traven died with her.

There is strong evidence that Traven had, or was, a writing collaborator. Original manuscripts may have been written in English by an American and then translated into German by Traven, who added his own philosophy in the text.

Traven became world famous in 1948 with the success of John Huston's film, *The Treasure of the Sierra Madre*, adapted from a book Traven first published in 1927. The film won Academy Awards for Best Picture of the year and for the acting performance of John's father, Walter Huston.

The Bridge in the Jungle, also published in 1927, is regarded as B. Traven's finest novel, a story of simple, desperately poor people coming together in the face of a death that affects them all. The locale is "huts by the river," a nameless Indian settlement deep in the Mexican jungle. A festive gathering is about to begin when death arrives. A small boy has disappeared. As the intimation of tragedy spreads among the people gathered in the jungle clearing, they unite, first to find the lost boy, and then to console the grieving mother.

Between 1931 and 1940, Traven published six interrelated novels of the jungle, forming an epic history of Southern Mexico and the birth of the Mexican Revolution. They included: *Government, The Carreta, March to the Montería, Trozas, The Rebellion of the Hanged,* and *General from the Jungle.*

Traven had great sympathy for the indigenous people of the Chiapas region of Southern Mexico. In his stories he describes the terrible plight of those working in the mahogany forests. During the reign of the dictator Porfirio Díaz, greedy plantation owners manipulated the laws of peonage through the use of debt-slavery. *The Jungle* series tells of an incredibly dark period of Mexico's history.

As for his obsession for keeping his identity a secret, Traven once stated that his writing was for the public, but his private life was his alone.

REVISTA DE REVISTAS — LUPITA TOVAR EN "RESURRECCION", DE CLASA FILMS, S. A.

CINEMA REPORTER

MAYO 7 de 1943

30¢

Lupita TOVAR
ESTRELLA de
RESURRECCION
PELICULA de
CLASA *films*

49

"FORGIVE ME"

My father was not like other men; something inside him made him angry and resentful. He never praised us or encouraged us. He couldn't express love. We were afraid of him. Guillermo, my only brother who survived childhood, was not at all like him. Guillermo was kind and patient. He liked to draw and paint. In the evenings he took classes in art at the Academia San Carlos. Even though Guillermo was nineteen he still had to be home by a certain hour. One evening he had coffee with the other fellows and he was late. When he got home the front gate was locked and my father would not let him in.

Guillermo disappeared and wasn't heard from for months.

I can't explain my father's actions, even in context with Latin-American machismo. He was vain and he was shorter than my mother and maybe that had something to do with it. I suspect my mother didn't love him. She was afraid of him, too.

* * *

I got a phone call in Los Angeles from my mother telling me that Guillermo had gone to Veracruz and joined the army. But something had happened during training and he'd gone blind. The army was sending him home. I took the next train.

One station before Mexico City, my father met me and we went the rest of the way by car. My father didn't want me to face the reporters, who invariably knew when I was arriving, and have to tell them what had happened.

I couldn't believe my brother was blind. We took him to a doctor. "Aren't you Lupita Tovar?" he asked. The doctor wanted to talk about how much he admired me and my work. I asked him about my brother. The doctor said there was nothing wrong with his eyes, that the problem was psychosomatic. Apparently the soldier next to him had accidentally been shot in the face. Guillermo was traumatized and that was why he could no longer see.

My brother slowly regained his eyesight. I bought him a suit and got him a job with the Ford Company. He seemed to be doing well, so I went back to California.

It happened again; he came home late and Father locked him out. After that he disappeared and I didn't see Guillermo again for twenty years.

* * *

In 1947, my mother wrote that my father was ill and had only a month to live. I told Paul, "I have to go and take care of him."

John Huston was going to Mexico to direct *The Treasure of the Sierra Madre*, and he was leaving that night by plane. In those days it took twelve hours to fly to Mexico City with stops on the way, but the train took three days! I traveled with John and the crew. We arrived at five in the morning.

I first went to see my sister Lucy and her husband, Jesús Inaraja Aristi. Jesús came from San Sebastián, Spain. They had a business in the working-class area called Peralvillo,v where on Sundays people could go to bathe. You could bathe small children in a tub in the kitchen with water heated over coals, but homes in the poorer neighborhoods did not have real bathrooms with a shower. It was a common belief that it was healthy to eat gelatin after bathing and Lucy was already up making Jell-O®. Their first daughter, Christina, was five; Isabel was only two; their third daughter, María de la Luz (Lucy), hadn't been born yet.

My mother phoned there, looking for me. "Your father said the plane that flew over the house at five this morning was carrying you," she said. "He woke up with a start and said, 'Lupita's on that plane!'"

Lucy took the phone. "She's here, but she's going to have breakfast with us first and then she'll go to you." Only my sister Sarita still lived with my parents at 29 Agustin Melgar in the Colonia Condesa. My youngest sister, Mary, had married a professional soccer player who had started a printing business. They lived in the Colonia Pedregal, close to the university campus.

It was a shock to see my father looking so frail. He had always been a robust man. He saw me and said, "Look at me. I'm a shell of what I was." He was gaunt and very weak.

I said, "Don't worry. You'll get your weight back." I gave my father the excuse that I was there doing interviews for a new picture. I did not want to say I had come because he was dying. The doctor had said there was no hope; he had cancer of the liver and pancreas. We did not tell my father; he thought he was going to get well. From that day, I did not leave his bedside.

One morning he wanted a blood transfusion. The doctor said, "It won't do any good, but okay." They were going to get somebody, a donor, but my father said, "No, I want it from my daughter, Lupita. She is going to give me life!"

When Lucy had been pregnant with her daughter Isabel, she was close to death with a burst appendix. I had given her blood with an arm-to-arm transfusion and she had pulled through, so he thought it would work for him, too.

They did the transfusion from my arm directly into his arm, right there at home. After the transfusion, he perked up. We sat him in a chair and I shaved him.

"You see," he said, "I knew she was going to give me back my life."

Well, that was only temporary; from then on, it went from bad to worse.

I gave him injections of morphine when the pains were very bad. I was by his side for one month. Three days before he passed away, he said he wanted to talk with me.

"I've been so wrong," he said. "I want you to forgive me."

"There is nothing to forgive," I said.

"It was my ignorance," he continued. "I respect you. From now on you will be the boss of the family." I felt nothing but sorrow for him.

When I gave him the last shot for the pain, the whole family was around his bed. He tried to say something, but he couldn't speak anymore.

His body stayed in the house and that evening there was a rosary. The next day, my mother did not go to the funeral. She stayed home with my sisters and her friend from Salina Cruz, Doña Menche. Paul was still in Los Angeles. He didn't fly in those days and the train trip would have taken him three days. I went to the cemetery with my cousin Roberto, who had come from Oaxaca. It was raining hard.

That night my mother told me that when she died she did not want to be buried next to my father. She never did visit his grave.

Now I was the head of the family.

* * *

Months later, a man came to the house. He was dressed in peasant clothes and wore a large sombrero. He said he was from the village of Chinconcuac and he wanted to speak to Don Egidio, my father. My mother turned him away. She simply told him that Don Egidio was dead. Perhaps she was unaware that my father had bought many *hectares* of farmland in Chinconcuac with money I had sent. That stranger was probably his tenant. As soon as my father died, my mother cleaned out all of his papers and used them to light the furnace. If there was a deed to that land, it went up in smoke.

FINALLY MEETING B. TRAVEN

Susan and Pancho celebrated their First Holy Communion in Mexico, in a church called La Professa. Afterwards, there was a breakfast at Dolores del Río's house. Dolores and Pancho Cabrera were Susan's godparents; Mauricio and Pikye de la Serna were Pancho's.

Dolores was a great beauty. She had already made several movies in Hollywood by the time I arrived. When she saw *La Voluntad del Muerto*, her secretary, Charlotte Brown, called and invited me to have tea with Miss del Rio, at her house on Outpost Drive in Beverly Hills. I was younger than Dolores, and at that first meeting I felt like a kid next to her. She and her parents were very nice to me and we became lifelong friends.

Several years later, when I was married and Paul and I moved back from Europe, Dolores was living with Orson Welles, just up the street from us on Stone Canyon Road.

Dolores and Orson were madly in love for a while; then Orson became involved with Rita Hayworth. I had known Rita since she was twelve when her father, Eduardo Cansino, was teaching me to dance. I had given Rita my practice costume when I left for Europe to be married. Orson eventually married Rita, and Dolores moved back to Mexico.

Emilio Fernández, Dolores del Río, and Lupita

Lupita and Orson Welles

* * *

After my father died, and I was still in Mexico helping my sisters, I finally met the mysterious B. Traven.

I got a call from Dolores who said, "Lupita, come over for tea. Traven is here; he calls himself Hal Croves, but I know he's Traven."

So Dolores sent a car for me. I first went to say hello to Señora Asúnsolo, Dolores' mother. Then I was introduced to several men, and as we were talking, a thin, tall man in white shoes ended up next to me.

Traven had once said to me in a letter, "One day when we meet, you will know me." These were love letters that he sent me. As he got close to me, he quoted something from that letter: "You are like an orchid caught in the early morning dew." When he said that, I knew that this man was B. Traven.

He said, "You look sad, dressed all in black."

"Yes, I buried my father."

"Where is your husband?" he asked.

"He's in Hollywood, at work."

"I wouldn't leave such a beautiful lady alone, especially at a time like this."

I knew who he was, but I didn't say so. Several months earlier, Paul had arranged for Traven to sign a contract at the American embassy for John Huston to film *The Treasure of the Sierra Madre*.

I met Traven one last time in 1968, when my son Pancho was preparing to make a film based on Traven's book, *The Bridge in the Jungle*. Paul and I met Traven with his then-wife, Rosa Elena Luján, at their house on Río Mississippi. When I entered the room he stood up and said, "*Endlich!*" (Finally!)

I said, "It wasn't my fault."

He put his arms around me. He was old now and very frail.

Traven died in March 1969, just before the start of Pancho's film. His funeral was postponed from the customary twenty-four hours so the international press would have time to arrive. Pancho was one of the pallbearers who took turns

Lupita, B. Traven, and Paul

standing guard by the body while photographers and cameramen from all over the world filmed this world-renowned recluse for the first time.

Two days later we went to the cemetery, the Panteon Civil de Dolores. Their crematorium was a crumbling brick structure, more like an old incinerator used to burn trash; it had a small cast-iron door that could be raised for the body to be inserted. There were narrow railway tracks that started at the base of the brick crematorium and ran a dozen feet uphill. Traven's body was placed headfirst on a flat trolley.

With newsreel cameras whirring, the metal door was raised. We could see the roaring flames. Then the trolley was let go from ten feet away and banged to a stop, letting the body shoot into the flames. I had seen this before; the sudden heat causes the body to contract. I told Pancho, "Watch now, he'll sit up facing us before they close the door."

Just before the iron door slammed shut, Traven's body sat up. Of course, this caused a big excitement from the crowd.

"He's saying good-bye to you," Pancho said.

We waited and waited. It was an old kiln and it took several hours before the body was reduced to ashes. Then, a dark native woman who Rosa Elena Luján said was María de la Luz Martínez, the woman Traven had lived with near Acapulco in the 1930s, ran into the little building where they were grinding up what was left of his bones to add to the ashes, and she grabbed a handful. The press and cameramen caught that and filmed her as she ran from the place clutching a fistful of Traven's ashes close to her heart.

When it was finally over, we went back to my mother's house and had double tequilas.

"YOU CHANGED MY WHOLE LIFE"

Over the years I have met most of the presidents of Mexico and I was often invited to Los Piños, the president's official residence. I knew the daughters of President Elias Calles; we were students together at the Parque Lira School, and I had my picture taken with their father in 1928.

Lupita and President Ortiz Rubio's sons

I met other presidents, too, and most asked for my picture or signed pictures to me: "To the Sweetheart of Mexico." It started with President Pascual Ortiz Rubio, whose two sons were in Hollywood at the first screening of *La Voluntad del Muerto*. President Ortiz Rubio gave me a letter that said I could do anything, anything at all, and the police were not to arrest me!

Manuel Ávila Camacho was Mexico's president from 1940 to 1946. He started an ambitious program called "Teach Somebody." He asked everyone who could read to take the time to teach somebody who could not. He himself took an hour out of his day to teach.

Lupita and President Manuel Ávila Camacho, 1943

Miguel Alemán Valdés was Mexico's president from 1946 to 1952. In 1951, his son, Miguelito, a movie producer/director, was in charge of the twentieth anniversary celebrations of *Santa*. We were invited to participate and we went from one event to another with motorcycle police escorts

217

and wailing sirens. The children were with us and they had fun.

When Miguelito Alemán married the actress Christiane Martel, he bought up all the prints of *Rosa Blanca* (*White Rose*), based on a B. Traven novel, because Christiane had bared her breasts in the film. And for many years, *Rosa Blanca* was on a list of *enlatadas* (forbidden films).

President Miguel Alemán, inscribed to Lupita and Paul

* * *

In 1970, Luis Echeverría Álvarez was campaigning around the country for the presidency. He and busloads of the press and followers stopped in Tapachula, Chiapas, at the river location where Pancho was directing *The Bridge in the Jungle*. Luis and his entire entourage walked across the movie's temporary bridge over a dangerous river at night to watch the filming. It was great publicity for the film as well as for Luis Echeverría, who won the election. Pancho was just happy that his "movie bridge" hadn't collapsed. Luis' brother, Rodolfo Echeverría Landa, had acted with me in the film *María*, when I was pregnant with Pancho.

Pancho and President Luis Echeverría Álvarez on the set of *The Bridge in the Jungle*

* * *

I used to do many things for the poor in Mexico. I would arrange to donate the money from an evening's screening to buy toys for children. Then we would go to the poorest sections on a Sunday morning; children would come and they would each get a toy. One time there was a child (he must have been about eight or nine) who did not want the toy. I asked him, "What do you want?" He said he wanted a kiss on the cheek. I talked to him for a moment, kissed him, and gave him a toy. I thought nothing of it.

Many years later I was with Paul in Mexico and we went to a screening of *Santa* on one of its anniversaries. As we came out of the theater a young man, very well-dressed with a coat and tie, approached me, and said, "May I have a word with you?"

The young man said, "I am the child to whom you gave a toy and kissed on the cheek many years ago. You told me to study hard and to make good. I did just that; I have a career. I read in the paper that you would be here today, so I wanted to thank you in person because you changed my whole life."

Paul was listening and understood why I had tears in my eyes.

52

GRANDMOTHERS

Southern California has wildfires and floods. Our house on Stone Canyon has a creek running through the front garden. Every year when it rains that creek floods with water and every year we have to clean out the leaves and fallen branches so it won't get blocked up. The winter of 1946, it rained very hard. The creek was not a problem, but somebody had wanted to build a house on the mountain above us. Bulldozers had leveled the site, pushing dirt over the side. When the rains came, it washed three feet of mud right through our house!

Paul and Lupita—mud at Stone Canyon

* * *

The next summer, when Pancho was seven years old, we were on a train on our way to visit my family in Mexico. Always curious and friendly, he had wandered off. I went to look for him and found him talking to some people in another carriage.

I said, "I'm sorry, I hope my son is not disturbing you."

The lady said, "Your son says his grandmother is Lucy Slocum Sullivan. My mother was a bridesmaid when Lucy Slocum married John Wallace Sullivan in El Paso, Texas." I got her address, and for years after that Grandma wrote back and forth to her childhood friend from their convent school days. Grandma Lucy lived with us at Stone Canyon until she died at the age of eighty-nine.

My mother-in-law, Helene Kohner, had her own apartment nearby in Beverly Hills. Her apartment was very nice, but she resented that my grandma lived with us. Helene was a difficult woman. She didn't like me from the beginning; I wasn't Jewish, and I hadn't brought a dowry to the marriage. But Paul wouldn't tolerate her talking against me. I once overheard him yelling at her, "All the happiness I've ever had, *she* has given to me, not *you*!" My sister-in-law, Hanna Bloch Kohner, was her favorite. Helene's three sons always kissed her hand and took very good care of her, but there was always yelling in her house.

Helene used to come to us every Sunday. I taught the children to respect their *grossmutter* Helene.

When she was ill, I would give her a bath and take care of her. When she died in 1952 after an appendix operation, the only thing her sons could say about her was, "She loved apple strudel." Helene's sister, Tante Clara, was her complete opposite. She was kind and sweet; it was Tante Clara who had put the money in Paul's prayer book when he first went to America. Lovely Tante Clara died in Auschwitz.

Susan, Grandma Helene, Paul, Lupita, Grandma Lucy, and Pancho

53

THE FIFTIES

In the 1950s, I stayed close to home. There was a worldwide polio epidemic that left thousands of children paralyzed, or worse. It was a terrible disease that increased in the summer months, and there was no cure. We were afraid to let our children go anywhere near a swimming pool. It wasn't until 1953 that a vaccine was developed, and immediately every child in America received it.

We were also at war with Communist North Korea, and there was a "witch-hunt" in the Hollywood film community.

For many years there had been an ongoing investigation by a Congressional House Un-American Activities Committee (HUAC), led first by J. Parnell Thomas, and later by John S. Wood. By 1951, the hearings were synonymous with Senator Joseph R. McCarthy. The HUAC was afraid that Communists and their way of thinking could influence motion picture people, who might pass on this "subversive" thinking to an audience. Writers, actors, directors, and producers were subpoenaed to appear before a congressional committee where they were asked, "Are you now or have you ever been a member of the Communist Party?" They were also asked to name anyone who might be a Communist. Some named names; others had the courage not to. Scared of being implicated, the studios created an infamous "blacklist." Those who refused to answer were labeled "unfriendly" witnesses. Blacklisted, they could no longer find work in Hollywood and there was a reverse migration of talented filmmakers moving back to Europe. At the Academy Awards, several Oscars were awarded to fictitious names or to people who had loaned their names to front blacklisted writers.

John Howard Lawson, who had written *Blockade*, was one of those investigated by the HUAC. Because he refused to answer their questions, he was cited for contempt of Congress and sentenced to twelve months in prison. He was one of the so-called "Hollywood Ten," important writers who were blacklisted by the studios. When he was released from prison, he moved to Mexico, where under a pseudonym, he wrote the anti-apartheid movie, *Cry the Beloved Country*.

After our last trip to Mexico for one of the *Santa* commemorations, Susan asked her classmates to call her Lupita. She had decided she wanted to be an actress. Susan got her first part in a professional play while she was still in high school. She was a natural.

Paul and I had gone to see a play one evening with Susan at a very small theater, what might be described as theater-in-the-round. During intermission, the producer told Paul that he was looking for a young girl for his next play.

"What type of girl?" Paul asked.

"Just like that girl sitting there in the first row," the producer said.

"Oh, *no*," Paul said. "That's my daughter!"

The next day, the producer called and asked Paul if he would let Susan come in for a reading, an audition. I went with her and she got the part in *The Girl on the Via Flaminia*. Every evening I would sit with her backstage and, between her scenes, she would do her school homework.

54

A MEMORABLE TRIP

In the summer of 1954, we took Susan and Pancho with us on a trip through Europe to visit Paul's clients and to attend several film festivals. We arrived at Le Havre after crossing the Atlantic on the French ocean liner, S.S. *Liberté*. In Paris, Erich von Stroheim and Denise Vernac invited us to lunch at their house. There, Erich tried to shock me by showing me his collection of erotic sculptures that he kept in a barn. Erich was a naughty man.

Erich von Stroheim and Lupita

The next evening, Eric and Denise picked us up at our hotel and drove us through Paris in a red Cadillac convertible with the top down. When he drove through the narrow streets of the Latin Quarter, students from the Sorbonne recognized Erich, as he knew they would. At dinner in a small restaurant, Erich's dog sat with us on his own chair. Another night, we went to the *Folies Bergère*; Line Renaud was the headliner. When asked what he thought of all the bare breasts on stage, Pancho said, "I've seen better at home."

Paul Henreid rented us his American Chevrolet and we drove south, through the center of France, to Cannes on the Mediterranean. We were going to attend three film festivals that summer, so we had many changes of clothes in thirteen pieces of luggage tied on the roof of the car. It wasn't until after several unpleasant incidents, rude gestures, and comments, that we realized our car had German license plates. It was not so long after the war, and many people assumed we were rich German tourists.

On our way south to Aix-en-Provence, Paul had his mind set on having lunch at the four-star restaurant, La Pyramide, also known as Chez Point, in the town of Vienne. We got a late start that morning and by mid-afternoon the children and I were hungry. I insisted that we stop to buy bread, ham, and cheese for a picnic. Like many Europeans, Paul enjoyed a gourmet meal, and he was not going to just drive past Monsieur Point's restaurant. So when we finally arrived at four in the afternoon, Paul went in by himself to eat his incredible French meal that he had been looking forward to. The rest of us finished our picnic and took a siesta in the car. That evening when we arrived in Aix-en-Provence, our Chevrolet's axle broke, so we stayed several days in that lovely town.

Our Chevrolet in France

Cannes is on the French Riviera, the Cote d'Azur. It's a jewel of majestic hotels and hillside villas overlooking the blue Mediterranean. The concierge at the Carlton Hotel, on the Croisette, greeted us with enthusiasm and a stack of phone messages. The Carlton's crowded lobby and terrace are where film projects were pitched and deals were made, and Paul was everyone's friend and facilitator.

From the moment we arrived until we left ten days later, we were constantly with old friends and business people, meeting at favorite restaurants, or watching films. Day and night, Paul was on the phone speaking in five languages. This was what Paul enjoyed most, being in the center of things, helping producers and directors put together the elements of a movie. Mornings in small screening rooms, we saw films by new directors and films that did not yet have distribution. Evenings, we dressed up to see films in competition at the elegant festival theater. Afterwards, we would go to parties given by producers and distributors to promote their films, usually with movie stars flown in just for the evening.

We saw Maurice Chevalier perform at the Palm Beach Casino, down the coast from Cannes. The next morning, Paul met him for a long walk on the beach.

They immediately established a friendship and Maurice agreed to have Paul represent him in America. Maurice had been one of Europe's most important entertainers, but his career was in trouble. During the war he had entertained French prisoners held by the Germans, and as a result he was unjustly attacked in the press as a Nazi collaborator.

Leaving Cannes, we drove along the coast to Nice and Monte Carlo and on into Italy. For many years, it was our habit to go to the resort town of Montecatini near Florence, for Paul's birthday after the festival. Shirlee and Robby Lantz and many other friends would come and celebrate with us. We always stayed at the Grand Hotel La Pace, where a doctor would recommend a special diet and certain waters. Mornings, we would walk to the park in the center of town, where guests of the various hotels drank the water from different fountains as a small orchestra played. Many European health spas prescribed drinking an assortment of smelly waters to cleanse the system. That meant getting back to your hotel room and bathroom very quickly. From Montecatini, we took day trips to Florence and the surrounding hill towns. After a week, we drove across Northern Italy to Venice.

The Venice Film Festival is held on Lido Island, which is on the far side of the lagoon, facing the Adriatic Sea. This festival was so popular that the organizers had built a long tunnel under the street to get from the hotel to the festival theater, where the huge crowd of Italian fans and photographers clamored to see their idols.

Venice is magical and it was especially so when we showed it to our children for the first time. For me, Venice—with its gondolas, cafés and orchestras on the Piazza San Marco—is the most beautiful city in Europe.

Next, we drove over the Dolomites into Austria on our way to the Berlin Film Festival. We were going to spend the night with our dear friend, Luis Trenker, in South Tyrol, halfway between Bolzano and Munich. There was an unusual summer snowstorm as we drove over the Grossglockner Pass and our Chevrolet had a bad habit of popping out of gear. By the time we arrived, it was snowing hard and the brakes were letting out an awful smell. Luis' first words when he saw us were, "*Ostia Madonna*! Who was driving in this weather?" I had been driving as Paul was uncomfortable with heights. We stayed the night and the next day Luis led us down the mountain to Innsbruck, driving his huge, elegant pre-war Mercedes-Benz convertible befitting the movie star that he still was.

We met up with George and Hilda Marton and their son, Peter Stone, at the small resort of Wolfgangsee, close to Bad Ischl, where the famous Zauner's Konditorei was known for having the best pastries in Austria.

George Marton was Hungarian by birth. He had produced pictures in Hollywood, which is where he met and married Hilda Stone. They lived in Paris, where George had a literary agency. Peter, Hilda's eighteen-year-old son from her previous marriage, was infatuated with Susan. To impress her, he played "Smoke Gets in your Eyes" on the hotel piano, but that was the only piece he knew, so he played it over and over. Peter became a very successful writer. He was awarded an Emmy, an Oscar, and a Tony Award, and he was president of the New York Dramatists Guild.

We visited the Robinsons, who lived in an overgrown farmhouse. In typical Austrian fashion, the cow barn was underneath the bedrooms; that way the cows' bodies heated the rooms above in winter. Not so usual was the secret room behind a movable bookcase used to hide people during the war. In 1935, Armin Robinson had written the screenplay for *Forbidden Music*, which starred Richard Tauber, Diana Napier, and Jimmy Durante.

We continued on to Salzburg, where we stayed at the old Goldener Hirsch Hotel. That night we saw an outdoor performance of the fifteenth century morality play *Jedermann*. We visited Silvia and Gottfried Reinhardt, who were living in a small *Schloss* (castle). Gottfried, a writer, producer and director himself, was the son of Max Reinhardt, who created the Salzburger Festspiele (Salzburg Theater Festival). Max was called the greatest theater director in Europe. He had inspired Fritz Lang, F.W. Murnau, Ernst Lubitsch, William Dieterle, Otto Preminger, and many more directors. From Salzburg we drove to Munich on our way to Berlin.

In 1954 Berlin was an island surrounded by Soviet-occupied Germany. The Russians had tried to isolate the city by not allowing any transport by land, so a round-the-clock stream of French, British, and American planes had supplied the city with everything from coal to milk. The Berlin Airlift had ended in 1949, and it was now possible to drive to Berlin through a corridor of Russian-occupied Germany. But this was still the time of the Cold War with the Soviets, and it didn't seem like a good idea to risk our Chevrolet breaking down in that corridor. You were not allowed to stop for any reason. So we flew from Munich to Berlin.

The city was divided into four sections that were controlled by the Russians, French, British, and Americans. Our plane landed in the middle of the city at Tempelhof Airport.

This was our first time back to Berlin since 1935. The city still showed a lot of damage from the war; many buildings had only their façade standing, with nothing behind. We took a taxi ride past the places where we had lived. Many buildings were missing; others were burnt-out shells from the allied bombing. The grand boulevards looked naked. The trees were gone and the shops that were open were very drab. It was sad to see this once-exciting city now in ruins. I'm sure Paul had mixed feelings; he had loved Berlin, but this had also been the heart of Hitler's Third Reich.

Lupita with Artur and Maria Brauner

We could only cross from the American sector into the Russian-occupied east sector at Berlin Friedrichstrasse, the famous "Check-point Charlie" featured in many spy movies. Artur and Maria Brauner took us to a restaurant/nightclub in the Russian sector, where the entertainment was Cossack dancers performing and singing. Artur, a Polish Jew, had spent the war years in Russia. Rumor had it that he arrived in Berlin at the end of the war with a mysterious suitcase full of cash. He bought an old gas factory, because it was cheap, and turned it into the CCC Film Studio, where he personally produced hundreds of films.

On the gala evening of the Berlin Film Festival, we came out of the theater with Horst Buchholz and his beautiful wife, actress Miriam Bru. Their fans crowded around us, trying to get a closer look, wanting to touch them. There were too many people and the pushing got out of hand. We had to split up and run to find taxis to get back to the Kempinski Hotel. It was scary.

It was the end of summer when we finally flew back to California. It had been a memorable trip, but it felt very good to get back to our home on Stone Canyon Road.

Pancho, Miriam Bru, Horst Buchholz, and Lupita

55

MAURICE CHEVALIER

After the war, Maurice Chevalier had performed in Stockholm at a Communist benefit against nuclear arms and had participated in Communist demonstrations in Paris. Consequently, he had been denied a visa to enter the United States. Now, after Senator McCarthy's downfall, Paul was able to arrange a visa for Maurice to come to Los Angeles. He was to perform at the Greek Theater, an eight-thousand-seat outdoor amphitheater, similar to the Hollywood Bowl.

On opening night, Maurice appeared on stage in his usual tuxedo and top hat, but when the orchestra began to play, he froze; he could not say or sing a word. After several false starts, the orchestra stopped playing and Maurice left the stage. Paul and I ran to his dressing room. Maurice was terribly upset. We talked to him, trying to bolster his confidence. We told him how this could happen to anyone, and often did. I had once panicked when I played in *Don Juan Tenorio*. I looked out at the audience and was overwhelmed. They had to bring the curtain down and it took me fifteen minutes to gather my courage to go back out on that stage.

François and Madeleine Vals were there to help. François was Maurice's manager. Together, we convinced Maurice that this American audience loved him, and that was true. Americans knew Maurice from his films of the thirties, like *One Hour With You, Love Me Tonight*, and Franz Lehár's operetta, *The Merry Widow*.

When Maurice came back on stage the audience gave him a thunderous applause. He sang all of his old favorites: "Valentine," "Louise," and "Mimi," and at the end of the evening he was given a standing ovation.

Paul next represented Maurice to star in Billy Wilder's film *Love in the Afternoon*, with Audrey Hepburn, and then Maurice starred in Vincente Minnelli's *Gigi*, with Leslie Caron. *Gigi* won ten Academy Awards, including Best Picture. Maurice was awarded a special Academy Award for his contributions to the world of entertainment and he performed his one-man show on every continent to sold-out performances. Maurice was an international star again. In France, Josh Logan directed him in *Fanny* with Leslie Caron, Horst Buchholz, and Charles Boyer. The story was based on the trilogy, *Marius, Fanny and Cesar*, by Paul's longtime friend, Marcel Pagnol. Horst and Charles were also Paul's clients.

There were many stories of Maurice's penny-pinching ways. Every Christmas he would make a big fuss about a present for us which invariably turned out to be a new photo of himself, not even in a frame.

François and Madeleine Vals are lovely people. They traveled with Maurice on his world tours, leaving their daughter in the care of relatives. The year when Pancho was studying at the Sorbonne, they were like surrogate parents, helping him find an apartment and often having him to their home just outside of Paris. The following year, when we were in Paris, they invited us to dinner. We were surprised to find that a painting hanging over their fireplace was signed by Pancho! And it was quite good. As a student, he had been living in Montmartre, the artist's quarter, and to make extra money he had painted and sold many canvases. We convinced François and Madeleine to give us the painting, and now it hangs in our house.

Maurice Chevalier, Lupita, and Paul

56

THE BEL AIR FIRE AND OTHER TRAGEDIES

In the beginning of Susan's career, I coached her. Then she studied with Salka Viertel, Sanford Meisner, and Lee Strasberg. Susan was studying at UCLA and performing in *The Rose Tattoo* with Jody McCrea at the Player's Ring in 1957, when she was called to New York to audition for a role in *The Quiet Place* with Tyrone Power. She got the part.

During rehearsals, Susan and I stayed at the Park Chambers Hotel, where we had a hot plate in the room to cook light dinners. *The Quiet Place* opened in Boston and got very good reviews. At first Susan and Tyrone took separate curtain calls, but it was embarrassing because Susan got a much bigger round of applause. So Tyrone started taking Susan by the hand so they could share the curtain calls and applause.

In April 1958, I was in New York again with Susan. She was performing in *Love Me Little* on Broadway with Joan Bennett; that's where producer Ross Hunter saw Susan and asked her to audition for his upcoming film, *Imitation of Life*.

Susan and I were already asleep in our hotel room when the phone rang. It was Paul in Los Angeles. One of his clients, Lana Turner, had called him, hysterical, saying that Johnny Stompanato was lying on the floor of her bedroom, dead!

Lana, the "sweater girl," had been famously "discovered" at the soda fountain of a drugstore by Billy Wilkerson, owner of the *Hollywood Reporter*. She became a movie star overnight. Her first husband was Steve Crane, who owned the Luau Restaurant in Beverly Hills. Then she married millionaire Bob Topping. Her third husband was Lex Barker, who played Tarzan in the movies. For a while now, she had been carrying on with Johnny Stompanato, a gigolo who worked for Mickey Cohen, a Los Angeles mobster and nightclub owner. Now, Lana said Stompanato had a knife in him and she begged Paul to "Please come over right away!"

When Paul got to Lana's house, her doctor, her lawyer, and the Beverly Hills Police were already there. It seems that Stompanato had been regularly hitting and threatening Lana. That night, Lana's fourteen-year-old daughter, Cheryl Crane, heard another violent argument coming from Lana's bedroom. Cheryl went to the kitchen and came back with a large knife. When she entered her mother's bedroom, Stompanato turned and rushed toward her; he was impaled on Cheryl's knife. That, anyway, was the official explanation.

Paul suggested that I send Lana a telegram of support. The morning papers had photos of Johnny Stompanato lying in Lana's bedroom in a pool of his own blood. His death was ruled self-defense and Cheryl was not prosecuted; she went to live with her grandmother.

Johnny Stompanato's death was a shocking scandal, but Hollywood was used to scandal. Walter Wanger, producer and past president of the Motion Picture Academy, had been married to actress Joan Bennett for many years and they had two daughters. When Walter found out that

Joan was having an affair with her agent, Jennings Lang, Walter confronted them and shot Jennings in the "privates" in the parking lot of a restaurant! Jennings survived, and Walter went to jail for a short time.

Hollywood was used to tragedies, too. I'll never forget going to the airport with Paul to meet Charles Boyer, who was returning from Paris to bury his son; he had accidentally killed himself while playing Russian roulette.

Charles Boyer was a very handsome leading man, a major European star. In the early thirties, he had made foreign-language versions of American films, the same as I had. He was in films opposite Claudette Colbert, Greta Garbo, and Hedy Lamarr. He starred opposite Ingrid Bergman in *Gaslight*. Charles was nominated several times for his performances. In 1942, the Motion Picture Academy awarded him a special Oscar for his achievements. He lived in Los Angeles with his wife, Pat, until she died in 1978. Two days later, Charles took his own life.

Five months after her lover died at the hands of her teenage daughter, Lana went back to work, filming *Imitation of Life* with John Gavin, Sandra Dee, Juanita Moore, and my daughter, Susan. The Motion Picture Academy nominated Susan for her supporting role as Juanita Moore's light-skinned daughter who tries to pass for white. And Susan was awarded a Golden Globe for her performance by the Foreign Press Association. Douglas Sirk, her director, was awarded the Outstanding Directorial Achievement in Motion Pictures by the Directors' Guild members.

* * *

On November 6, 1961, Paul was at his dentist's office, where the nurse told him she had heard on the radio that guests at the Bel-Air Hotel were being evacuated because of a brush fire. The hotel was just down the street from us, so Paul rushed home immediately.

When I heard the first fire engines race past our house, I ran outside. They were heading toward the reservoir at the end of the canyon. My mother and Nina Laemmle were staying with us. We could see a tremendous column of black smoke rising from the ridge that separates the San Fernando Valley from Bel-Air and Beverly Hills. It had been a dry summer; we hadn't had any rain since February.

Susan and Pancho were both in Munich, where Susan was playing opposite Montgomery Clift in John Huston's film, *Freud*. Pancho was an assistant to John and production manager "Doc" Erickson.

By the time Paul got home, the whole sky was turning black with smoke. I took my mother and our dog, Scrabble, to Paul's office on Sunset Boulevard. Driving back, there was a police roadblock on Sunset at the entrance to Bel-Air. I told them where I lived and they let me drive through. Flying embers had landed on dry roof shingles and there were houses burning on both sides of the canyon. There were fire engines everywhere. At our driveway a woman tried to stop me, shouting, "You can't go in there!" I could see the fire had not reached us yet, and anyway, our house had a tile roof! I told the woman in no uncertain terms that *she* could leave—I was staying! When she wouldn't move, I pushed her out of the way and kept going. Just then Wayne Smith, a good friend of Pancho's, ran up. He had a hose in one hand; his face was beet-red and he was perspiring heavily.

"Mrs. Kohner!" he shouted. "That's a policewoman!"

There was so much excitement that Paul felt he should take a Valium to calm down. By mistake he took a strong sleeping pill instead. I found him sound asleep in the kitchen!

Wayne and our neighbor, Herbert Sturdy, used garden hoses to wet down our roof and walls. Nina and I watched as flames burned right down to our patio, consuming all the vegetation, and then retreated. For the moment we were safe.

As it got later, many of our neighbors from farther up the canyon walked down to our house; they were in a daze, their homes had burned to the ground. Walter and Hanna, with their daughter

Julie, came to us. Their house on Roscomare Road, two canyons away, had burned; they hadn't been able to save a thing.

Toward evening, the sky turned red. It looked and smelled like the end of the world. There were helicopters overhead, fire engines, and sirens wailing everywhere. The canyons and hills were thick with tall dry brush. As night fell, we saw red embers blowing with the wind, starting new fires wherever they landed. On the hill behind us and across the canyon we could see small animals on fire—rabbits probably—running through the dry brush, starting new streaks of fire as they ran.

All around us houses burned, but we were lucky. With our tile roof and with help from several friends, our house was saved. When it was all over, the Bel-Air Fire had destroyed 484 homes.

57

A "BOUTIQUE" AGENCY

By the sixties, the Paul Kohner Agency had become the premier Hollywood "boutique" talent agency. It was small compared to the goliath William Morris Agency, but Paul's client list was very prestigious. He had several agents working for him, including his brother, Walter. But in fact, the Paul Kohner Agency was a one-man show. The force of Paul's personality was what made his agency a success.

There is a saying, "When you learn another language, you gain another soul." Paul could speak to his European clients in their own languages; he gained their trust and inevitably they became close friends. That was why he was so successful in a business that depends so much on personal relationships. Nevertheless, he was working too hard. The constant pressure of negotiating deals for his clients eventually took its toll. He was overwhelmed.

* * *

Early in 1962, when Paul was sixty-four, he had a breakdown. He fell into a deep depression; his eyes were glazed, and he barely spoke. At night he didn't want to fall asleep; he was afraid of dying. This lasted for several months. During that time, he didn't go to the office. His lawyer, Mark Cohen, would call at night to discuss business matters on the phone; so did Irene Heyman, his secretary, who was also his trusted right hand. They might as well have been talking to air as Paul had completely shut down. Paul liked to take pills and he took a lot of them. He was taking pills to go to sleep and pills to wake up, pills to settle his stomach, and pills that a friend may have recommended; who knows what they were for. I emptied our medicine cabinet and flushed them all down the toilet; Paul was furious. It was a gruesome time. I didn't know where to turn. Both of his brothers had had periods of depression, but why did this happen to Paul, and why now? I didn't know.

Hanna's brother, Friedrich Bloch, was a psychiatrist; I wanted Paul to go see him. He was reluctant, saying, "I don't need help!" But he went. It was a slow journey of many months, but Paul recovered from his bout with depression.

During this time Susan was in New York, working in the theater and on television. She had just been in Thornton Wilder's play, *Pullman Car Hiawatha,* at the Circle in the Round Theater. Pancho was living in Italy.

That summer, Paul made a trip to Europe alone. He said he needed to know that he could stand on his own two feet, so to speak. His first stop was to visit Pancho who was working with Franz de Blasi, an Italian talent agent in Rome. This was the year that producer Walter Wanger and director Joseph Mankiewicz were at the Cine Città Studios filming *Cleopatra,* a very expensive movie that went way over budget. The large cast was headed by Elizabeth Taylor and Richard Burton; their love affair made news around the world.

The cafés on the Via Veneto were suddenly full of American actors. European producers wanted Americans in their films to make them easier to sell to other countries, maybe even to Hollywood. Many found work in "Spaghetti Westerns," so called because they were made by Italian filmmakers. Sergio Leone was the most successful of these directors, with Clint Eastwood in *A Fistful of Dollars* and *The Good, The Bad, and The Ugly*, and Charles Bronson in *Once Upon a Time in the West*. These two actors were relatively unknown at the time.

Paul tried to talk Pancho into leaving Italy to come work with him in Los Angeles. Pancho was hesitant because he loved Italy and his independence there. His fluency in several languages gave him an important edge in business in Europe, just as that same talent had served his father. Perhaps, having just recovered from his bout with depression, Paul really did need him. He said that they were going to merge the business with a New York talent agency and Pancho would be in charge of implementing that. He was convincing, and Pancho finally agreed to return to California.

* * *

Paul's style at work was to keep things very much to himself. He expected Pancho to sit quietly and learn by observing. But Pancho was used to working closely with his Italian partner. Two months after returning to California, Pancho called Franz in Rome to ask why he hadn't heard from him, and what was happening to the deals they had been working on.

It seemed that Franz had written. When Pancho asked Paul's secretary, Irene Hayman, where that correspondence was, she answered, "You'd better ask your father."

Paul thought he was doing the right thing by trying to keep Pancho from returning to Italy. But the resulting argument proved the opposite. Pancho realized that trying to work with his father was harming their relationship. He decided to go back to Europe, this time to Spain, where Doc Erickson was now running the Samuel Bronston Studio. Pancho had worked for Doc in Germany and continued their friendship in Rome, where Doc was production manager on *Cleopatra*. With his fluency in Spanish, he was sure he could get a job at the studio in Madrid.

On the day Pancho was to leave again for Europe, he and Ellen Picking, his steady girlfriend since they were teenagers, decided to get married. Ellen had been studying at Sarah Lawrence College in New York, and had spent the previous year studying in Paris. Ellen and Pancho were now twenty-one and twenty-three, respectively. That same evening we flew with Ellen's mother and stepfather, Mary and Allan Jones, to Las Vegas, where Pancho and Ellen were married in a church and Allan, an opera and Broadway performer, sang the "Lord's Prayer." From there the newlyweds went directly to Spain.

It was hard for me to see Pancho leave, but I understood his need to live his own life away from the shadow of his father. Paul had a more difficult time accepting his failure to bring his son into his business, but he respected Pancho's decision, and our lives went on.

* * *

We had a large circle of friends in Los Angeles, some from Europe, and others we met here. I first met Armando del Moral when he interviewed me in 1947. Armando had left Spain in 1938 because he was in conflict with General Francisco Franco and the fascists. He first went to Mexico, where he taught school while he waited for an American visa. After serving in the U.S. Army, he edited the evening edition of the Spanish-language newspaper, *La Opinión*, and in 1947 he founded *Cine Gráfica*, the first Spanish-language magazine in the United States. Paul and I immediately became friends with Armando and his wife, Amelia. We went together to the bullfights in Tijuana, and on my birthdays Armando would tell amusing, risqué stories about my life. He was my biggest fan.

In 1963, Armando asked me to be a part of his group of actors performing in a Spanish-language soap opera for radio. The story was called *María Elena*. It was about a Latino couple who lived in the San Fernando Valley. We met twice a week in the evenings in Armando's office behind Paramount Studios; we recorded one hundred and fifteen shows! Late at night, Paul would come by with donuts and coffee. One day, when I took a pair of Paul's shoes to be repaired, the shoemaker said to me, "I know that voice! You're María Elena!" He told me that his mother listened to our program every morning, and the rest of the family were not allowed to say a word while the show was on. I was very flattered.

* * *

Afectuosamente Lupita Tovar *(María Elena)*

Lupita, Ricardo Montalban, and Armando Del Moral

With my children grown up and far away, I had extra time. So I went to the UCLA hospital and asked, "Can you use a pair of hands?" Eleanor Wasson was in charge of volunteers. With my Spanish, German, and some French, she was very eager to have me on their staff. I started by translating for doctors and patients and their families, but I also got to watch operations with the medical students. I had always been fascinated by medicine. If I hadn't been an actress, I would have liked to have been a doctor. My family often asked for my advice on medical matters, but they also called me "*La Curandera*" (the quack).

Every day from eight to four, I did whatever was needed at the hospital. I stayed with a woman who was giving birth to her thirteenth child.

Her husband was outside and I translated for the doctor who wanted permission to tie her tubes. The husband refused and I couldn't convince him otherwise. Another time, a doctor wanted permission to circumcise a baby boy for hygienic reasons. I was talking in Spanish and with my hands. I guess I looked funny because the doctors had to stifle a laugh. The father said nobody was going to cripple his son that way.

I usually stayed in the operating room until the patient had anesthesia. But when a Czech lady needed an operation, the doctor asked me, "How strong is your stomach—do you mind blood?" They couldn't put the woman completely to sleep. They wanted me there to ask her where it hurt while they were operating. I'd never seen such an operation before. It was an intricate, fascinating procedure. My stomach didn't fail me.

There was a young patient from Tijuana, a boy who wore leg braces as a result of polio. He was there for an operation to remove a tumor near his heart. At Christmas, the hospital tried to send most children home, but this boy had no family in Los Angeles.

I asked, "Would you like me to take him home with me?"

We sent for his mother who came from Tijuana and she stayed with us, too.

At the end of the year, the hospital held a holiday party honoring the volunteers. When I was introduced as their Russian translator, Paul was so surprised he burst out laughing.

"*Russian?*"

There had been a sweet, elderly Russian patient who spoke Yiddish. Nobody understood him. Yiddish is very close to German. I understood the man wanted Jewish rye bread. He didn't like the soft white bread they were giving him. Paul's office assistant went to a deli and brought us rye bread. I solved his problem.

Sometimes when I was needed late into the night, Paul would come and keep me company, reading scripts in the hallway. I volunteered at UCLA for eight years, until I felt Paul needed me to be home more.

* * *

Paul needed a cataract operation and he was nervous about it. So to prove how easy it was, I offered to go first. However, something went wrong. A mistake had been made by the eye surgeon and I had lost the sight in that eye. I didn't tell Paul; I didn't want him to feel guilty that I had gone first as a guinea pig. He never did know that I was blind in one eye. I took Paul to the Jules Stein Eye Institute at UCLA, where he had his successful cataract operation.[25]

A few years later, Paul also lost his sight in one eye when he neglected to take his glaucoma condition seriously. We were flying to New York on our way to Europe, but when we landed in New York, Paul had a terrible pain in one eye. We checked into the Plaza Hotel. Early the next morning Paul woke up in excruciating pain. At that moment, Roberto Haggiag, an old friend from Rome who also had an apartment in New York, happened to call. I told him that Paul was having trouble with his eyes and Roberto immediately called his friend, Dr. Ramon Castroviejo, a leading eye surgeon in New York. We went straight to his office; the doctor was able to relieve the pain, but it was too late to save Paul's sight in that eye. We canceled our trip and stayed in our suite at the Plaza with the curtains drawn for several days before flying back to Los Angeles. Paul was devastated. Billy Wilder tried to cheer him up in a note referring to his position in Hollywood, quoting the proverb, "Among the blind, the one-eyed is king."

* * *

On one of our trips to Europe, we continued on to Israel. For several days, we had a guide show us all of the historical sights, but Paul was searching for a particular man, Dr. Weiss, the rabbi from Teplitz who had married us. We had heard that he had

---

[25] Jules Stein, an ophthalmologist-turned-agent, was the founder of MCA Booking Agency. When MCA merged with Universal Studios, Jules became its board chairman.

survived the war. We found Dr. Weiss on a kibbutz near Jerusalem. When we knocked on his door and he saw me, he said, *"Das schönste Mädle, das jemals nach Teplitz gekommen ist!"* (The most beautiful girl who ever came to Teplitz!)

On that same trip, we went to visit the new museum in Jerusalem, and who should we see there but Sam Spiegel. He was speaking Yiddish with another man. As they passed by I said, "Sam, you have a terrible accent." He was so surprised to see me.

He said, "That's all I need, criticism from a *schickse*." Then he threw his arms around me. We had first met in Berlin and in London before the war; then again in Mexico, Cannes, and Hollywood. Now, as he hugged me in Israel, halfway around the world, I realized that the years were starting to hurry by.

58

OUR SCANDINAVIAN FRIENDS

Paul had met the brilliant Ingmar Bergman and his lead actor, Max von Sydow, at several European film festivals. In 1965, Paul brought Max to Los Angeles to play the part of Jesus Christ in George Stevens' film, *The Greatest Story Ever Told*. As usual, Paul took great care to make his foreign client feel at home in Hollywood. Our house was again a meeting place for dinners and—in summer—lunch by the pool. Max became a close friend, and that friendship is just as strong today.

This was the beginning of Paul's "Scandinavian connection." We made frequent trips to Stockholm and eventually Paul represented most of the Swedish film industry. That included directors Ingmar Bergman, Jan Troell (*Zandy's Bride*), Bo Widerberg (*Elvira Madigan*), and Kjell Grede (*God Afton, Herr Wallenberg*), who was married to the actress Bibi Andersson. There was also Ingrid Thulin, Harriet Andersson, Erland Josephson, and the lovely Norwegian actress Liv Ullmann. In summer, Sweden is full of my favorite lilacs, and whenever we were there, Max always sent bunches of lilacs to our hotel room.

Paul admired Ingmar Bergman's talent and wanted to represent him, not just for a commission but to facilitate this great artist's vision. Paul wanted to arrange financing for Ingmar's films. More generous budgets would free Ingmar to concentrate on the artistic side of filmmaking. It took several years of dinners and social visits to gain the trust of Ingmar, who was a very private person.

The first time Paul wanted to discuss business with Ingmar, he left me at the hotel. Arriving at Ingmar's house at the appointed time, Ingmar asked, "Where is Lupita?" He insisted on sending a car back to the hotel for me to join them. Ingmar liked the company of women and was especially attentive to me.

In 1971, Paul arranged for ABC Pictures to finance and release Ingmar's *The Touch*. Then, Paul convinced Roger Corman to buy not only Ingmar's *Cries and Whispers,* but also Federico Fellini's film, *Amarcord*. Paul told Roger that it would be good for his soul, as well as his business, to elevate the caliber of films he was identified with. Roger was a prolific director, producer, and distributor of very low-budget films. His minimal financial risk allowed him to nurture young filmmakers, many of whom went on to achieve stellar careers.[26]

Cries and Whispers was nominated for five Academy Awards. *Amarcord* won an Oscar for Best Foreign Film and, to Roger's surprise, both films also made a profit.

Ingmar was notoriously shy, but he did come to Hollywood in 1975 with his wife, Ingrid. When Ingmar visited the set at Warner Bros. Studio, where Pancho was filming *St. Ives* with Charles Bronson, the American crew all stood and applauded him.

It was a very successful trip for both Paul and Ingmar. They met with Dino de Laurentiis, who immediately offered to finance Ingmar's next film,

---

26 The Academy of Motion Picture Arts and Sciences awarded Roger Corman with an Honorary Lifetime Achievement Oscar in 2009.

The Serpent's Egg. That evening we were all going to dinner, but Ingmar balked at the door of the restaurant. It was too crowded for him. He had already moved from the Bel-Air Hotel to the Beverly Wilshire because he had trouble sleeping. Now, he insisted on going back to his hotel room to have dinner. But after dinner he did come to Pancho's Venice production office, where he screened my 1931 film, *Santa,* for Ingmar.

After he saw the movie, Ingmar asked me, "Why did you ever stop acting?!" From Sweden, Ingmar sent me a beautiful letter, saying that he fell

INGMAR BERGMAN
FÅRÖ

Dear Lupita,

This is a little loveletter written to a young girl whom I met by accident during my stay in Los Angeles. It was a very short encounter, I could not even talk to her. I saw her during about hundred minutes in the evening of October 24th and instantly fell in love. (I have confessed to Ingrid, who is very understanding).

I am, you know, an old professional and I have seen thousands of girls, talented, beautiful, original, delicate. But never have I seen a young woman with such an atmosphere of a warm and pure heart combined with such an intuitive talent for acting. So I fell in love both humanly and professionally.

Dear Lupita, I know that you know this young lady very well. Will you now do me a great service! But be careful! Talk to her in all secrecy. She seems to be married to one of the most powerful men in Hollywood, who is also told to be very jealous!

Tell her that I love her and that she, during our short meeting, gave me a great experience of beauty and talent. Show her this letter and tell her that I am sorry that I am writing to her in a for me foreign language. I would like to use my own language and I would like to write all the beautiful and strong words used in my language to express tenderness.

Tell her that I will never forget her.

Tell her that that is true.

LOVE
Ingmar.

in love with me when he saw me on the screen.

Many men have fallen in love with me; most didn't even know me. And too often I was told that I was beautiful. It should have gone to my head; it didn't. But this lovely letter from Ingmar touched me deeply, coming from a friend whose talent I respected above all others.

Paul, Ingmar, and Lupita

59

A TROUBLED YEAR

In May 1968, the Cannes Film Festival was shut down by student demonstrators—young filmmakers took control of the festival theater and prevented directors from showing their films. These protestors, rebelling against the conservative morality of the time, then instigated a series of strikes at universities. When the De Gaulle government countered with riot police, battles broke out in Paris streets, and workers throughout France went on strike in sympathy with the students. This mini-revolution almost succeeded in toppling the De Gaulle government. It did have a great impact on the way French people thought about human rights and respect for authority.

That same year, the Soviet Union had relaxed its grip on Czechoslovakia. It was a time known as the Prague Spring, and the Barrandov Film Studio in Prague was open for business, if you had hard currency.

Pancho was supervising two productions for United Artists, *The Last Escape* in Munich, and *The Bridge at Remagen* in Prague. When Paul heard that Pancho was going to be in Czechoslovakia, he asked him to visit Teplitz and go to the family house. There had been a painting hanging over the living room fireplace and Pancho was to try and buy it from the current resident.

Pancho drove to Teplitz and afterwards told us the elegant old house was still there and the garden and trees were still beautiful. An elderly woman had let him look inside the house. Of course, the walls were completely bare of any paintings. There were mattresses on the floors of each room and old shoes lined the walls. Several families lived there now.

Paul never wanted to go back to his birthplace after the war. At first, it was under Soviet Communist control and later, when he could have gone back, Paul found it too painful. His childhood friends and so many of his family had died in the Holocaust.

* * *

That same year the summer Olympic Games were being held in Mexico, and I hadn't seen my family in a while, so Paul and I went for a visit. We were so excited by the spectacle of the games and by the city, which was all spruced up, that as we were leaving for the airport I said, "I think we should spend more time here." Paul agreed.

We were unaware then of the student demonstrations and the roundup and jailing of dissidents that preceded the Olympic Games. On the night of October 2, in the Plaza de las Tres Culturas at Tlatelolco, soldiers had opened fire on thousands of unarmed students and workers. That night came to be known as *La Noche Triste* (The Sad Night). These demonstrators were supporters of the socialist movements in many third-world countries such as Cuba and China; they wanted to create change in Mexico, away from the dominant PRI political party led by President Díaz Ordaz. That night, more than three hundred were killed and several thousand students were held in jail until after the games were over and the international press had left. I was shocked when I heard this and I almost regretted buying a house in Mexico.

* * *

Cuernavaca is just one hour from Mexico City. You drive high up, out of the valley of Mexico, before dropping down five thousand feet into the state of Morelos. Descending on the left, you can see two snow-covered volcanoes, Popocatépetl and Iztaccíhuatl. An Aztec legend says that Popocatéptel (Smoking Mountain) watches over Iztaccíhuatl, (Sleeping Lady); Popocatépetl represents a warrior who was in love with the daughter of a king who would only allow them to marry if the warrior proved himself in battle. Popocatépetl was victorious but he was away so long, Iztaccíhuatl died of grief. When he returned, he laid her body on top of a mountain range and climbed to the top of an adjacent mountain, where he stands with a smoking torch, forever watching over her.

We had visited Cuernavaca, known as The City of Eternal Spring, when John Sturges was filming *The Magnificent Seven* in 1960. That time we had stayed with Horst and Miriam Buchholz. The villa they had rented had a magnificent garden. Yul Brynner, Charles Bronson, Steve McQueen, and Eli Wallach were all staying in lovely private houses with large tropical gardens, hidden behind high walls.

Paul loved Mexico and he had promised to retire soon, so I stayed behind and found a house in Cuernavaca. The property had a large garden and a swimming pool. I knew Paul would fall in love with it just as I had, so I sold some stock I owned and bought it.

One morning during the war years, as Paul was leaving for the office, the phone rang. He answered it and heard a man's voice asking for me.

"Who's calling?" he asked.

"Mr. Grant."

"Cary Grant?" Paul asked.

"No," he chuckled, "I'm Mrs. Kohner's stock broker."

Paul was laughing as he handed me the phone. He thought it was amusing that I had a brokerage account. Over the years I had learned to save money and invest it. Once, I almost bought a vacant lot on Wilshire Boulevard on what was to become known as The Miracle Mile. Unfortunately, Paul and his lawyer, Mark Cohn, talked me out of it. I would have made a lot of money if I had ignored their advice. I had had to work hard to convince Paul to buy our house on Stone Canyon Road; now, I was able to buy the house in Cuernavaca by myself. What a great feeling of independence that was!

* * *

When I returned to Los Angeles, I brought Sarita with me. We had been out shopping and came back to find Paul already home. He put his arms around me and said, "Darling, I have something very difficult to tell you. Your brother, Guillermo, is in very bad shape."

"Where is he?" I asked. I hadn't seen Guillermo in more than twenty years.

"He is in Guaymas. His wife sent a telegram to my office."

"I want to go," I said.

Sarita and I drove to Tijuana and caught a plane to Guaymas, a small port on the west coast, three hundred miles south of California. It seems Guillermo was a deep-sea salvage diver. He had had a diving accident and he was at a clinic; that's all we knew.

We took a taxi from the airport to the Sisters of Guadalupe Charity Clinic. I walked in and found Guillermo with his family around him. I was shocked to see my once-robust brother looking so frail and in pain. It was a very traumatic meeting; I hugged him, and we both cried. Guillermo had simply disappeared; he had isolated himself from our family.

The doctor said they could not save his leg—it was gangrenous. It looked and smelled terrible. The leg had to go, but they couldn't do the operation there. The doctor suggested the military hospital. Guillermo's wife was a peasant, a woman with no education and unable to cope with the situation. She was hysterical and of no help, so Sarita and I took Guillermo in a taxi to the military hospital. That was the worst place you could ever hope to see, with patients lying on the floor in the hallways, rats running around everywhere; just awful.

The military doctor said Guillermo's situation was dire. They had to cut off his leg immediately, but there was no nurse to help.

So I said, "I will help." And I held my brother's leg while they sawed it off! It's a wonder I didn't faint. The place was so filthy that a few days later we took my brother back to the clinic so the sisters could nurse him.

I think Guillermo never got in touch with me or his sisters because of his male pride. He was only eight when I left Mexico. My mother never defended him against my father; if she had, things might have been different.

Guillermo recovered and got a job as a night watchman, but he couldn't adjust to the loss of his leg. A year later, he shot himself with a revolver.

I sent money to Guillermo's wife and I arranged for his eldest daughter to go live with my mother in Mexico City, but she wouldn't go to school; she ran away with a bricklayer and returned to Guaymas a year later with a baby.

60

GRANDCHILDREN

Our daughter Susan married John Weitz in our garden in 1964. They had met in Palm Beach, Florida, where she was performing with Jon Voight in the play *Sunday in New York*. John Weitz was movie-star handsome and a very successful menswear designer. Born in Berlin, he had been sent to school in England. He emigrated in 1940 when he was seventeen, arriving in New York via Shanghai and Canada. John, who spoke German, English and French, was quickly recruited by the OSS, the precursor of the Central Intelligence Agency. He became a naturalized American citizen and rose to the rank of captain. Toward the end of the war, he was sent to help in the reconstruction of the German government.

John and Susan lived in Manhattan, where they had a very active social life. Their first son, Paul Weitz, was born November 14, 1965. Early in the following year, when Susan and John had to go to Japan on a business trip, Paul flew to New York to pick up four-month-old baby Paul and brought him back to stay with us for two weeks. The proud grandfather hardly went to the office during that time, preferring to stay at home and play with his first grandson.

* * *

We often visited Ellen and Pancho in Spain, where Pancho was working for producer Samuel Bronston on films such as *The Fall of the Roman Empire* with Sophia Loren and *Circus World* with John Wayne. Then we saw them in Paris when Pancho worked for Les Artistes Associés, the French production company of United Artists. And we would see them every May in Cannes during the film festival.

Paul always had many clients at the festival; his days were busy negotiating deals, but Cannes was also where we saw old friends and visited favorite restaurants. We liked to go to Saint Paul de Vence, a small quaint town in the hills above Cannes. We would have lunch at the Colombe d'Or, where Simone Signoret sat by the front door greeting guests. Her husband, Yves Montand, would often be playing *boule*, with the local men in the town square. Yves was handsome and had known many women. I heard that he once said, "A man can have two, maybe three, affairs while he is married. But three is the absolute maximum. After that, you're cheating." The Colombe d'Or had a wonderful collection of paintings by artists who, over the years, had paid for their meals with their art. Close by was the Gallery Maeght, with its impressive Giacomettis and Calders in their sculpture garden.

In spite of all the commotion of the festival, we enjoyed those European trips immensely. The lifestyle in Europe was so different from the pace of life in America.

* * *

In 1969, Pancho decided to leave United Artists to produce his own independent films. He had met B. Traven in Mexico and had acquired the rights to film his book, *The Bridge in the Jungle*. Pancho wrote the screenplay and he and Ellen left immediately to look for locations, before the rainy season made the jungle in Southern Mexico impassable.

As the short "dry season" approached in Chiapas, twenty-four actors and a very young, physically fit crew followed Pancho into the jungle near the border with Guatamala. Among the actors were Chano Urueta, John Huston, and my good friend, Katy Jurado. Chano Urueta never told Pancho that he had directed me in *María*, twenty-nine years earlier, when I was pregnant with Pancho. He was there as an actor, and, I'm sure, to be of whatever help he could be to my son. John had emphysema and carried an oxygen tank with him on the set. He was especially generous to suffer the heat and oppressive humidity of the rain forest, to be a part of Pancho's first film. John played the character his father, Walter Huston, created in *The Treasure of the Sierra Madre*, which was also a B. Traven story.

Pancho's daughter, Melissa Sullivan Kohner, was born in Los Angeles on October 30, 1969, just before filming was to begin—just one week after Susan gave birth to Christopher John Weitz in New York.

When photography was completed, Pancho and Ellen returned to Paris (with six-month-old Melissa) to edit the film.

Filming on locations around the world and working in several languages was fun and challenging, but after twelve years of living abroad, Pancho and Ellen decided to move permanently back to Los Angeles.

When they first got back, Pancho worked for Roger Corman, directing second unit; then he adapted and produced *The Lie* from a story by Ingmar Bergman for CBS television.

Alexander Paul Kohner, our fourth grandchild, was born in Los Angeles on January 12, 1972. Pancho and Ellen were living in the Venice Beach community. That's where Pancho wrote, produced, and directed *Mr. Sycamore*, with Jason Robards, Sandy Dennis, and Jean Simmons, a story about a man who turns himself into a tree rather than face the reality of his crumbling marriage—a prophetic subject for Pancho. Pancho and Ellen had been childhood sweethearts, but after thirteen years of marriage they divorced in 1975.

My grandchildren, Melissa, Chris, Alex, and Paul

61

LENI RIEFENSTAHL

Paul's relationships with the people he worked with naturally became part of my life. Most were very positive experiences but there were others.

When Leni Riefenstahl was still acting, Paul had made two films with her: *Die Weisse Hölle vom Piz Palü* (*The White Hell of Pitz Palu*) in 1929, and the big-budget *S.O.S. Eisberg* (*S.O.S. Iceberg*) in 1933. During that time they had a cordial relationship. Subsequently, Adolf Hitler commissioned Leni to direct two films: the infamous *Triumph of the Will*, which was the Nazi propaganda film of the Nuremburg Party Rally of 1934, and in 1936, *Olympia,* an epic record of the Berlin Olympic Games. Although she did film African-American Jesse Owens' accomplishments alongside blond, blue-eyed Aryan athletes, when the film was completed it was boycotted by the American anti-Nazi League. This was largely because of her close association with Hitler and the Third Reich. In 1938, when Leni wrote to Paul, asking for his help in finding distribution for *Olympia* in America, he refused to do so.

In 1939, Leni Riefenstahl followed Hitler's army into Poland, filming the invasion. She continued directing films during the war, once using gypsies from "internment camp" Maxglan, as extras for her film *Tiefland*. After filming these same extras were transported to Auschwitz—Birkenau, the "death camp."[27]

In 1948, screenwriter Tom Reed, who had worked on *S.O.S. Iceberg*, wrote to Paul, asking him to send CARE packages to Leni. Paul's response was a resounding "No."

In 1974, Paul got a phone call from Leni Riefenstahl. She was coming to America and wanted to meet with him. She wanted him to help her with introductions to Hollywood studio executives. Paul told me he had again turned her down, and I agreed wholeheartedly.

---

[27] Leni Riefenstahl was later cleared of charges of collaboration by the German denazifying court and was, instead, labeled a "sympathizer."

May 17, 1948.

Mr. Tom Reed,
633 The Esplanade,
Redondo Beach, Calif.

Dear Tom:

I am sorry that I cannot agree with you in regard to your statements about Leni Reifenstahl. It is too bad that by reason of the fact that she, like many other Nazis, have been cleared by a de-Nazification court - and probably by one in the French zone - she now appears to be an object of pity rather than of scorn. However, in this particular case, I am too well informed about her activities to be hoodwinked as you apparently have been.

Miss Reifenstahl was a self-admitted Nazi and, as such, was one of the prime elements and prime forces in the development of the Nazi movement. I, for one, will never forget how she stepped out on the stage of the Ufa Palast in Berlin at the opening of "S.O.S. ICEBERG" and, for the first time on any stage in Berlin or Germany, gave the Nazi salute, and started a demonstration which emptied the house which was filled by at lease one half of my co-religionists in five minutes flat. Outside of the theatre, an "honor guard" of 16 SS Storm Troupers cleared the way for her exit.

Do I have to remind you of the many "valuable contributions" she made to the rise of the Nazi party with the direction and over-all production of some pictorially very beautiful pictures? No Tom, from me as one, Miss Reifenstahl shall not receive any CARE packages. I have to leave that to people whose families and relatives were not put to death in the torture chambers and death camps created by the diabolical Nazis.

With kindest regards, I remain

Sincerely,

PAUL KOHNER

PK/r

62

THE FAMILY IN MEXICO

As with all large families, there was often a crisis happening in ours. My brother-in-law, Jesús Aristi, suffered a debilitating stroke in 1976 and was bedridden. He and my sister Lucy moved out of the family house in the Colonia Condessa to live with their daughter, Isabel, in Pedregal near the National Autonomous University of Mexico, which is the second-oldest university in the Americas. For the next seven years, Lucy, her daughter, Isabel, and Isabel's children took care of Jesús.

My youngest sister, Mary, had married Fernando González, a football player who went on to own the Mexico City team. Fernando had a personality larger than life. He liked to say you could drop him in any city in the world without a penny in his pocket and he would achieve success. And I believed him. With his company, Lithographica Juventud, Fernando became the most important printer of books and magazines in Mexico.

Mexico City used to shut down for three hours at midday. Shops would close and everyone would go home for their siesta. Our family had been renting the old house on Agustin Melgar for fifty years. It was where our family gathered every day at lunchtime.

With the expanding population of the city, traffic now made that daily gathering impossible. My sister Lucy had her own apartment and my niece Christina, moved out. That left just Sarita, who had never married, and my mother. I bought them a modern apartment on the Avenida Revolución where, typically, *Abuelita,* as we affectionately called our mother, refused to take the clear plastic wrapping off the new sofas.

My mother loved Paul just as my grandma, Lucy Sullivan, had. She often came to see us in California, and we took her with us on vacations. Her favorite destination was Hawaii; she loved the islands. She loved sweets, but she had diabetes and had to watch her diet. Of her nine children, there was only myself and my three sisters left. Five brothers had died, four of them as infants. Sarita had been taking care of our mother all her adult life.

When Pancho was planning to drive from Los Angeles to New York, and from there take his car on the S.S. *United States* to Europe, we called Sarita and asked her if she would like to take a vacation and travel with Pancho. She said, "Yes, of course!" Sarita was always very young at heart.

The next day she arrived in Los Angeles and she and Pancho drove cross-country in a two-seater sports car. They looked like brother and sister and I'm sure they were laughing all of the way. In Paris, Sarita met up with her niece Isabel and Isabel's husband, Manolo Canibe, while Pancho went on to Germany to work on the movie *Freud*.

* * *

In July 1979, I got a midnight call from Sarita in Mexico. Our mother's heart had given out. Paul and I drove to Tijuana in order to catch the only plane that would get us there in time. We arrived at the Gayosso Funeral Home, which for some strange reason is on Sullivan Street, my mother's maiden name, just as they closed the coffin. It was raining at the cemetery, appropriate weather for a funeral. She would have been furious if she knew we buried her next to my father. A few days later, Paul flew back to Los Angeles while I stayed with Sarita to help her pack up our mother's clothes to give away.

Sarita worked in an antique shop. That's where she met and fell in love with Fred Tardif, whose son owned the beauty shop next door. The Tardifs are from France so Sarita has learned to speak French. Sarita and Fred were married in our house in Cuernavaca by a very pregnant judge. One of our guests that day was John Gavin, who was the American ambassador to Mexico at the time. As an actor, John had starred in many films, including *Imitation of Life* with our Susan and Lana Turner.

Lupita and Ambassador John Gavin

We loved going to Cuernavaca. The garden was beautiful, and Sarita spoiled Paul terribly. He liked the town plaza with its traditional covered band stand in the center and children running all about. On the weekends, there were musicians, and in the evenings, boys and girls still walked in groups of twos and threes around the plaza in opposite directions, flirting under the watchful eyes of parents and grandparents. Mornings, Paul liked to go to the bakery to choose his favorite morning *pan dulces* and *bizcochos*.

On several occasions Susan and Pancho brought their children to visit, and my sisters and their children and grandchildren would visit us. We became friends with our neighbors, Pilar Ochi across the street, the Watkins next door, and Robert Brady, whose four hundred-year-old house backed up to the cathedral in town. Robert would serve us delicacies, such as *quesadillas de huitlacoche,* made with zucchini blossoms and blue mushrooms that sprout on ears of corn and, for dessert, mangoes with a flaming tequila sauce! Robert's guests were often Barbara Hutton, the Woolworth heir, and Helen Hayes, the First Lady of the American Theater. Malcolm Lowry wrote *Under the Volcano* in Cuernavaca, and art deco painter Tamara de Lempicka spent her last years there.

There is a part of Cuernavaca known as "Gringo Gulch," where they joke that at sunset the sound of ice cubes in cocktail shakers is deafening. We preferred a quieter vacation. Mexico had a soothing effect on Paul, away from the pressure of clients and negotiations. We were always happy there.

* * *

With an eye to spending more time in Mexico, Paul tried to lighten his workload by merging his agency with that of Michael Levy. But on the contrary, he found himself working even harder, competing with Michael, wanting to show that he still had what it took to be a powerhouse in Hollywood. The Kohner/Levy Agency hired more agents and doubled their office space. Maggie Abbott joined them; she brought in British talent, including Mick Jagger and Twiggy. Michael Marcus joined the agency; he later became president of M-G-M. Frank Wulliger, Pearl Wexler, and Gary Salt joined the agency. Paul became exhausted with the pace of work; it was no longer fun. After three years he dissolved the Kohner/Levy partnership and the business went back to being just the Paul Kohner Agency.

* * *

Over the years many younger agents came to work for Paul, and his influence on their careers was substantial. Richard Kahlenberg came to him from the American Film Institute. Paul Davids started as a reader; his critiques of stories were so good that he became Paul's valued right hand, until he moved on to writing and directing his own films. Bob Stein went on to the William Morris Agency, where he represented our now-governor, Arnold Schwarzenegger. John Burnham became a president of the William Morris Agency. Ron Meyer began his career as a messenger at the Paul Kohner Agency. Since 1997, Ronnie has been the president and chief operating officer of Universal Studios, the studio where Paul began his career.

Frederick, Walter, and Paul Kohner

* * *

Paul's brother, Frederick, wrote serious plays, novels, and screenplays. He also wrote the *Gidget* books that became very successful films and a television series. The character of Gidget was based on his daughter, Kathy Kohner Zuckerman, who learned to surf at Malibu long before girls did that sort of thing. Because she was small, the surfers—boys with names like Moondoggie and The Great Kahuna—gave her the nickname Gidget, from girl-midget.

Frederick collaborated with his brother and sister-in-law on a wonderful book, *Hanna and Walter: A Love Story*. The book spans their teenage years in Teplitz, their separation during the terrible war years, to the happy emotional moment of finding each other again.

Frederick also wrote a biography about Paul. He called it *The Magician of Sunset Boulevard*. Paul's office on Sunset Boulevard, with his name on the front of the building, was a landmark of sorts for the film community. The book is a fond account of Paul's life, and touches on many of the highlights of his career.

63

COURAGE, HARD WORK, AND DESTINY

Paul and I celebrated our golden wedding anniversary in October 1982 with a party at the Bel-Air Hotel. There were toasts by friends we had known for a very long time. John Huston stood and said that on our tenth anniversary his father, Walter Huston, had sung the lovely, bittersweet "September Song." Now, John asked Andy Williams to sing it for us, which he did beautifully.[28] Fifty years of marriage seemed to have flown by. I was now seventy-two and Paul was eighty. It seemed like only yesterday that I'd met the handsome young studio executive.

Susan and Pancho had arranged a surprise for us that evening. Father Kevin Larkin, a Roman Catholic priest, invited us to stand before him and repeat our wedding vows. Now, we had been married by a rabbi *and* a priest. Our different religions had never been an issue with us. Paul would accompany me to Easter services and Midnight Mass at Christmas, and I would go with him to temple on High Holy Days. Love for each other and respect for each other's beliefs was all that it took. Army Archerd, the dean of Hollywood columnists, wrote about our anniversary party in *Variety*:

* * *

Tues., Nov. 2, 1982

Just for Variety
By ARMY ARCHERD

GOOD MORNING: Literature Nobel Prize winner Gabriel Garcia Marquez, tabbed the most popular Spanish-language writer since Cervantes, has consistently nixed pic offers. But he (and his agent) will meet "shortly" with John Huston and Paul Kohner in Mexico City. Marquez's chef d'oeuvres include, of course, "One Hundred Years Of Solitude," well as "The Autumn Of The Patriarch." Kohner and Huston have been huddling here the past few days and will only admit, "Something is in the wind." Huston, who last week got word he'll receive the AFI's Life Achievement Award, winged up from his hideaway down the coast from Puerto Vallarta to join longtime friends of Lupita and Paul Kohner at their 50th wedding anni party at the Bel Air, hosted by Pancho Kohner and sister Susan (K.) Weitz. It was one of the warmest occasions seen in these parts. Paul called it "the last remnants of a bygone era" — but what great "remnants" and what an "era!" Huston claimed "I'm Paul's oldest client — I've been with him 50 years — just like his wife. Forty years ago, my father sang a song at their 10th anniversary party, I'd now like to ask Andy Williams to sing it for you." Williams sang (beautifully) "September Song" and there wasn't a dry eye in the house. Writer Walter Reisch delivered bon mots along with Armando del Moral; brother Frederick Kohner wrote a poem, "Lupita." And Walter Kohner did a "This Is Their Lives" which was nothing short of brilliant, parodying tunes, "Old Man Laemmle," "Bei Mir Bist Du Schoen," "Get Happy," "Oh Mine Papa," "There's No Office Like Their Office," "I Lost My Heart In Cuernavaca" and "Thanks For The Memory" (joined by Pancho's two children) . . . The Kohners, who had been married by a rabbi in Czechslovakia, repeated their vows Saturday before Father Kevin Larkin of Sherman Oaks' St. Francis de Sales . . . Among pals-clients on hand, Max Von Sydow winged in from Toronto filming "Strange Brew." "Tin Drum" director, Volker Schloendorff is prepping a contemporary comedy-drama, "Cafe de la Paix" (as in Peace). Also among those there: Bronsilau Kaper, Rudi Fehr, Milton Gunzbergs, Harold Nebenzals, Billy Wilders, Eric Weissmans, Charles Bronsons, Jerry Perenchio, George Wasson, Gottfried Reinhardt, Robert Lantz and Sarita Tovar.

* * *

Showbiz and politics: Chuck Heston spent yesterday winging from L.A.-San Fran-San Diego pitching for Pete Wilson and other GOP'ers. Despite the thesp's repeated denials of political aspira-

---

28 Walter Huston first sang that song in Kurt Weill's Broadway musical, *Knickerbocker Holiday*, in 1938.

In 1986, after a seventy-six year tour around the heavens, Halley's Comet returned—that meant I was seventy-six years old. I had always kept myself in good physical shape but Paul was a large man and in his later years he did not exercise very much. One morning I tried to help him out of the bathtub; he laughed while I pulled. The result was a hernia and I had to have an operation. Pancho was in Mexico filming, but Susan came from New York to help out.

As we were leaving to go to the hospital, Paul wanted to take a picture of our neighbor's home which had just been sold. He had heard that the new owners were going to demolish the beautiful old colonial house. He was looking through the camera lens and backing up when he fell into a five-foot-deep well surrounding a big sycamore tree. He was very embarrassed. His leg was cut and bleeding so badly that when we got to the hospital we first had to take him to emergency, where they sewed him up with twenty stitches. Then I went in for my hernia operation.

We had planned to visit Pancho in Guadalajara, but this was my fifth operation over the years. My first was the tubal pregnancy in Berlin, when I nearly died. Then there was the Caesarean section when Pancho was delivered, the removal of my appendix, a hysterectomy, and now the hernia. I was forced to accept that I was no longer a "spring chicken," and it took a while before I was up and moving again.

Sarita was in Guadalajara with Pancho, working as continuity and translator for the second unit director, Ernie Orsatti. Ernie is the nephew of Frank Orsatti, who lived on Stone Canyon Road and influenced Paul to become an agent fifty years earlier. They were filming *The Evil That Men Do* with Charles Bronson; J. Lee Thompson was the director. Pancho, J. Lee, and Charlie made eight pictures together, they were good friends, and the atmosphere on their set was very congenial.

In 1988, Paul began having serious health problems. He was still working every day and he never complained, but he suffered from what the doctor called uremic poisoning. His kidneys functioned at only fifteen percent. Earlier, he had a tumor on the side of his neck treated at UCLA with radiation, and he had had several T.I.A.s (ministrokes), from which he had fully recovered.

Harvey Kohner, Paul's loyal assistant for ten years, was with us in Cuernavaca when one of these incidents happened. I immediately called our doctor in Los Angeles and we decided to bring Paul back home. We drove to Mexico City and took the first plane. Paul recovered and there was no sign afterwards that anything had happened.

Then, at age eighty-five, Paul's body simply gave up. We had lunch with Pancho on a Sunday at the Bistro Garden in Beverly Hills, and the next day he was suddenly in trouble. I called our doctor, who came to the house. Paul refused to ride in an ambulance so Pancho drove us to UCLA Hospital, where he was rushed to intensive care; all of his vital organs were shutting down. His kidneys were failing and he was having trouble swallowing.

Susan came from New York, where her husband, John, was still recovering from a lung cancer operation. For several weeks, Paul was alert and could talk to me; then he slipped into a coma that lasted another month. Our family took over the sixth-floor waiting room at the hospital, taking turns being with Paul. Sarita came from Mexico; Nicola Lubitsch was there with us every day and my good friend Ulla Courant came and stayed with me at the house.

The saddest day of my life was March 16, 1988. Paul died that day.

* * *

There were several hundred people at Paul's funeral: old friends like Robert Laemmle and his family; Pat and Walter Mirisch; Eli and Anne Wallach; and Rosa Elena Luján, B. Traven's widow. After the eulogies by Susan, Pancho, and Charles Champlin, we went to the grave-site, a beautiful small garden in the upper part of the cemetery. We had asked Jerry Perenchio, Billy Wilder, Charles Bronson,

Carl Esmond, Rudi Fehr, John Weitz, Jerry Thor, and Harvey Kohner to be the pallbearers. As we waited, eight somber dark-suited men approached carrying the coffin. The first man was a very large Samoan; I didn't recognize him. I looked around to see if there was another funeral nearby. Then I saw Jerry Perenchio walking beside the large Samoan; with his bad back, he had had to substitute his chauffeur in his place.

Jerry has been one of our best and most loyal friends. He is thoughtful and terribly generous; he takes me to lunch and celebrates my birthdays, always arriving with Mariachi musicians. I think Jerry made a promise to Paul that he would always look after me.

When Paul died, many friends said I should move to a smaller house or maybe an apartment. I decided not to move. The house on Stone Canyon holds too many memories for me and the large garden keeps me active all year long. Besides, my children and grandchildren think of this house as their home; it gives them an anchor, a place to come back to. After fifty-six years of marriage to Paul, fifty of them in this house, I wanted to stay here.

Ryan O'Neal, the son of my friend Patricia O'Neal, said, "You're still a very attractive woman, Lupita; you'll be married again in no time." That was lovely of him, but Ryan didn't know me very well. I could never love another man.

Going through old photographs I found an eight-by-ten of Paul with Pancho, who must have been five years old at the time. That would place the date around 1944 when I was in Mexico filming *Miguel Strogoff*.

On the back of the photo Paul had written me a love letter:

Pancho and Paul, 1944

Back side of photo (love letter)

My darling—Here I sit, thinking about you—missing you—and re-thinking again in my mind as so many times before all the many thoughts which somehow when I'm with you never seem to come over my lips. I think them often. What keeps me from expressing them? I don't know and I can't explain it. But in the stillness of this night—and with you very far away I can try at least to tell you some of these things which have moved me silently, inwardly so often before. I love you very much my darling; you have given me such a great deal of happiness in all the years that we've been together. How happy a man must be to find the one human being in the world that from the very first moment of their meeting becomes so much a part of his own self, as you have been. I know there have been times when I have made you unhappy; but what great love you must have for me, always to have forgiven me—and come back to me with more and even greater love. That in those trying times, when I stretched your love to the breaking point you still stood by me—and came back to me, I'll always remember. I love your gentle directness, your lovely soul, your inner strength, your almost unerring judgment of things, right or wrong, your intuitive feeling for good or evil. I love all of it. The happiness you have given me in our sweet little angels Susi and Pancho whose love we will share, I hope for many more years to come I can never repay. Does this give you an inkling of what I want to say? What I feel about you, that you are a wonderful marvelous dear, dear human being. I love you with all my heart—even though my mouth does not have the ability to say all this when I'm with you? This poem, though in German, expresses what I feel. I tried to translate it just now but it didn't work. So here goes:

[What Paul transcribed in German, was Elizabeth Barrett Browning's 43rd poem of her *Sonnets from the Portuguese*.]

> How do I love thee? Let me count the ways.
> I love thee to the depth and breadth and height
> My soul can reach, when feeling out of sight
> For the ends of Being and ideal Grace.
> I love thee to the level of everyday's
> Most quiet need, by sun and candlelight.
> I love thee freely, as men strive for Right;
> I love purely, as they turn from Praise.
> I love thee with a passion put to use
> In my old griefs, and with my childhood's faith.
> I love thee with a love I seemed to lose
> With my lost saints, I love thee with the breath,
> Smiles, tears, of all my life! and, if God choose,
> I shall but love thee better after death.

It's such a long time since I've written you a love letter but in my heart and in my mind, silently, I have often composed many of them. That you must believe me. What made me write this one down, I do not know. But believe that I mean every word.
I kiss you in my dreams!

—Paul.

There will never be another man like him.

Paul, 1928

* * *

It has taken a long time to adjust to living alone, but I am fortunate to have a close family and many friends. I have six grandchildren (including Maggie's children, Emily and David Olsen) and six great-grandchildren. I look forward to many more.

Fate has been good to me. I was plucked from an obscure life in rural Mexico to a life of good fortune and some fame. My acting career included thirty-five movies. I have traveled all over the world with a man who loved me and took wonderful care of me. My nature is to be happy and live life to the fullest; I have never been envious of anyone. My greatest good fortune was meeting and falling in love with Paul. That was our destiny.

AUTHOR'S NOTE:

EULOGY

A eulogy for Paul Kohner was written by Charles Champlin, film critic and arts editor for the *Los Angeles Times,* on March 20, 1988. It reads:

The movies are not much older than Paul Kohner was. They've been through a lot, but compared to sculpture, painting, poetry, and drama they're still in their infancy.

This has meant that we're still in the presence of the men and women who have helped to shape the motion picture and the motion picture business.

Paul was one of those founding fathers of the movies. He was one of those who helped to say whether they would remain a toy and a perishable item of commerce forever, or whether they would qualify as both art and commerce.

No one did more than Paul to assure that American films would reflect the arts and the artists of the world beyond our borders. I've always thought of him as a kind of one-man United Nations or a cultural ambassador. He brought to Hollywood the most gifted actors and actresses and the most thoughtful directors from Europe and Latin America.

But to turn it around, he was also a principal ambassador from Hollywood to the international world of filmmaking.

One of the pleasures of my life was meeting with Paul and Lupita during the Cannes Film Festival when I was attending regularly in the 1970s. Although he was then in his own 70s, Paul's energies and his devotion to the telephone were awesome. In those days the French telephone system demanded the patience of saints. But Paul as always seemed majestically unruffled and keenly interested to hear what films anybody had been excited by in that blizzard of screenings. After a while in Cannes, some of us would begin to look pale and glassy-eyed but Paul – often to Lupi's concerned exasperation – would keep to his stately and ceaseless rounds.

All of you are familiar with Paul's extraordinary life. Many have shared that life far longer and more deeply than I have, and how I envy you.

It's a wonderful, even a cinematic story – stalking Carl Laemmle during his ritual cleansing at the Karlsbad spa and arranging an interview that was really a job-seeking, then arriving in New York at only 18 to begin work in the movie business.

There's a story that Billy Wilder was remembering when we spoke yesterday. Paul and William Wyler, his young pal in the Foreign Publicity Department at Universal (they had arrived from Europe on the same boat), were not grandly paid. And they came up to one weekend, stony broke.

"Let's go to synagogue," Paul said. "It couldn't hurt." They went, and when Paul opened his prayer book, an envelope fell out containing money and a note from his aunt saying, "If you opened this book, you deserve a reward." The money saw them through the weekend and may have left them with a deeper appreciation of the workings of Providence.

Billy also remembered that Paul, who was by then overseeing production in Europe for Universal, had handled the German version of Lewis Milestone's *All Quiet on the Western Front*. The right-wing militarists, the Nazis-to-be, did not like the novel or the book's pacifist message and they disrupted Paul's premiere in Berlin by releasing 300 white mice 10 minutes into the first reel.

Later generations have known Paul specifically as an agent. But the several dozen films he produced before 1938 are significant. They reveal his taste, his versatility, his familiarity with fine literary works in several languages. Above all they reveal his aspiration to see how much the film form could do, and whether there was life after slapstick comedy, chases and exotic romances.

What seems clear to me and I'm sure to many of you is that Paul's optimism about the possibilities of the motion picture was at the heart of his long and unprecedented success as an agent.

From the start he was nothing so simple as a bargainer or a deal-maker, although it is obvious from Frederick Kohner's lively biography, *The Magician of Sunset Boulevard*, and from a lot of collateral evidence that Paul was as wily, tough, and persuasive a salesman as could be found in Hollywood.

The difference was that he saw the agent as a creative catalyst. He had a genius for matching material to the men and women who should be involved with it. He was also, I know, an invaluable Early Warning System against the script that was likely to cause a client more grief than satisfaction.

It may well have been the European heritage that enabled Paul to take the longer view of careers – the long-term development versus the instant gratification and the gimcrack undertakings. He did his own reading – a heretical concept that I understand had not yet swept through Hollywood's power centers.

You don't wonder that directors from abroad, anxious about all the dark legends of Hollywood, sought out Paul to represent them. They knew Paul spoke their artistic language as well, in most cases, as their mother tongue. And of course they were right.

The European Film Fund, which Paul and Ernst Lubitsch formed to help wartime exiles re-establish themselves in Hollywood, is another measure of the man. I understand that the archives of the fund have been presented to the new German Cinematheque in Berlin, and I hope that one day the full story of the fund and Paul's part in it will be preserved in book form.

Thursday morning when Pancho called me with his melancholy news, I tried to remember just when I had first met Paul. But I couldn't. It seems to me that, once met, he was one of those rare and indelible figures you feel that you have known forever.

But I've been remembering lunches at the Cock 'N Bull, now also of blessed memory, to talk about films, naturally, and a dinner with Susan and John and their sons and Ingmar Bergman, and the wonderful nonsensical toasts Paul liked to make at George Rees' wine lunches and dinners. And, of course, I remember the screenings at the Beverly Hills Hotel and elsewhere, films that Paul was representing in every case I can think of because of his admiration for the film and its maker.

I've always thought that if you were fortunate in this life, we become acquainted with men and women who, by the force of their example, change our own lives in ways large and small, subtle and obvious.

They may help us see that there is strength in gentleness, or that it is possible to operate from idealism rather than cynicism, and that following generous and humanistic instincts may well be more rewarding than keeping to a narrow and sour self-interest. They may also remind us that in a life of furious devotion to work there are ways of preserving space for wife and children and grandchildren and the enjoyment of a backyard full of wild strawberries.

Paul Kohner was in all these ways a model: a delightful companion, a charming raconteur, a loyal friend, a man who left his mark on his profession and the art-form he loved.

On this sad day, it is impossible not to feel as well a joyful gratitude for the pleasure and the privilege of Paul's company. On behalf of all of us, I extend great love and sympathy to Irene and Paul's colleagues and most especially to Lupita and the family.

64

FILM FESTIVALS AND A RETURN TO BERLIN

In the summer of 1991, the Mexican Cineteca celebrated *Santa*'s 60th anniversary by re-enacting the first scene of the film in front of television cameras and an audience. It took place in the same village, the Plaza de Chimalistac in San Angel, where we had filmed *Santa* sixty years earlier. I felt so proud that our film was still remembered.

Lupita Tovar and Juan José Martínez Casado in *Santa*

The quaint plaza with its church had somehow been preserved, even though it was now surrounded by the city. A young actress played my part: As she draws water from the well, a handsome cavalry officer rides into the square with his troops. Still on his horse, he asks Santa for a drink of her water. Eager to please, she approaches and lifts her pitcher of water to him. Their eyes meet and the seduction begins. There was a good reason *Santa* captured a large audience. It is a story of seduction and betrayal, of love and death.

* * *

The revival of my *Drácula* film began when David J. Skal interviewed me for his book *Hollywood Gothic*, a history of Dracula films and, in particular, a comparison of Universal's *Dracula* with Bela Lugosi and the Spanish-language *Drácula* in which I starred with Carlos Villarías. In his book, David praised our version and soon after Universal restored the original thirty-five millimeter negative and reissued *Drácula* on video and DVD. That started a steady arrival of fan mail from all over the world and requests to speak at many film festivals.

I was invited to attend the USA Film Festival in Dallas, Texas, in 1991. My grandsons, Paul and Christopher, came from New York; they were twenty-one and twenty-five. The Spanish-language *Drácula* had not been seen in a movie theater in many years. Now, there I was on a huge screen wearing a low-cut, thin nightgown with nipple bumps! I had forgotten how risqué the film was. My grandsons got an eyeful that night. In the English-language *Dracula*, Helen Chandler wore clothes that covered her up to her neck.

A few years later, Paul and Chris reminded me of that sheer nightgown when I watched their film, *American Pie*.

Lupita and Barry Norton in *Drácula*

* * *

In 1992, I was invited to Spain to attend a screening of *Drácula* at El Escorial, an hour north of Madrid. Maruchi Fresno was there; she had acted with me in *Vidas Rotas*, and José Crespo, who had worked in Hollywood in the 1930s.

Pancho accompanied me to Spain but we hurried back because that June, Pancho and Dr. Maggie Olsen were to be married in my garden. Maggie's children, Emily and David, are just a couple of years younger than Melissa and Alex.

That same year Pancho, Maggie, and her daughter Emily went with me to a film festival in Guadalajara, Mexico. *Drácula* was screened and I gave a short speech about the different mores of that time that made *Drácula* such a shocker.

* * *

Next we traveled to the Santa Fe Film Festival in New Mexico, where I was invited to speak before screenings of both *Santa* and *Drácula*.

At all of these film festivals, the commonality is a love of movies. If a celebrity is present, all the better; but it is the films with all the love, hard work, and talent that go into making them that are the stars that will live on for generations of fans to enjoy.

I have been very fortunate to be a part of the movies.

* * *

In September 2000, I was invited to the opening of the Berlin Film Museum, the Stiftung Deutsche Kinemathek. One room of the museum has a permanent exhibit, dedicated solely to the life of my hero and my love, Paul Kohner. Gero Gandert, a representative of the museum, spent a lot of time during the previous years going through Paul's correspondence and the many documents from storage files at the Paul Kohner Agency. Gero chose the most important papers that told Paul's story—his place in the history of the motion picture industry, his part in the history of German filmmakers in exile, and especially Paul's creation of the European Film Fund, which helped so many German refugees in Hollywood. The Paul Kohner Collection comprises a large, catalogued, and well-preserved assemblage of letters, photographs, and documents, available to students and researchers.

Pancho, Maggie, and Maggie's son, David Olsen, traveled with me to Berlin. I spent the first day giving interviews. I've always loved giving interviews. That evening, a group of us, with several German officials from the museum, walked across the Potsdamer Platz to the new steel and glass Sony Building which houses the state-of-the-art Film Museum.

It was evening and the city lights were just coming on. The newly rebuilt Reichstag Building was lit by giant spotlights. Germany's distinctive red, black, and gold flags were flying from its four corners. It was just like 1934. I could not help having mixed feelings about Germany, and Berlin in particular. As we stopped to cross the street at a signal light, David innocently asked Maria Riva, Marlene Dietrich's daughter, what it was like for her coming back to Berlin.

Maria said, loud enough for everyone to hear, "My favorite trip to Berlin was in 1946, when this was all rubble . . ." No one said a word. The light changed and we continued walking.

As we approached the museum, we could see a sea of guests in the open courtyard. Pancho leaned over and said to me, "Mom, I think you're going to have to sing for your supper." So I'd have to give a speech. That didn't bother me; I was used to public speaking.

We sat in the front row with other distinguished guests: Maria Riva with her son, Peter, Nicola Lubitsch and her daughter, Amanda, Monique Blanke, the daughter of Henry Blanke. The lives of Paul Kohner, Marlene Dietrich, Ernst Lubitsch, and Henry Blanke, are all represented in the museum.

The event was televised and Senta Berger, who had been a client of Paul's, was the hostess for the evening. Maria was asked to speak first and she chose to speak in English. Then Nicola spoke, also in English. I was next. The platform was several steps up and it was dark. I was helped to the microphone and there, at the last moment, I decided to speak in German. I never prepare beforehand; I just begin talking and say what is in my heart.

I started by saying that I was ninety years old and I had lived through a lot. I had many good memories of Berlin; after all, this was where I had started my life with the man I loved. Back then, in the 1930s, Berlin had been a very exciting place, with nightclubs and elegant restaurants; that had soon changed with the rise of the Third Reich. I told my audience that Paul and I had gone into exile with many of our friends. But I still had fond memories of our time here. I told stories about my struggles with the language as a young bride and how exciting a time it had been for me, sixty-eight years earlier, when I was just twenty-two. I mentioned the many Berliners Paul and I had known who had not left in time and consequently died.

I'm told that I spoke fluently in German for twenty minutes, but afterwards I could not remember a word of what I had said. I do remember everybody standing up and applauding at the end. Many old friends came up to congratulate me. I had known Horst Buchholz since he first came to Hollywood to act in *The Magnificent Seven*, in 1960. Artur Brauner greeted me; since the war he has produced many pictures at his Berlin CCC Studio; he is still a busy producer. Volker Schlöndorff, the Academy Award–winning director of *The Tin Drum*, is an old friend. He congratulated me and the next day he drove us to his house in Babelsberg to have lunch with his wife, Angelika, and their lovely young daughter. Volker told us that the demarcation line, the wall between East and West Germany, used to run through their back garden.

I hadn't been to Berlin since the wall was built in 1961. At that time there were still empty bombed-out shells of buildings, especially in the eastern sector, where Paul and I had once lived. Now, there was new construction everywhere. Despite the Nazi years of terror and the deaths of so many friends and Paul's family, it felt good to be back in the city where we had started our life together.

Angelika and Volker Schlöndorff, Lupita, and Horst Buchholz

THE GOLDEN ARIEL

In December of 2001, the Academia Mexicana de Artes y Ciencias Cinematográficas, A.C. awarded me a Golden Ariel for my lifetime achievement in cinema. This was the equivalent of receiving an Oscar in Hollywood. The ceremony took place on the stage of the Bellas Artes, the same beautiful opera house that my sister and I passed in a streetcar back when I was sixteen. Back then, I had boldly told her that someday I would dance on that stage. Well, I danced the tango with Pedro Rubín on that stage when I was twenty, while I was filming *Santa*.

Now, I was going to stand on that same stage to accept this great honor. I was ninety-one and I was having trouble with my eyesight. My sister Mary had taken the precaution of having a bottle of oxygen at home in case I felt the effects of Mexico City's high altitude. My sisters and many of their children and grandchildren were there, as well as my grandchildren Melissa, Alex, his lovely wife Ali, and of course, Maggie and Pancho.

At the theater, Pancho and I were taken backstage, where we waited for my cue to go forward to accept the Ariel. At the center of the stage there was a giant revolving platform with a high partition down the center. The front of the partition was a giant movie screen and the audience was viewing clips of my films. All I needed to do was walk to the back of the platform, in the dark, and the platform would revolve to bring me front and center in the spotlights, facing the huge audience. I wanted Pancho to go with me, but he felt I should show my strength by walking out alone. Had he forgotten I was ninety-one? I could hear the master of ceremonies give me a wonderful introduction; then it was time.

Well, the platform malfunctioned. It did not revolve and I had to make my way alone in the dark, stepping over electrical cables to the front of the stage. When I got there and the spotlight found me, the audience rose to their feet. There was tremendous applause. My family was seated in the front row and I knew that many of my old colleagues and friends were there, too. I thought of Paul and how proud he would have been of me. It was a very emotional moment.

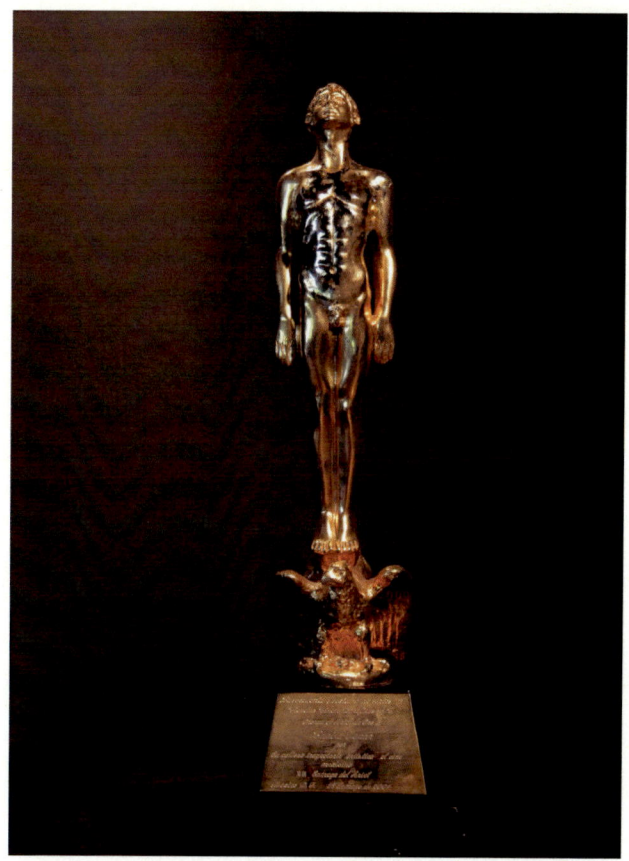

The Golden Ariel. Photo courtesy of Fabricio Espasande

Then I was handed the Ariel statue, which must weigh at least twenty pounds! At the same time, I was given a hand microphone. It took both of my hands just to hold the heavy statue and even if I could have raised the microphone, I was so overcome with emotion that I could hardly speak. I wanted to say how much this moment meant to me, to be honored in Mexico by the industry I had been a part of at its beginning, seventy years earlier. Whether it was my emotion or the weight of the statue—I simply couldn't. All I could say was "Thank you from the bottom of my heart."

The audience responded with thundering applause that went on and on. I had the feeling that this moment was as emotional for everyone in the theater as it was for me.

* * *

Today, many of my friends in Mexico are no longer alive. The list is long. Dolores del Río and her husband, Lou Riley; María Félix, her husband, Jorge Negrete, and even her son, Enrique, who stayed with us on weekends when he was in boarding school in Los Angeles. Pedro Armendáriz and his wife, Carmelita; Pedro had taken his own life with a pistol at the UCLA Hospital, ending a long battle with cancer. He had been in constant pain while acting in his last film, *From Russia with Love*. Mario Moreno "Cantinflas," Mexico's beloved clown who played Passepartout in *Around the World in Eighty Days*. Mario, who was also a pilot, once flew us from Acapulco, where we were staying with Teddy Stauffer, to San Miguel de Allende where we watched Mario fight a *toro bravo* (fighting bull) in the ring. Teddy Stauffer was Swiss; he was a nightclub owner, a bandleader, and had once been married to Hedy Lamarr. Now he owned an exclusive Acapulco resort called Villa Vera with private bungalows and individual swimming pools. Teddy graciously traveled to Chiapas to give a cameo performance in *The Bridge in the Jungle*.

Mario Moreno's producing partner was Jack Gelman; he was Russian. His wife, Natasha, was Czech. They had a spectacular house in Acapulco; in their Mexico City home in the Lomas de Chapultepec, they had an important collection of Mexican art. Alex Phillips, Gabriel Figueroa, and Jorge Stahl, Mexico's great cameramen who had helped create the Golden Age of Mexican cinema in the 1940s and 50s; all had passed away.

Gone also are directors José Bohr, Gilberto Martínez Solares, Chano Urueta, Roberto Gavaldón, and Emilio "El Indio" Fernández, who directed *Enamorata, Flor Silvestre*, and John Steinbeck's *The Black Pearl, La Perla*. Emilio also directed *María Candelaria*, one of Mexico's finest films that combined the talents of cameraman Gabriel Figueroa, with Dolores del Río and Pedro Armendáriz in the lead roles. Producers Gregorio Wallerstein, Mauricio de la Serna, and Francisco (Pancho) Cabrera all left their mark with great films that will live forever.

* * *

In 2005, Larry Ceplair interviewed me at length for the UCLA Oral History Department. I felt privileged to participate in this prestigious program which focuses on the history of Southern California and includes the diverse lives of working-class people, scientists, activists, politicians, musicians, artists, and more. It was Larry who suggested to Ellen Harrington at the Motion Picture Academy that they screen *Santa* for the general membership. The Academy embraced the idea and arranged for the film laboratory in Mexico to create a new print with a restored sound track and, for the first time, English subtitles. My good friend Bob Dickson was asked to talk about the film with me on stage. I have known Bob many years and I felt very safe in his hands. On December 7, 2006, the Academy held a party for me and screened *Santa* at their theater in Beverly Hills. I was overwhelmed. I only wish Paul had been there. He would have loved the acclaim and all the fuss being made over a film we had made seventy-five years earlier.

AUTHOR'S NOTE:

AN EVENING TO REMEMBER

On October 13, 2006, the Academy of Motion Picture Arts and Sciences in Beverly Hills opened an exhibit, "Made in Mexico; the Legacy of Mexican Cinema." The invitation reproduced the 1931 poster for *Santa* with then twenty-one-year-old Lupita Tovar's photo on the cover. The exhibit, which spanned the history of the Mexican film industry, was organized by Ellen Harrington, curator and special events programmer for the Academy, with the help of Alejandra Espasande of the Cervantes Institute.

On opening night, Sid Ganis, the president of the Motion Picture Academy, congratulated Lupita as she was overwhelmed with photographers and television cameras. Lupita has always enjoyed a good relationship with the press and her public, and this night was no exception. For three hours she gave interviews and posed for pictures in front of memorabilia from her film career, and her grandchildren saw their ninety-six-year-old grandma Lupi in a new light.

* * *

December 7, 2006, was another very special evening to remember. The Academy of Motion Picture Arts and Sciences held a "Salute to Lupita Tovar" with a reception for guests in the main lobby of the Academy building in Beverly Hills and then held a screening of a new, subtitled 35mm print of *Santa,* commissioned by the Academy Film Archive in conjunction with the *Filmoteca* of the Universidad Nacional Autónoma de México (UNAM). Pepe Romay, the son of Joselito Rodríguez, the original sound recording engineer of *Santa*, had re-mastered a new sound track.

Bob Dickson (film historian, author, and authority on Mexican cinema) was the moderator for the evening. For several weeks prior, Bob had been offering to go over the evening's schedule and talking points with Lupita. Bob and Lupita have known each other for many years, but Bob was unaware that Lupita did not "prepare." She is a terrific spontaneous speaker, as she had proven in Berlin when at the last moment she was asked to speak before several thousand people at the opening of the Berlin Film Museum.

The evening was a big success. The Academy invited guests and press to a reception. As Lupita entered the large lobby, she was blinded by a barrage of electronic flash strobes and the clatter of cameras clicking. Television cameramen and reporters with microphones pushed forward. The *Los Angeles Times* had printed an interview with Lupita the week before, so the public was very aware of this historic evening when *Santa* would be screened with Lupita Tovar in attendance.

At eight o'clock, in the main theater, Academy members and guests filled the one thousand seats. Ellen Harrington introduced Bob Dickson. Bob then acknowledged the presence of Alejandro Pelayo, the cultural attaché from the Mexican Consulate in Los Angeles, and two of Mexico's most distinguished film historians, Aurelio de los Reyes and Eduardo de la Vega Alfaro, who had come to lecture at the University of Southern California the previous night.

Pepe Romay was thanked for his help in re-mastering the soundtrack and the Film Library of UNAM was acknowledged for their work in restoring this new print of *Santa*.

Onstage, Bob Dickson started with a general overview of the importance of *Santa* to the Mexican film industry and the delight of having its star present to discuss the film on its 75th anniversary. Bob and Lupita talked about the serendipitous development of events that brought her to Hollywood just as silent films were coming to an end, and her chance meeting with Paul Kohner, himself an immigrant, who fell in love with her at first sight. Bob told how Paul convinced Carl Laemmle to film Spanish-language versions of current films in order to keep Lupita from returning to Mexico. Lupita's success in those first movies, filmed at night at Universal Studio, won her the starring role in *Santa*.

When Bob asked her how she felt this evening she answered, "I tell you, it's like a dream... Who could have guessed, seventy-five years ago, that this would happen, that I would be here at this Academy tonight? It's such an honor. I am very grateful, very grateful to all the wonderful people who have helped me through the years."

For this audience of friends and film enthusiasts, the evening was a very big treat. At the conclusion, there was again a standing ovation. As she left the stage, Bob said spontaneously, "What a remarkable lady!"

The following month, as the Academy Awards were seen by over one billion viewers around the world, mention was made of this special evening and Lupita's picture was on their TV screens. Afterwards, our phone rang off the hook.

66

ANOTHER BIRTHDAY!

Susan and Pancho just gave me a marvelous birthday party. There were grandchildren, great-grandchildren, and almost a hundred friends and family members present. Jerry Perenchio came with mariachi players, the best I've ever heard. Chuck and Peggy Champlin came; Father Larkin, who blessed our marriage on our fiftieth anniversary, came to wish me a happy birthday. David Wyler came; he looks just like his father when he rode his motorcycle through our house on Toluca Lake.

* * *

I never imagined I would live so long. I have friends who are coy about their age, but I'm proud to be a survivor. I've always been a fighter and I refuse to let my age slow me down. I continue giving interviews, talking about the wonderful times I've been a part of.

It hasn't always been an easy life. There were lean times, too. I told my daughter-in-law, Maggie, at dinner one evening, "In this business, some years you buy the jewelry, and some years you sell the jewelry." She laughed, but I was serious.

Paul and I were married fifty-six years. I still say goodnight to him before I fall asleep. Paul loved children. He would have been joyfully beside himself with our grandchildren and great-grandchildren.

Pancho and Susan each have two children. My granddaughter, Melissa, has published a book, *Inspired Philanthropy*, and is studying for a Ph.D. in psychology. My grandson, Alex, is a partner in an entertainment law firm. He and his wife, Ali, have twins, Charlotte and Daisy. Susan's sons, Paul and Chris Weitz, are writing and directing films; they have been nominated for an Academy Award for their screenplay, *About a Boy*, which they also co-directed. Paul and his wife, Patricia, have a young daughter, Jane, and baby Maxwell. Chris and Mercedes have a son, Sebastian. Maggie has two children from her first marriage. Her daughter, Emily, is married to Jonathan Hunt, a vice-president at Goldman Sachs in New York, where Emily is a first-grade teacher; their daughter is named Riley Elizabeth. Maggie's son, David, is a lawyer and also has a successful business on the Internet. He is married to lovely Michelle and their daughter is named Sophia Rose. We also have a special relationship with Katrina Holden, whom I consider one of my grandchildren. Katrina was just twelve when her mother, Hilary Holden, died; leaving a letter asking Pancho to be Katrina's guardian in just such an event. Katrina grew up in Jill and Charles Bronson's large household along with their children, but she and her son, Charlie, are part of our family, too.

* * *

Pancho once asked me how, in an era when love rarely lasts *forever*, my marriage withstood the test of time. I told him, "Ours was not just a grand adventure across cultures and continents, we lived for each other, and we had a very happy life together. Your father was a very romantic man, and I loved him very much."

* * *

I have a loving family and wonderful memories of my life with Paul. I have been to China. I have ridden a camel in Egypt and lit a cigarette by touching it to flowing lava at the Paricutin Volcano in Mexico. I have had an amazing life. My niece, María Esther, says that I am an "Adelita" (a woman soldier of the Mexican Revolution), a symbol of the emancipation of subservient Mexican women, a pioneer. I was pleased and very proud to hear that. It's funny; my family in Mexico bakes American-style lemon pies, a legacy from our grandmother, Lucy Sullivan. And my favorite foods here in California are chilaquiles, arroz con pollo, frijoles, and platanos fritos; foods I remember from my childhood in Oaxaca.

Recently, Matt Beckoff interviewed me for a book he is writing. Referring to the continuing popularity of *Drácula*, he asked me what I thought of being a cult figure among horror genre aficionados. I said, "I'm surprised. I still get fan mail from all over the world. Don't they realize that I am almost a hundred years old?"

Matt said, "Well, Dracula bit your neck—you're going to live forever."

I am fiercely proud of my Mexican heritage, but I also love my adopted country. I got my first immigration green card in 1928 when I was just eighteen. One of my most thrilling patriotic experiences was having dinner at the White House with President Jimmy Carter. I hope my children and grandchildren and great-grandchildren appreciate what a wonderful country they live in. When we get together for a birthday or holiday, the youth and energy that flows from my family makes me feel young again. Then I know I'm ready for anything that comes my way.

Yesterday, Pancho mentioned that a friend of his is starting a picture in two weeks. Of course, I asked, "Is there a part in it for me?"

LUPITA TOVAR FILMOGRAPHY

The Veiled Woman, 1929   Fox Film Corporation
    Presenter: William Fox
    Director: Emmett Flynn
    Story: Julio De Moreas and Lia Torá
    Writer: Douglas Z. Doty
    Cast: Lia Torá, Paul Vincent, Walter McGrail, Kenneth Thompson, André Cheron, Ivan Lebedeff, Maude George, Lupita Tovar

The Black Watch, 1929 (aka King of the Khyber Rifles, UK) Fox Film Corporation
    Producer: Winfield R. Sheehan
    Director: John Ford
    Story: Talbot Mundy
    Writers   James Kevin McGuinness and John Stone
    Cast: Victor McLaglen, Myrna Loy, David Rollins, Lumsden Hare, Roy D'Arcy, Mitchell Lewis, Cyril Chadwick, Claude King, Francis Ford, Walter Long, David Torrence, Frederick Sullivan, Richard Travers, Pat Somerset, David Percy, Joseph Diskay, Joyzelle Joyner, Lupita Tovar (uncredited)

Joy Street, 1929   Fox Film Corporation
    Presenter: William Fox
    Director: Raymond Cannon
    Story: Raymond Cannon
    Writers   Charles Condon and Frank Gay
    Cast: Lois Moran, Nick Stuart, Rex Bell, Sally Phipps, Lupita Tovar, Maria Alba

The Cock-Eyed World, 1929 Fox Film Corporation 118 minutes
    Presenter: William Fox
    Director: Raoul Walsh
    Story: Maxwell Anderson, Tom Barry, Wilson Mizner, and Laurence Stallings
    Writers: Raoul Walsh and William K. Wells
    Cast: Victor McLaglen, Edmund Lowe, Lili Damita, Leila Kennedy, El Brendel, Bib Burns, Jeanette Dagna, Joe Brown, Stuart Irwin, Ivan Linow, Jean Laverty, Soledad Jimenez, Curley Dresden, Joe Rochay, Lupita Tovar

La Voluntad del Muerto, 1930 (aka The Cat and the Canary) Universal Pictures
    Presenter: Carl Laemmle

Producer:	Paul Kohner
Director:	George Melford
Writers:	John Willard (play)
	Gladys Lehman
	Baltasar Fernández Cué
Cast:	Antonio Moreno, Lupita Tovar, Andrés de Segurola, Roberto Guzmán, Paul Ellis, Lucio Villegas, Agostino Borgato, Conchita Ballesteros, Maria Calvo, Soledad Jiménez

Sólo un Sueño, 1930 (short) Universal Pictures
- Cast: Lupita Tovar and Romualdo Tirado

Caprichos de Hollywood, 1930 (short) Universal Pictures
- Director: Kurt Neumann
- Cast: Lupita Tovar and Martín Garralaga

El Rey del Jazz, 1930 Universal Pictures
- Directors: John Murray and Kurt Neumann
- Cast: Lupita Tovar

Drácula, 1931 Universal Pictures 104 minutes
- Presenter: Carl Laemmle
- Producer: Paul Kohner
- Director: George Melford
- Writers: Bram Stoker (novel)
  - Baltasar Fernández Cué
- Cast: Carlos Villarias, Lupita Tovar, Barry Norton, Pablo Álvarez, Rubio, Eduardo Arozamena, José Sonano Viosca, Carmen Guerrero, Amelia Senisterra, Manuel Arbó

Yankee Don, 1931 Universal Pictures
- Director: Noel M. Mason
- Producer: Richard Talmadge
- Writer: Madeline Allen
- Cast: Richard Talmadge, Lupita Tovar, Julian Rivero, Sam Appel, Gayne Whitman, Alma Real, Victor Metzetti

East of Borneo, 1931 Universal Pictures 77 min
- Director: George Melford
- Story: Dale Van Every
- Writer: Edwin H. Knopf
- Producers: Paul Kohner, Carl Laemmle Junior, George Melford

    Cast: Rose Hobart, Charles Bickford, George Renavent, Lupita Tovar, Noble Johnson

Border Law, 1931   Columbia Pictures
- Director: Louis King
- Cast: Buck Jones, Frank Rice, Lupita Tovar, Jim Mason, Don Chapman

El Tenorio del Harem, 1931   Universal Pictures
- Director: Kurt Neumann
- Producers: Stanley Bergerman, Paul Kohner
- Writers: Gabriel Argüelles, Francis Martin
- Cast: Slim Summerville, Tom Kennedy, Lupita Tovar, Eduardo Arozamena, José Peña, Manuel Arbó

Carne de Cabaret, 1931   Columbia Pictures Corporation 88 min
- Directors: Eduardo Arozamena and W. Christy Cabanne
- Producers: Juan de la Cruz Alarcón
- Story: Jo Swerling
- Writer: René Borgia
- Cast: Lupita Tovar, Ramón Pereda, René Cardona, Carmen Guerrero, Soledad Jiménez, Aurora del Real, Maria Calvo, Nancy Torres, Ralph Novarro, Juan Duval, Felipe de Flores, May O'Keefe, Rodolfo Hoyos

Estamos en París, 1931 (short) Universal Pictures 20 min
- Director: Kurt Neumann
- Writers: Francis Martin and James Mulhauser
- Cast: Slim Summerville, Harry Gribbon, Lupita Tovar

Santa, 1931   Compañía National Productora de Peliculas 81 min
- Director: Antonio Moreno
- Story: Federico Gamboa
- Writer: Carlos Noriega Hope
- Music: Agustin Lara
- Cinematographer: Alex Phillips
- Cast: Lupita Tovar, Carlos Orellana, Juan José Martinez Casado, Donald Reed, Antonio R. Frausto, Mimi Derba, Rosita Arriaga, Joaquin Busquets, Feliciano Rueda, Jorge Peón, Alberto Martí, Ricardo Carti, Sofia Álvarez, Rosa Castro, Nena Betancourt, Jorge Marrón, Carlos Bocanegra, Fernando Rivero, Lupita Gallardo, Ismael Rodríguez, Raúl de Anda, Parkey Hussian, Cube Bonifant

The Invader, 1933 (An Old Spanish Custom) British and Continental – M-G-M 61 min
    Director: Adrian Brunel
    Producer: Sam Spiegel
    Writer: Edwin Greenfield
    Cast: Buster Keaton, Lupita Tovar, Lyn Harding, Esme Percy, H. Malandrinos, Clifford Heatherley, Hilda Moreno, Webster Booth

Vidas Rotas, 1933   Inca Film
    Director: Eusebio Fernández Ardavín
    Producers: Géza Pollatschik and Erich Darmstaedter
    Story: Concha Espina
    Writer: Wenceslao de Francisco
    Cast: Lupita Tovar, Maruchi Fresno, Cándida Losada, Fernando de Cordoba, Pepe Isbert, Enrique Zabala, Paco Álvarez, María Amaya, Manuel Arbó, Arturo Girelli, Manuel Paris, Luisa Sala, Dolores Valera

Alas Sobre el Chaco, 1935   Universal Pictures
    Director: W. Christy Cabanne
    Producers: Paul Kohner and Maurice Pivar
    Story: W. Christy Cabanne and Elliot Gibbons
    Writers: René Borgia, Alberto DeMond, Frank Wead, and Eva Greene
    Cast: José Crespo, Lupita Tovar, Antonio Moreno, Romualdo Tirado, Julio Peña, Barry Norton, Juanita Garfias, Juan Torena, José Rubio, Luis Diaz Flores, Francisco Moreno, George J. Lewis, José A. Caraballo, Lucio Villegas, Hans Heinrich von Twardowski, Alma Real

El Capitán Tormenta, 1936   Metropolitan Pictures 75 min
    Director: John Reinhardt
    Producers: George A. Hirliman and Louis Rantz
    Story: Gordon Ray Young
    Writers: José Luis Tortosa and Crane Wilbur
    Cast: Fortunio Bonanova, Lupita Tovar, Juan Torena, Movita, Romualdo Tirado, José Luis Tortosa, Roy D'Arcy, George J. Lewis, Barry Norton, Francisco Moreno, Agostino Borgato, José Peña, Alberto Gandero

Marihuana, 1936 (aka El Monstruo Verde) 90 min
- Director: José Bohr
- Producer: Duquesa Olga
- Writer: José Bohr
- Cast: José Bohr, Lupita Tovar, Barry Norton, Angel T. Sala, Alberto Marti, Sara Garcia, Emilio Fernandez, Manuel Noriega, Carmelita Bohr, Arturo Manrique, Virginia Ramsey, Carlos Baz, Pilar Fernández, Consuelo Segarra, Roberto Cantú Roberto, Guillermo Cantú Roberto, Clifford Carr, Max Langler

El Rosario de Amozoc, 1936
- Director: José Bohr
- Producer: Vicente Saisó Piquer
- Writers: José Elizondo, Pepe Nava, Arturo Ávila Gandolín, and Ramón Perez Diaz
- Cast: Lupita Tovar, Emilio Tuero, Carlos Orellana, Alpiste, Daniel Arroyo, Paco Astol, Arturo Ávila Gandolín, Carolina Barret, Manuel Buendia, Juana Campo, Clifford Carr, Enrique Carillo, Ernesto Cortázar, Juaquin Coss, Elena D'Orgaz Eufrosina Garcia, Leonor Gómez, Raul Guerrero, Daniel 'Chino' Herrera, Agustin Isunza, Félix Medel, Alicia Reyna, Consuelo Segarra, Victor Velázquez

María, 1938   PIPSA 83 min
- Director: Chano Urueta
- Producer: Miguel León R.
- Story: Jorge Isaacs
- Writers: José Lopez Rubio and Chano Urueta
- Cast: Lupita Tovar, Rodolfo Landa, Miguel Arenas, Josefina Escobedo, Mimi Derba, Gonzalo D. Luque, Eduardo Aroamena, Maritza Nieto, Linda del Moral, Ricardo Mondragón, Dolores Camarillo, Arturo Turich, Paco Martínez, Celia Ortiz, Luis López Somoza, Maria Teresa, Mondragón, René, Estela, Juan José Laboriel

Blockade, 1938   United Artists
- Director: William Deterlie
- Producer: Walter Wanger
- Writers: James M. Cain and John Howard
- Cast: Madeleine Carroll, Henry Fonda, Leo Carrillo, John Halliday, Vladimir Sokoloff, Robert Warwick, Reginald Denny, Peter Godfrey, William B. Davidson, Katherine DeMille, Fred Kohler, Carlos De Valdez, Nick Thompson, George Houston, Rosina Galli, Lupita Tovar

Tropic Fury, 1939   Universal Pictures 62 min
- Director: W. Christy Cabanne
- Story: Maurice Tombragel and Ben Pivar
- Writer: Michael L. Simmons
- Producer: Ben Pivar
- Cast: Richard Arien, Andy Devine, Beverly Roberts, Lupita Tovar, Samuel S. Hinds, Charles Trowbridge, Leonard Mudie, Adie Kuznetzoff, Nobel Johnson, Frank Mitchell, Milburn Stone

The Fighting Gringo, 1939   RKO Radio Pictures 59 min
- Director: David Howard
- Producer: Bert Gilroy
- Cast: George O'Brien, Lupita Tovar, Lucio Villagas, William Royle, Glenn Strange, Slim Whitaker, LeRoy Mason, Mary Field, Martin Garralaga, Dick Botiller, Bill Cody, Cactus Mack, Chris-Pin Martin

South of the Border, 1939   Republic Pictures 70 min
- Director: George Sherman
- Producer: William Berke
- Story: Dorrell McGowan and Stuart E. McGowen
- Writers: Betty Burbridge and Gerald Geraghty
- Cast: Gene Autry, Smiley Burnette, June Storey, Lupita Tovar, Mary Lee, Duncan Renaldo, Frank Reicher, Alan Edwards, Claire Du Brey, Dick Botiller, William Farnum, Selmer Jackson

Green Hell, 1940   Universal Pictures
- Director: James Whale
- Producer: Harry E. Edington
- Writers: Frances Marion and Harry Hervey
- Cast: Douglas Fairbanks, Jr., Joan Bennett, John Howard, George Sanders, Alan Hale, George Bancroft, Vincent Price, Eugene Gericke, Francis McDonald, Mala, Peter Bronte, Lupita Tovar

The Westerner, 1940   The Samuel Goldwyn Company
- Director: William Wyler
- Producer: Samuel Goldwyn
- Story: Stuart N. Lake
- Writers: Niven Busch and Jo Swerling
- Cast: Gary Cooper, Walter Brennan, Doris Davenport, Fred Stone, Forrest Tucker, Paul Hurst, Chill Wills, Lilian Bond, Dana Andrews, Charles Halton, Trevor Bardette, Tom Tyler, Lucien Littlefield, Lupita Tovar (uncredited)

Recordar es Vivir, 1940   Documentary Short POSA FILMS
    Director: Fernando A. Rivero
    Cast: Cantinflas, Sara Garcia, Lupita Tovar, Lupe Velez

Two-Gun Sheriff, 1941   Republic Pictures 56 min
    Director: George Sherman
    Producer: George Sherman
    Story: Bennett Cohen
    Writer: Doris Schroeder
    Cast: Don "Red" Barry, Lynn Merrick, Jay Novello, Lupita Tovar, Milton Kibbee, Fred Kohler, Jr., Marin Saïs, Fred "Snowflake" Toones, Dirk Thane, Arch Hall, Sr., Charles Thomas, Lee Shumway

Resurrección, 1943   CLASA FILMS MUNDIALES
    Director: Gilberto Martínez Solares
    Producer: Mauricio de la Serna
    Story: Leo Tolstoy
    Writers: Gilbert Martínez Solares, Eduardo Ugarte, Rodolfo Usigli
    Cast: Sara Garcia, Lupita Tovar, Julio Ahuet, Victoria Argota, Rafael Banuells, Alejandro Cobo, Lupe de Castillo, Elena D'Orgaz, Edmundo Espino, Eugenia Galindo, Enrique García Álvarez, Rosario García, Cinsuelo Guerrero de Luna, Carmen Montejo, Amparo Morillo, José Pulido, Arturo Soto Rangel, José Torvay

Miguel Strogoff, 1944   CIMESA
    Director: Miguel M. Delgado
    Producer: Joseph N. Ermolieff
    Story: Jules Verne
    Writers: Joseph N. Ermolieff and Mauricio Magdaleno
    Cast: Julian Soler, Lupita Tovar, Julio Villarreal, Anita Blanch, Andrés Soler, Luis G. Barreiro, Francisco Jambrina, Victoria Argota, Salvador Quiroz, Manuel Dondé

Gun to Gun, 1944   Warner Bros. Pictures 20 min
    Director: D. Ross Lederman
    Producer: Gordon Hollingshead
    Story: Lanier Bartlett and Virginia Stivers Bartlett
    Writer: Ed Earl Repp
    Cast: Robert Shayne, Lupita Tovar, Pedro de Cordoba, Harry Woods, Tom Tyler, Anita Camargo, Roy Bucko, Julian Rivero

Crime Doctor's Courage, 1945 Columbia Pictures 70 min
    Director: George Sherman
    Producer: Rudolph C. Flowthow
    Story: Eric Taylor
    Writer: Max Marcin
    Cast: Warner Baxter, Hillary Brooke, Jerome Cowan, Mark Roberts, Lloyd Corrigan, Emory Parnell, Stephen Crane, Charles Arnt, Anthony Caruso, Lupita Tovar

INDEX

A

Academy of Motion Picture Arts and Sciences. 29, 53, 117, 171, 191, 200, 208, 223, 229, 231, 232, 241, 269, 272, 275, 276, 279
A House Divided, 94
Abbot, Maggie, 254
Anderson, Maxwell, 6
Agrasánchez, Rogelio, Jr. 10, 107
Aguglia, Mimí, 109
Alarcón, Juan de la Cruz, 12, 42, 57, 58, 60, 61, 63, 71, 72, 77, 78, 81, 87, 207
Alba, María, 30, 91
Alcañiz, Luana, 87
Alemán, President Miguel, 200, 217, 218
Alemán, Miguel, Jr., 217, 218
All Quiet on the Western Front, 53, 264
Alpar, Gitta, 134
Álvarez Rubio, Pablo, 65
Álvarez, Sofía, 87
An Old Spanish Custom, 135
Andergast, Maria, 143
Anderson, Marian, 159, 160
Andersson, Bibi, 241
Andersson, Harriet, 241
Annikin, Ken, 121
Arbó, Manuel, 65, 90
Archerd, Army, 257
Arenas, Miguel, 171
Argota, Victoria,191
Ariel, Golden, 271
Aristi, Jesús Inaraja, 159, 211, 253
Arlen, Richard, 179
Arliss, George, 53
Armendáriz, Pedro, Jr., 81
Armendáriz, Pedro, 154,172
Arno, Sig, 68
Arozamena, Eduardo, 65,71,90
Arp, Jean, 125
Arriaga, Guillermo, 291
Arriage, Rosita, 285
Arruza, Carlos, 197
Ascárate, General Juan, 191

Astor, Mary, 27, 154
Auer, John, 42, 43, 47, 51, 152
Auerbach, Norbert, Dasha, Helga, 151
Auerbach, Olga & Josef, 115, 116
Autry, Gene, 179, 185, 191
Avalos, Enrique Tovar, 50, 65
Ayres, Agnes, 21

B

Bader, Dave, 109
Bhabi, Alex, 166
Baker, Josephine, 125
Baker, Mel, 162
Ballesteros, Conchita, 187, 284
Barker, Lex, 231
Barrymore, Lionel, 71
Basserman, Albert, 168, 180
Baum, Vicky, 167
Baxter, Warner, 192, 290
Béamt, Caroline, 110, 111, 147, 169, 183
Beckoff, Matt, 280
Bell, Alfonso, 162
Benjamin, Carl, 170
Bennett, Joan, 231, 288
Bergendahl, Erling, 161, 162
Berger, Senta, 269
Bergman, Ingmar, 241, 242, 243, 250, 265
Bergman, Ingrid, 232
Bernhardt, Curtis, 144, 167
Berkovici, Eric, 165
Berkovici, Konrad, 165
Berkovici, Leonardo, 165
Bickford, Charles, 75, 157, 285
Black Watch, The, 31, 283
Blanch, Anita, 191, 289
Blanke, Henry, and Ursula, 94, 107, 167, 269
Blanke, Monique, 269
Bloch, Gottfried, 195, 235
Blockade, 171, 223, 287
Bloomberg, Colonel von, 146
Blue Angel, The, 116, 121, 125
Bohr, Carmelita, 154, 287

Bohr, José, 154, 171, 272, 287
Bolaños, Aicia, 81
Booth, Webster, 136, 286
Borden, Olive, 27
Border Law, 70, 71, 285
Boyd, Stephen, 121
Boyer, Charles, 144, 229, 232
Bradley, Mary, 162
Brady, Robert, 254
Brauner, Maria and Artur, 228, 269
Brecht, Bertolt, 125, 129, 167
Brent, George, 154
Bridge in the Jungle, The, 181, 210, 214, 218, 249, 272
Bronson, Charles, 236, 241, 246, 258, 279
Bronson, Jill Ireland, 279
Bronston, Samuel, 236, 249
Brook, Clive, 91
Brooke, Hillary, 192, 290
Browning, Tod, 65, 70
Bru, Miriam, 228
Brunel, Adrian, 135, 136, 286
Brynner, Yul, 246
Bryson, Mary, 254
Buchholz, Horst, 228, 229, 246, 269
Burnette, Smiley,179, 288
Burnham, John, 255
Burton, Richard, 235

C

Cabanne, W. Christy, 71, 153, 179, 288
Cabinet of Dr. Caligari, The, 116
Cabrera, (Pancho) Francisco, 81, 137, 159, 179, 213, 272
Cabrera, Hazel King, 9, 13, 24
Calderón, Rafael, 87
Calles, President Plutarco Elias, 17, 18, 217
Camacho, President Manuel Ávila, 200, 217
Canibe, Manolo, 253
Cansino, Eduardo, 28, 153, 213, 253
Cansino, Marguerita Carmen, 28
Cansino, Volga, 32, 41, 42
"Cantinflas", Mario Moreno, 189, 272
Caprichos de Hollywood, 71, 284
Cárdenas, President Lázaro, 17, 18, 174, 177, 178, 183, 201
Cardona, René, 71, 154, 285
Carne de Cabaret, 71, 73, 94, 285

Carol, Sue, 29
Caron, Leslie, 229
Carranza, Venustiano, 8
Carroll, Madeleine, 171, 287
Casablanca, 186, 187
Casado, José Martínez, 78, 267, 285
Cat Creeps, The, 46, 45, 49, 69
Cedillo, General Saturnino, 33, 74, 157, 158, 159, 160, 171, 174, 175, 177, 178
Ceplair, Larry, 272
Cereijo, Maestro, 82
Champlin, Charles, 258, 263, 279
Chandler, Helen, 65, 66, 134, 267
Chapman, Don, 71, 285
Chevalier, Maurice, 226, 229, 230
Chafino, Mrs., 19
Chimalistac, San Angel, 77, 81, 267
Churchill, Marguerite O'Brien, 27
Churchill, Winston, 185
Cinemateca de Cuba, 69
Circus World, 249
Clasa Films, 189, 289
Clift, Montgomery, 232
Cock-Eyed World, The, 31, 94, 283
Cohen, Mark, 235, 246
Cohen, Mickey, 231
Cohn, Harry, 95, 96
Colbert, Claudette, 232
Colman, Ronald, 91, 107
Canseco family, 5
Cooper, Gary, 185, 228
Corman, Roger, 241, 250
Covarrubias, Miguel, 201
Cowan, Jerome, 192, 290
Crespo, José, 87, 153, 154, 268, 286
Crime Doctor's Courage, The, 192, 290
Croves, Hal, 209, 214
Cuando La Vida Florece, 154, 155
Curtiz, Michael, 186

D

D'Orgaz, Elena, 287
Damita, Lili, 31, 94, 283
Dantine, Helmut, 186
Darmstetter, Eddie, 137
Darrieux, Danielle, 144
Davenport, Doris, 185, 288
Davids, Paul, 255

De Anda, Raúl, 87, 285
De Cordoba, Pedro, 191, 286, 289
De la Serna, Mauricio, 189, 191, 213, 272, 289
De Laurentiis, Dino, 241
Dee, Sandra, 232
Deitrich, Marlene, 116, 125, 268, 269
Del Moral, Armando, 236, 237
Del Rio, Dolores, 160, 199, 213, 272
Delahaye, Herbert (Tío Baby), 3, 30, 134
Delgado, Miguel M., 191 289
DeMille, Cecil B., 116
Dennis, Sandy, 250
Der verloren Sohn, 143
Derba, Mimí, 78, 285, 287
Deutsche Kinemathek, 168, 268
Devine, Andy, 179, 288
Deyers, Lien, 132, 165
Diaz, Felix, 7, 8
Diaz, Porfirio, 7, 210
Dickson, Bob, 272, 275, 276
Diessl, Gustave, 121
Dieterle, William, 144, 160, 167, 171, 179, 180, 227
Dieterle, Charlotte, 167, 179
Dietrich, Marlene, 116, 125, 268, 269
Disraeli, 53
Divorcee, The, 53
Döblin, Alfred, 125, 136, 167
Don Juan Tenorio, 229
Doomed Battalion, The, 66, 135, 141
Drácula, 63, 65, 66, 67, 68, 69, 70, 77, 134, 267, 268, 280
Durbin, Deanna, 165

E

East of Borneo, 75, 76, 284
East of Java, 257
Eastwood, Clint, 236
Echeverría Landa, Rudolfo, 218
Echeverría Álvarez, Luis, 87, 218
Ecstasy, 96, 100, 115, 116
Edwards, Ralph, 196
Eggerth, Mártha, 134
Eichberg, Richard, 149
El Capitán Tormenta, 154, 286
El Choclo, 83
El Rosario de Amozoc, 171 ,287
El Tenorio del Harem, 71, 90, 285

Ellis, Paul, 49, 51, 87, 284
Epstein, Julius J., 186
Erickson, C.O. "Doc", 282, 236
Ernst, Max, 126
Escalante, Esteban V., 87
Escobedo, Josefina, 174, 287
Esmond, Carl, 168, 259
Espina, Concha, 137, 286
Estamos en Paris, 89, 285
European Film Fund, 166, 167, 180, 183, 264, 268

F

Fábrigas, Virginia, 65
Fairbanks, Douglas, Jr., 288
Fairbanks, Douglas, Sr., 91, 288
Fanck, Dr. Arnold, 107, 121
Farrell, Charles, 27
Fehr, Rudi, 120, 144, 259
Félix, María, 85, 272
Fellini, Federico, 241
Fernández Cué, Baltazar, 49, 284
Fernández, Esther, 85, 160
Fernández, Emilio, 81, 213, 272, 287
Fife, Jack, 186
Fighting Gringo, The, 171, 172, 288
Figueroa, Carmen Lopez, 21
Figueroa, Gabriel, 207, 277
Fisher, Heinrich, 110
Flaherty, Robert, 19, 20, 21, 25, 26, 28, 29, 30, 81, 135
Flynn, Emmet, 31, 283
Fonda, Henry, 157, 171, 287
Foolish Wives, 35, 37
Ford, John, 31, 283
Forest, Carl, 186
Forst, Emil, 99
Forst, Willi, 134
Fouce, Frank and Anita, 71, 86, 87, 94, 96
Franco, Francisco, 236
Frank, Leonhard, 167
Fresno, Maruchi, 137, 268, 286
Friede, Lita, 99, 100, 101, 107
Freud, Sigmund, 129, 232, 253
Freulich, Jack, 47, 49, 63, 73, 74, 75, 89, 99
Fröhlich, Gustav, 134
Fry, Mrs. Gertrude, 45. 49. 63. 73. 75, 89, 99

G

Gable, Clark, 186
Galindo, Alejandro, 206
Galindo, Eugenio, 289
Galindo, Marco Aurelio, 206
Gamboa, Federico, 77, 85, 285
Gandert, Gero, 268
Ganis, Sid, 275
Garbo, Greta, 66, 93, 232
Garcia, Sara, 189, 287
Garden, Tilla, 149
Garland, Judy, 186
Garson, Greer, 186
Gavaldón, Roberto, 272
Gavin, John, 232, 254
Gaynor, Janet, 27, 53
Gelman, Jacques, 272
Gide, André, 129
"Gidget" Kathy Kohner Zuckerman, 255
Goebbels, Joseph, 126, 128, 129, 131, 143
Gonzalez, Fernando, 253
Gonzalez, Maria Esther, 280
Grandma Lucy, Slocum Sullivan, 1, 2, 3, 5, 11, 12, 13, 20, 23, 24, 25, 26, 27, 28, 30, 31, 32, 41, 42, 43, 44, 45, 46, 50, 51, 53, 54, 57, 60, 61, 67, 71, 73, 77, 89 92, 94 95, 96, 99 112, 119, 159 169, 191, 221, 223
Granach, Alexander, 168
Grant, Cary, 186, 246
Grede, Kjell, 241
Greenberg, Julie Kohner, 232
Greenfield, Edwin, 135, 286
Guerrero, Carmen, 284
Guggenheim, Peggy, 126
Gumbert, Josephine, 166
Gun to Gun, 191, 289

H

Hakim, Raymond and Robert, 200
Hamsun, Knut, 161, 162
Harding, Lyn, 136, 286
Harrington, Ellen, 272, 275
Hayes, Helen, 254
Hays Office, 69
Hayward, Leyland, 157
Hayworth, Rita, 28, 213
Heatherly, Clifford, 136, 286
Hemingway, Ernest, 129
Henreid, Paul, 191, 192, 225
Hepburn, Audrey, 229
Heston, Charlton, 121
Heyman, Irene, 235, 265
Himmler, Heinrich, 195
Hitler, Adolf, 116, 119, 125, 126, 128, 129, 130, 131, 132, 143, 144, 147, 149, 150, 166, 170, 183, 227, 251
Hobart, Rose, 75, 285
Holden, Katrina, 279
Hollywood Gothic, 267
Hope, Carlos Noriega, 58, 77, 285
Howard, David, 171, 288
Huerta, General Victoriana, 7, 8
Hunter, Jeffrey, 196
Hunter, Ross, 231
Huston, John, 95, 160, 163, 165, 166, 197, 201, 205, 209, 210, 211, 214, 232, 250, 257
Huston, Walter, 72, 155, 163, 165, 210, 250, 257

I

I am an Incurable European – Letters from Exile, 168
Ibáñez, Mrs., 77
Inaraja, Christina de Caballero,
Inaraja, Isabel de Canibe,
Invader, The, 135, 136, 137, 286
Isaac, Jorge, 171, 287

J

Jannings, Emil, 116, 125
Jaray, Hans, 134
Joe Schenck, 197
Johann, Zita, 96
Johnson, Leroy, 47, 54
Jones, Allan, 236
Jones, Buck, 71, 89, 285
Josephson, Erland, 241
Joy Street, 28, 283
Juan Silveti, 197
Juarez, Benito, 7, 160
Julian, Rupert, 49, 50
Julissa, 85

K

Kahlenberg, Richard, 255
Kahlo, Frida, 199, 200, 201
Kandinsky, Wassily, 125
Keaton, Buster, 135, 136, 286
Keller, Fred and Margo, 113
Kennedy, Tom, 71, 90, 285
Kiepura, Jan, 134
King of Jazz, The, 89
King of the Khyber Rifles, The, 30, 31, 283
Klee, Paul, 126
Klimt, Gustav, 125
Knopf, Edwin H., 101, 121, 284
Kohler, Fred, Jr., 185, 287, 289
Kohner Alexander Paul, 250, 268, 271, 279
Kohner, Frederick, 33, 108, 133, 255
Kohner, Hanna Bloch, 169, 195, 221, 235
Kohner Harvey, 258
Kohner, Helene, 33, 110, 147, 169, 221, 222
Kohner, Julius, 33, 34, 109, 110, 113, 117, 128, 14, 147
Kohner, Melissa Sullivan, 250, 268, 271, 279
Kohner, Paul, 31, 32, 35, 36, 37, 38, 41, 42, 43, 44, 45, 46, 47, 49, 50 and throughout the book
Kohner, Ruthie, 108, 163
Kohner, Walter, 33, 108, 169, 186, 195, 232, 235, 255
Kortner, Frederick, 168
Koster, Henry, 144, 167
Kraly, Hans, 90

L

La Paloma, 107
La Plant, Laura, 71
La Roque, Rod, 121, 122
Laemmle, Carl, 33, 34, 35, 36, 42, 45, 46, 47, 50, 58, 60, 63, 96, 100, 108, 119, 122, 144, 157, 162, 186, 263, 276, 283, 284
Laemmle, Carl, Jr., 91, 153, 284
Laemmle, Ernst, 42, 47, 50, 94, 95, 96, 163, 164, 176
Laemmle, Gregory, 150
Laemmle, Max, 122, 143, 150,
Laemmle, Nina, 163, 164, 232
Laemmle, Robert, 150
Laemmle, Rosabelle, 33, 62
Laemmle, Siegfried, 164
Lahn, Ilse, 186
Lamar, Adriana, 87
Lamarr, Hedy, 115, 116, 232
Landa, Rodolfo, 171, 218, 287
Lang, Fritz, 125, 167, 227
Lang, Jennings, 231, 232
Lantz, Robert, 226
Lara, Agustín, 82, 85, 285
Laurel and Hardy, 30
La Voluntad del Muerto, 46, 49, 52, 54, 58, 59, 66, 72, 77, 94, 199, 213, 217, 283
Lawson, John Howard, 171, 223
László, Paul, 166
LeBeau, Madeleine, 186
Lebedeff, Ivan, 28, 283
Lederer, Francis, 153
Lederman, D. Ross, 191, 289
Leise flehen Meiner Lieder, 134
Leni, Paul, 65
Leone, Sergio, 236
Levy, Michael, 254
Litvak, Anatole, 144
Logan, Ben, 21
Logan, Josh, 229
Lombard, Carole, 186
Lowe, Edmund, 194, 283
Loy, Myrna, 31, 283
Lubitsch, Ernst, 66, 90, 93, 116, 117, 167, 180, 227, 264, 269
Lubitsch, Nicola, 258
Lugosi, Bela, 65, 66, 69, 267
Luján, Rosa Elena, 214, 215, 258
Lupino, Ida, 191

M

Machatý, Gustav, 115
MacKenzie, Aeneas, 160, 165, 166
Madero, Francisco, 7
Magaña, Delia, 29, 30
Malandrinos, Andreas, 136
Mandelik, Lucien, 117, 162
Mankiewicz, Joseph, 235
Man Who Laughs, The, 37
Mann, Heinrich, 125, 167
Manners, David, 65
Marcus, Michael, 254
María, 171, 172, 174, 218, 250, 287

295

Maria Elena, 237
Marihuana, 154, 287
Maris, Mona, 87
Marton, Andrew "Bandi", 121
Marton, George and Hilda, 227
Mason, Jim, 71
Massary, Fritzi, 168
Mateos, Adolfo López, 207, 210
Mateos, Esperanza López, 207, 210
Maximilian von Habsburg, 13, 78, 158, 160
May, Joe, 167
Mayer, Louis B.,116, 165
McCarthy, Senator Joseph, 223, 229
McCrea, Jody, 231
McKenna, Miss, 27
McLaglen, Victor, 31, 94
McQueen, Steve, 246
Meisner, Sanford, 231
Melford, George, 49, 50, 52, 54, 65, 66, 70, 75, 284
Mercedes Ortega Lozana, 207, 208
Merrick, Lynn, 185, 289
Mexican Movies in the United States, 85
Meyer, Ron, 255
Miguel Strogoff, 150, 191, 259, 289
Minnelli, Vincente, 229
Mirisch, Walter, 258
Moana, 135
Mocambo, 96
Mojica, José, 67, 87
Monroe, Marilyn, 197
Montalban, Ricardo, 160, 237
Montand, Yves, 249
Moore, Juanita, 232
Moos, Sigmund, 43, 44, 51
Moran, Lois, 28, 283
Moreno, Antonio, 49, 50, 51, 54, 72, 81, 85, 87, 153, 159, 197, 284
Moreno, Hilda, 29, 30, 136, 286
Mr. Robinson Crusoe, 91
Muni, Paul, 160
Murnau, F.W., 135, 227

N

Nájera, Ambassador Castillo, 128, 145
Navarro, Gabriel, 87
Nebenzal, Harold, 144
Nebenzal, Seymour, 144

Neppach, Robert, 127
Neumann, Kurt, 42, 47, 50, 71, 89, 90, 284, 285
Next Time we Love, 157
Nissen, Greta, 95
Nolan, Mary, 42
Norton, Barry, 65, 87, 154, 267, 268, 284, 286, 287
Novarro, Ramon, 52, 87
Novello, Jay, 289

O

O'Brien, George, 171, 288, 289
O'Neal, Patricia, 259
O'Neal, Ryan, 259
Oakie, Jack, 95
Obregón, Alvaro, 8
Ocaranza, Doctor, 14
Ocaranza, Pepe, 14, 21, 24, 27, 57, 58, 60, 99, 198
Olsen, David, 262, 268, 279
Olsen, Emily, 261, 268, 279
Olsen, Maggie, 262, 268, 271, 279
Olympia, 251
Ophuls, Max, 167
Orellana, Carlos, 78, 87, 171, 285, 287
Orsatti, Frank, 165, 258
Orsatti, Ernie, 258
Ortiz Rubio, President Pascual, 52, 78, 199, 217

P

Pagnol, Marcel, 133, 229
Palmer, Ernest, 21
Parson, Louella, 95
Pasternak, Joe and Margie, 85, 197, 108, 113, 122. 165. 167
Pelayo, Alejandro, 276
Pena, Julio, 87, 286
Penizek & Rainer, 119
Péon, Ramón, 78
Percy, Esme, 136, 286
Pereda, Ramón, 71, 285
Peredo, Luis G. 85
Pérez, Silverio, 197
Pesqueira, Alfonso, 23, 27, 52, 157, 158, 183
Philbin, Mary, 36, 37, 38
Phillips, Alex, Jr., 81
Phillips, Alex, 81, 171, 272, 288

Pickfair, 91
Pickford, Mary, 60, 91
Polaty, Geza, 136
Pommer, Erich, 116, 117
Power, Tyrone, 231
Pressburger, Arnold, 136
Prince of Wales, 119
Prodigal Son, The, 141, 142, 143
Proust, Marcel, 129

R

Rebel, The, 66, 121, 138, 141,
Recordar es Vivir, 189, 289
Reed, Donald, 78, 84, 285, 289
Reed, Tom, 121, 251, 252
Reinhardt, John, 154, 286
Reinhardt, Max, 108, 167, 227
Reinhardt, Silvia and Gottfried, 227
Reinwald, Emma, 115
Reisch, Walter, 134, 167
Remarque, Erich Maria, 129, 167
Renaldo, Duncan, 129, 167
Resurrección, 189, 288
Reachi, Manuel, 21
Rice, Frank, 71, 285
Riefenstahl, Leni, 94, 121, 131, 251
Riley, Lou, 272
Riva, Maria, 268, 269
Riva, Peter, 269
Rivera, Diego, 160, 199, 200, 202
Rivero, Fernando A., 189, 285, 289
Robards, Jason, 250
Robinson, Armin, 227
Robinson, Edward G., 155
Robinson, George, 65, 70
Robitschek, Arthur, 186
Rodríguez, Joselito, 78, 275,
Rodríguez, Roberto, 78
Rogers, Will, Jr., 186
Roland, Gilbert, 297
Romay, Pepe, 275
Romero, Ernesto, 27, 43, 199
Roosevelt, Franklin D., 170, 183
Roosevelt, James, 170, 183
Ross, Jack, 119, 186, 188
Rubín, Pedro, 82, 271
Ryan, Jimmy, 25, 26, 31, 32

S

S.O.S. Iceberg, 94, 107, 110, 121, 122, 151
Salt, Gary, 254,
Sánchez Tello, Alfonso, 189
Schlöndorff, Volker, 269
Schneeberger, Hans, 121
Schubert, Franz, 134
Scott, Robert, 192
Segurola, Andrés de, 49, 71, 284
Selznick, David, 163
Shanghai Lady, 42
Shayne, Robert, 191, 189
Shearer, Norma, 53
Sheehan, Winfield, 25, 26, 283
Sheik, The, 21, 49
Sherman, George, 179, 185, 192, 288, 289, 290
Sherman, Vincent, 191
Shire, Dick, 95
Shultz, Franz, 107
Shultz, Jimmy, 75
Signoret, Simone, 249
Simmons, Jean, 250
Sinclair, Upton, 129
Siodmak, Curt, 144
Siodmak, Robert, 232
Sirk, Douglas, 267
Skal, David J., 267
Slocum, John Wallace., 1
Smith, Noel M., 71
Sokal, Harry, 180, 181
Sokal, Henry, 181
Solares, Gilberto Martínez, 189, 272, 289
Solares, Raúl Martínez, 189
Soler, Julián, 191, 289
South of the Border, 179, 180, 288
Spiegel, Sam, 135, 144, 172, 174, 239, 286
Stahl, Jorge, 272
Stanwyck, Barbara, 71
Stauffer, Teddy, 272
Stein, Bob, 255
Stern, Alfred, 121, 143
Sternberg, Josef von, 116, 121, 125
Stevens, George, 241
Stewart, Jimmy, 157, 191
Stompanato, Johnny, 231
Stone, Peter, 227

Storm Over the Andes, 153
Strasberg, Lee, 231
Stroheim, Erich von, 35, 36, 53, 225
Stuart, Nick, 29, 283
Student Prince in Old Heidelberg, The, 66
Sturges, John, 246
Sturges, Preston, 94, 164, 166
Sullavan, Margaret, 157, 166
Sullivan Carlos, 1, 2
Sullivan John, 1
Sullivan Mary, 1, 2
Sullivan, John Wallace., 1, 24
Summerville, Slim, 71
Sutherland, A. Edward, 91
Swanson, Gloria, 21
Sydow, Max von, 241

T

Tallichet, Margaret, 163, 164, 174, 191
Talmadge, Norma, 197
Talmadge, Richard, 71, 284
Tardif, Fred, 254
Tauber, Richard, 227
Taylor, Elizabeth, 235
Ten Cents a Dance, 71
Thalberg, Irving, 135, 162
Thompson, J. Lee, 258
Thor, Jerry, 259
Thulin, Ingrid, 241
Tiber, Doctor Leon, 134
Tora, Lia, 28
Torena, Juan, 71, 87, 154, 286
Tovar, Egidio, 1, 2, 212
Tovar, Guillermo, 57, 159, 211, 246, 247
Tovar, Lucy de Inaraja, 5, 9, 11, 12, 13, 14, 19, 57, 159, 211, 212, 253
Tovar, Lucy, Maria de la Luz Inaraja de Pascual, 5, 9, 11, 12, 13, 14, 19, 57, 159, 211, 212, 253
Tovar, Mary, de Gonzalez, 15, 20, 57, 112, 159, 166, 212, 253, 271
Tovar, Mary Alicia, Sullivan de, 1, 2, 3, 5, 9, 11, 12, 13, 14, 15, 20, 21, 23, 24, 33, 53, 57, 61, 67, 73, 159, 166, 177, 189, 211, 212, 215, 232, 247, 253, 254
Tovar, Sara Amparo, de Tardif, 14, 57, 159, 166, 212, 246, 247, 253 254, 258
Traven, B., 203, 204, 205, 207, 208, 213, 214, 215, 218, 250, 258

Treasure of the Sierra Madre, The, 230, 207, 208, 211, 214, 250
Trenker, Luis, 121, 135, 138, 141, 143, 181, 227
Triumph of the Will, 251
Troell, Jan, 241
Tropic Fury, 179
Trujillo, Rafael, 155
Tuero, Emilio, 171, 189, 287
Turner, Lana, 231, 254
Twelvetrees, Helen, 47
Two-Gun Sheriff, 185, 289
Tyler, Tom, 191, 288

U

Udet, Ernst, 94, 121
Ullman, Liv, 241
Ullrich, Luise, 134
Ulmer, Edgar, 167
Urbina, Mr., 73, 74, 75
Urueta, Chano, 171, 250, 272, 287

V

Valdez, Tommy, 65
Valentino, Rudolph, 21, 49, 66
Valenzuela, Elena Sánchez, 85
Valli, Virginia, 27
Vals, François and Madeleine, 129, 230
Van der Rohe, Ludwig Mies, 125
Van Dyke, W.S., 135
Veidt, Conrad, 36
Veiled Woman, The, 28, 283
Vernac, Denise, 225
Verne, Jules, 191, 289
Victoria, 161, 162, 163
Vidas Rotas, 136, 137, 138, 140, 268, 286
Viertel, Salka, 231
Vilches, Ernesto, 87
Villa, Francisco (Pancho), 8, 13
Villarías, Carlos, 65, 66, 68, 87, 267, 284,
Villarreal, Julio, 191, 289
Villavicencio, Jacobita, 28, 51

W

Wall, Fay, 114
Wallach, Eddie, 113

Wallach, Eli, 246
Wallerstein, Mauricio, 272
Walsh, Raoul, 31, 94, 283
Wanger, Walter, 171, 180, 231, 235, 287,
Warner, Jack, 120, 167
Wayne, John, 249
Weider, Joseph, 203
Weill, Kurt, 125, 257
Weinberg, Dr. Hugo, 133, 134
Weitz, Christopher, 250, 279
Weitz, John, 249, 259
Weitz, Paul, 249, 279
Weitzfelder, Doctor Friedrich and Annie, 53, 94, 95, 99
Wells, H.G., 129
Welles, Orson, 213, 214
Werfel, Franz, 167
West, Vera, 146
Westerner, The, 185, 288
Wexler, Pearl, 254
White Hell of Pitz Palu, The, 121, 181, 251
Whiteman, Paul, 89
Wicki, Bernhard, 121
Widerberg, Bo, 241
Wilder, Billy, 107, 120, 134, 144, 167, 229, 238, 258, 263
Wilkerson, Billy, 231
Williams, Andy, 257
Wilson, Ambassador Henry Lane, 7
Wilson, President Woodrow, 8
Wooding, Sam, 125
Woods, Harry, 191, 289
Wulliger, Frank, 254
Wyler, Bob, 42, 50, 51
Wyler, David, 279
Wyler, William, 33, 42, 47, 50, 53, 72, 93, 96, 100, 121, 263, 288

Y

Yankee Don, 71, 284

Z

Zanuck, Daryl, 121
Zapata Emiliano, 3, 7, 8
Zeisler, Alfred, 132, 165
Zinnemann, Fred, 167

Zolá, Emile, 85
Zuckmayer, Carl, 125
Zuckerman, Kohner Kathy, 255

Edwards Brothers,Inc!
Thorofare, NJ 08086
09 December, 2010
BA2010343